I0823876

A New Orleans Author in Mark Twain's Court

THE HILL COLLECTION

Holdings of the LSU Libraries

A New Orleans Author in Mark Twain's Court

LETTERS FROM GRACE KING'S NEW ENGLAND SOJOURNS

Edited by MIKI PFEFFER

LOUISIANA STATE UNIVERSITY PRESS   BATON ROUGE

Published by Louisiana State University Press

Manufactured in the United States of America
First printing

Designer: Barbara Neely Bourgoyne
Typeface: Garamond Premier Pro
Printer and binder: Sheridan Books

Grace King's letter to Olivia Clemens dated October 13, 1893, is located at the Henry E. Huntington Library, Art Collections and Botanical Gardens, San Marino, Calif. Other letters to the Clemenses are located at the Bancroft Library, University of California, Berkeley.

Other Grace King letters reproduced herein are located in the Grace King Papers, MSS#1282, Louisiana and Lower Mississippi Valley Collections, LSU Libraries, Baton Rouge, La.

Library of Congress Cataloging-in-Publication Data
Names: King, Grace Elizabeth, 1851 or 1852–1932, author. | Pfeffer, Miki, editor.
Title: A New Orleans author in Mark Twain's court : letters from Grace King's New England sojourns / edited by Miki Pfeffer.
Other titles: Hill collection.
Description: Baton Rouge : Louisiana State University Press, [2019] | Series: The Hill collection : holdings of the LSU Libraries | Includes bibliographical references and index.
Identifiers: LCCN 2019017927| ISBN 978-0-8071-6973-5 (cloth : alk. paper) | ISBN 978-0-8071-7281-0 (pdf) | ISBN 978-0-8071-7282-7 (epub)
Subjects: LCSH: King, Grace Elizabeth, 1851 or 1852–1932—Correspondence. | Authors, American—Louisiana—New Orleans—Correspondence. | Twain, Mark, 1835–1910—Friends and associates. | LCGFT: Personal correspondence.
Classification: LCC PS2178 .A44 2019 | DDC 813/.4 [B] —dc23

The paper in this book meets the guidelines for permanence and durability of the Committee on Production Guidelines for Book Longevity of the Council on Library Resources. ♾

For my daughter, Gretchen, of course,
and for the King family, who saved all those letters

And then, suddenly and unexpectedly, there was opened to me the path leading out of and beyond the life I was living, to the life of my secret hopes and prayers, for which I had been long and humbly waiting.

—Grace King, in *Memories of a Southern Woman of Letters*

Contents

Foreword

I was learning to be a guide at the Mark Twain House in Hartford, Connecticut, when I first heard of Grace King—or rather of what she had for dinner with Samuel and Olivia Clemens and other guests on the evening of June 19, 1887: "Olives, salted almonds, and bonbons in curious dishes were on the table and decanters of quaint shape and color held the wine. The soup was 'Claire'—the Clairest you ever saw, delicious flavor—sherry—Then fresh salmon in white wine sauce, Apollinaris water—sweet breads in cream served I vow, in what looked like pomatum pots—with covers (little flat round ones, exquisitely painted in blue)." She continued through the claret, the chicken, the peas, the potatoes, and the tomato salad, winding up with "Charlotte Russe and wine jelly with candied cherries in it, with whipped cream." I hadn't learned yet what Miki Pfeffer, the editor of the following collection of letters, later taught me—that King, a true daughter of New Orleans, had a keen interest in whatever food was being served.

Grace King was described to us simply as "a visiting southern writer." Later, working in the curatorial library, I came across a folder marked "Grace King," and in it an undated typescript by a Robert Bush. Bush had written an essay on King and Mark Twain and sent it to someone at the house for fact-checking. In Bush's excerpts, plucked from her letters and journals at Louisiana State University, I finally met this winsome, wry, brilliant, and ambitious author.

She had been invited to Hartford's Nook Farm neighborhood, where the Clemenses lived, by neighbor, newspaper editor, and author Charles Dudley Warner. I browsed through the anecdotes of her visit, and it quickly became apparent that this was much more than just a contemporary account of a visit to Mark Twain. King conveyed in detail what it was like to talk to Mark Twain face-to-face. From her journal:

> He is an easy man to get along with socially, in his own house, and with his own family. He is quick to catch your idea—and nice to it, after he catches it. He does not impose his opinions, at least on me he did not—and he listens—at least to me—with attention. His spirits rise easily—his fun is never asleep—at a wink he is alert. When he talks—there is something delightfully unpremeditated in the way he brings in his stories; good or bad, appropriate or inappropriate, egotistical or otherwise. [. . .] His fun is so personal; it is autobiographical. He cannot conceal—his frankness is startling. He simply doesn't care; he cannot stop to apologize or explain, and beg you not to consider him egotistical. And the absence of this uneasiness about the opinion of others, is perhaps the pleasantest trait in his intercourse, for it puts you also at your ease.

It was a conversation that few men might share with a woman in the nineteenth century, or, for that matter, in the twenty-first: "He treats ladies generally as if they were nice clever boys—like himself. [. . .] If they need his advice or protection—he treats them as if they were nice, good sorts of sisters—without any sentiment, or exaggeration of his services." His heart, she said, "had never been to dancing school."

Here was a new twist on the complicated author we at the Mark Twain House thought we knew. King's portrait in prose made it clear that she was a rare reporter. As I read further (including the excellent biography by Bush, a professor at the City University of New York), I learned how absolutely devastating she could be in her takedowns of stupidity among acquaintances, publishers, and northerners in general. I read more vivid descriptions of travel, of landscapes, of personalities. I sampled her fiction and, interestingly, an account of the Battle of New Orleans.

I also have to confess that when I first saw a picture of her—it accompanied an article about southern writers in the May 1887 *Harper's New Monthly Magazine*—I was captivated. It's a three-quarters profile. She leans forward, her nose slightly upturned, a wry smile turning up the corner of her mouth, as though something was secretly amusing her.

Into this infatuation stepped Miki Pfeffer, just before Christmas in 2015. Miki had published an absorbing account of the 1884 World's Industrial and Cotton Centennial Exposition, *Southern Ladies and Suffragists.* King was a bit player in, and observer of, that event and, in fact, had first met and cultivated

Warner there. Miki, like me, had been intrigued by King's wit, eloquence, perception, and biting commentary on things great and small.

Miki was now laboriously transcribing never-before-transcribed letters in the Louisiana State University library and other collections, and she got in touch with the Mark Twain House trying to see if anyone there could read Warner's nearly impenetrable handwriting. We couldn't, but she and I kept up a correspondence.

Finally we were able to host Miki as a speaker, and she tantalized us with her finds. King had not just been an occasional Hartford visitor. She and Olivia Clemens maintained an intimate correspondence; she wrote engaging notes to the Clemens daughters, and they wrote her affectionately back. She visited the Clemenses in Europe when they lived there in the 1890s. There is a particularly poignant exchange Miki has unearthed in which King and Olivia Clemens discuss whether or not the family should return to the Hartford house—the scene of daughter Susy Clemens's then-recent death at age twenty-four.

Miki brings persistence, good humor, and solid literary style to her work—and invaluable discovery. The interplay of literary figures between South and North is fascinating and will add much to historical and literary study of the period, of Reconstruction, of race, and of the role of female authors in that time. (After being stood up repeatedly in a New York publisher's office, King wrote, "I saw myself losing time & money, awaiting the convenience of a lot of men—which made me furious.")

This is also a tour of many nineteenth-century scenes, on two continents, which are unearthed like so many Pompeiis, with a splendid, sharp-tongued guide to explain it all.

An example: King takes a walk up a Hartford street to the home of Joseph and Harmony Twichell, Clemens's minister friend and his wife. She stops to chat with a local family: "They all seemed delighted to see me in fact had just been talking about me á propos of the youngest daughter complaining that there was nothing in life worth living for and I was being held up as an example. I believe the young lady like most young ladies of her age was blue on account of the scarcity of gayety and beaux in Hartford."

She describes vividly the massive "castle" and grounds of James Goodwin, the cousin of J. P. Morgan, at the next corner ("exactly like the pictures of old English Castles which have been added on Century after Century"), then continues to the Twichells' home: "Mrs Twichell is a very nice woman who has broken down suddenly in heart principally because she has had the foolishness to undertake to bring in the world and take care of nine children on a minister's salary."

She travels with the Clemenses to New York and deadpans her opinion of their accommodations: "The hotel rather overpowered me with the magnificence of its interior but I soon recovered my equanimity after seeing the bed rooms and eating lunch."

And yes, this critical interest in cuisine is again reflected as she leaves the elegant Clemens table and dines with a "puritan of puritans" on "a soup which seemed made of clear water with little floury balls in it, highly seasoned with salt and pepper. [. . .] How these people live on so little is a mystery to me."

But enough. It's time to immerse yourself in the energy, incisiveness, delight, and disdain of Grace King, as conveyed to us by another eloquent daughter of New Orleans.

STEVE COURTNEY
Curatorial Department
Mark Twain House & Museum

Preface

Historians are people who like to read other people's mail. The quip isn't mine, but I claim it. When I first encountered Grace King's letters, I knew these sirens would call me back. They are smart, snarky, aesthetically significant, and absolutely fascinating. In addition, who wouldn't want to know more of the intimate details about Mark Twain and his family that are revealed in her letters? Ten years ago, as I sat at an unwieldy machine in the microfilm room at Louisiana State University, I was struck by King's range of bold observations and vibrant expressions. I was then researching the Woman's Department at the 1884 World's Industrial and Cotton Centennial Exposition in New Orleans, and King nattered about it from the sidelines as an opinionated commentator rather than as participant. Not only did she remark on that world's fair but also on food, fashion, nature, manners, family, death and marriage, sermons, preachers and churches, politicians and elections, corruption, entertainment, transportation, architecture, female colleges and students, languages, literature, publishing, health, wealth, and the weather. These topics were also grist for her communiqués as she traveled and compared other places and people with those she knew so well in her beloved New Orleans. Her papers are cultural treasures.

The letters alone number well over a thousand, divided into two sizable collections in the Hill Memorial Library at Louisiana State University. The Grace King Papers are exchanges among family members, mentors, and friends, including many from Hartford editor and essayist Charles Dudley Warner, who was her special guide into the world of literature. The Selected Letters are mainly business correspondence but also include some exchanges with acquaintances old and new. Letters *from* the Clemenses, for example, are in both sets; letters *to* them are lodged in the Mark Twain Papers in the Bancroft Library at the University of California, Berkeley, many of which had never been transcribed until now. The hundreds I have chronicled offer a portrait of a sassy writer becoming an independent woman during changing times for her gender and region. They read like a cliff-hanging novel. Will the family regain its place in society? How will King find success? Whom will she meet next; where will she go? What outrageous thing will she tell in unfiltered letters to family and friends? And a question for me: Would she be amenable to having those private thoughts laid bare? That she herself relished reading volumes of letters of George Sand, George Eliot, Robert Browning, Balzac, and others, I take as her proxy to offer these.

My dream is to see all of the letters published, but multiple volumes of Grace King's correspondence are as yet unlikely. In the meantime, this volume's major cache bubbled up as a manageable suite that might whet appetites for more of her remarkable voice. King's manifold reports to her family from northern sojourns depict the literary and artistic world of the late nineteenth and early twentieth centuries. The letters also trace significant intersectional friendships, most often as seen through King's hungry southern eyes. They paint a partial picture of mentors and publishers who bolstered her budding career, and they render a complete portrait of her special friendship with the Clemenses. Here, all extant exchanges between King and the Samuel Clemens family are found in full, including never-before-published letters from Olivia (Livy) and daughters Susy, Clara, and Jean.[1] Here too are King's dazzling descriptions, as relayed to her own family, of the Clemenses' Gilded Age home and of others in the Nook Farm neighborhood. I make no claim of Twain expertise, but Grace King's unique voice can contribute to the scholarly storehouse of that literary lion. Her views as a southerner, a female writer, and a confidante of Livy serve up a portion of Twain's private world as a delicious morsel to be savored.

In the connecting narrative, I draw especially from letters that reveal the hues of King's character, tone, and complexity that might speak to a twenty-first-century audience. I take responsibility for the selected snippets which, after all, are made subjectively but only after having transcribed deeply and

1. Robert Bush's exceptional studies on Grace King prompted renewed interest in her as a writer and historian. His *Grace King: A Southern Destiny* (Baton Rouge: Louisiana State University Press, 1983) and "Grace King and Mark Twain," *American Literature* 44, no. 1 (March, 1972): 31–51, remain valid, as they are based so solidly in King's letters. For additional contextual works, see this volume's contextual bibliography.

broadly in the collections. I strive to have King's words heard rather than my own, but I occasionally assess or clarify in order to smooth the chronology or context, always from familiarity with the writer. These commentaries are meant to thread her professional development and growing self-regard and to annotate her relationships so that the reader is not distracted by holes in her story that, otherwise, could be filled only by the inclusion of innumerable and very long letters.

As a child of William Woodson King, a prominent attorney in New Orleans, Grace King had every reason to expect an upper-class urban existence. But the Civil War and Reconstruction intruded and stripped the family of existing assets and future prospects. Grace was an impressionable girl of ten when she watched Union troops take New Orleans. The family escaped to her father's working plantation, "L'Embarrass," to live out the war years until they could return to the city, but long resentments abided from her childhood fears. In addition, she attributed her father's death in 1881 to the stress of trying to rebuild the family's place in society.

Instead, the Kings became part of the genteel poor who devoted much energy to keeping up appearances of their former life. They valued hospitality, propriety, education, and ancestry; letters reflected those principles even when members of the family were exasperated with conditions at home. They preserved family correspondence long before Grace achieved celebrity as a writer. The collection is almost complete from all members with few obviously missing letters and perhaps only one purposely destroyed: an apparent account of wedding night "brutishness" for which an innocent May King was unprepared. Otherwise, because the letters are in archives for safekeeping, it is possible to know an entire family's saga of struggles, sorrows, and triumphs. The extensive Grace King Papers are the family's legacy, a gift to scholarship of which Grace would surely approve. My hope is that through this voyeuristic romp, readers and researchers will discover her papers anew as a wellspring to a historical age.

Letters in this volume cover a limited period of Grace King's long life (1852–1932). They begin in 1885, when she met Charles Dudley Warner, who became her most important promoter. They run through the blossoming of her career, the flowering of important relationships, and close with the death of her friend Samuel Clemens in 1910. The narrative here is gleaned solely from private correspondence with an occasional nod to King's public memoir, in which she tamps down emotions and remembers differently than in her real-time letters, where anger flies, worries mount, and moods swing. Grace King traveled far and often, but her core was always in New Orleans. She understood her one place well, and by remaining in her beloved city, she was a large fish in its small literary pond of the time. However, without the help of mentors, editors, and publishers in the North, surely her career would have been slighter. She applied southern wiles to capture and hold them as friends as well as business associates, and perhaps all of them gained from the bonds they formed. These enduring friendships enhanced her life, and the Clemenses were among the dearest.[2]

A NOTE ON THE TEXT

Transcriptions here are from handwritten letters on microfilm in the Grace King Papers in Hill Memorial Library at Louisiana State University. With a few exceptions, scanned handwritten texts are also used from the Bancroft Library at University of California, Berkeley. To transcribe letters from all members of the King family was a challenge. They wrote as idiosyncratically as they lived rather than having handwritings with a family resemblance, as in those of Olivia Clemens and her daughters. However, no hand was as inscrutable as that of Charles Dudley Warner, Grace King's mentor and Mark Twain's friend, so he is quoted only sparingly here. King's occasional left-handed writing was at first enigmatic but was eventually conquered. Like Louisa May Alcott and other writers including Twain, she resorted to her left hand to save her stiff right one for copying manuscripts. Also perplexing was the cross-writing typical of the nineteenth century when paper (or money) was so scarce that correspondents turned the page sideward and wrote across previous lines of script. Add a variety of unreliable pen nibs, ink types, and thin paper through which ink bled, and the need for intrepid transcribing is obvious.

In the interest of consistency and readability, I make minimal corrections. I standardize the appearance of the letters and take the liberty of using familiar names to introduce them. These educated writers employed vivid language, proper syntax, and somewhat systematized spelling so had little need to strike through words. I silently eliminate words they did scratch out except in the few

2. See this volume's contextual bibliography for relevant studies on Mark Twain.

cases where the mistakes reveal an interesting turn of mind. I keep their English spellings, eccentric punctuations, unsystematic contractions, and frequent use of the ampersand but correct their irregular use of *ei* and *ie*. When an occasional word is clearly intended but missing, I add it in square brackets; I silently remove accidentally repeated words. When I am unsure of a word or date, I add this: [?]. As a publishing convention, the writers' practice of underlining for emphasis is here replaced with italics.

Grace King used an abundance of short and longer dashes that inadvertently gave her letters a kind of breathlessness. She also used a very long dash when abruptly changing the subject. All of these lovely peculiarities are replaced here, in the interest of typesetting standards, by the more lackluster one-em dash (—). King wrote almost without paragraphs as if delivering a prolonged monologue; I maintain some of the practice to give that sense to these letters. When the context of a letter makes the date an obvious error, I correct the date and add a footnote. I use [. . .] for sections excluded within the narrative, but I use every complete extant letter of the Clemenses, noting those that are as yet incomplete in archives. Occasionally, a letter that is being answered is obviously missing. I indicate such in notes with the hope that eventually those absent gems will reappear.

ACKNOWLEDGMENTS

Four Men of Twain encouraged this volume. Steve Courtney, museum consultant at the Mark Twain House, was reading Robert Bush's biography of Grace King when I wrote begging help with Charles Dudley Warner's handwriting. Steve has become a friend and supportive reader of this project. By way of books and bibliographies, I found Robert Hirst, curator of the Mark Twain Project at the University of California, Berkeley. Bob has been an invaluable partner in helping to correct my transcriptions and in dating letters; his knowledge is deep and vast, and that was also reflected in his generous reading of this manuscript. Professor David Sloane of the Mark Twain Society insisted I must publish these letters after hearing me read from them at the conference of the American Literature Association, and Joseph Lemak, director of the Center for Mark Twain Studies in Elmira, New York, invited me to speak at Quarry

Farm and encouraged me to apply for a fellowship, for which I am grateful. These men validated the project with their enthusiasm for it, as did receptive audiences at the Mark Twain House and elsewhere.

Margaret Lovecraft, acquisitions editor at LSU Press, patiently sustained my meandering through a morass of transcribed letters to finally deciding upon the included corpus. She enriched the project with grace and affability and reminded me that this is Grace King's story. As my rock and touchstone, she prodded me to think more broadly and more precisely. Copyeditor Susan Murray treated the manuscript with respect and pleasure, and I thank her.

Heroic archivists and librarians assisted the project: Tara Z. Laver, Jenny Mitchell, and Germain Bienvenu, who went to extraordinary lengths, and photographer Margaret Albertine at the Hill Memorial Library; Lee Miller, Sean Benjamin, and Ann Case in the Louisiana Research Collection at Tulane University; Henry Arneth at Trinity College, and Matthew Turi at University of North Carolina, Chapel Hill Libraries. Library specialist April Rome at Nicholls State University assisted my Interlibrary Loan needs; archivists Clifton Theriot and Helen Thomas taught me their wonderful scanning machine. I thank the Kings and all families who save private papers, and I praise archivists everywhere who mind our treasures.

I am indebted to scholars who paved the way and to groups that scheduled readings in New England and south Louisiana that allowed me to gauge interest in my subject. I also thank Ann Maylie Bruce, who nurtured me and arranged an interview with Grace King's grandnephew, Rivers Richardson "Dick" King, whom I thank. I am appreciative of special favors: Sally Asher for photography; Joanne Ferriot for translations of French phrases; Polly Armstrong for willingness in Berkeley; Giselle Roberts and Melissa Walker for early interest in this project; Susan Tucker, who always makes connections happen, and Melissa Heidari, who gracefully let this one go.

I am grateful to those who squired me around Grace King's travel haunts: Rita White of the Blowing Rock Historical Society; residents Gary and Peggy Shore, who knew where May McDowell's cottage had been on their North Carolina hilltop; Rich West for the tour of landmarks in Northampton, Massachusetts, and Steve Courtney for the Nook Farm neighborhood in Hartford and the Elm Tree Inn in Farmington, Connecticut. Eileen Sweeney, David Smith, and Dennis Gleeson helped me tour Cheney Silk Mills properties in nearby South Manchester, and Carol Cheney was gracious in the style of her forebears. Kate Stickley and Richie Lasansky housed me in their Catskills home and transported me to "Olana" and the Hudson River valley. Zack Garceau of the Westerley Historical Society researched the Elizabeth Burnap house in Watch Hill, Rhode Island, and president Tom Gulluscio took me right to it. Lastly, Doreen Dolhun at a pleasant motel in Cooperstown, New York, told me exactly how to find "Lakelands." These kindnesses released emotional moments for me as I was able to stand where Grace King once stood.

I honor the community of writers and friends who cheer me on: Carol Gelderman, Anne Boyd Rioux, Teresa Tumminello Brader, Nigel Hamilton, Judy Pinter, Shauna Storey Grissett, Mary Ann Wegmann, Catherine Haws, Mary Ann Wilson, Rachelle Defillo, Mary Niall Mitchell, Pat Brady, Nancy Dixon, Chris Wiltz, Susan Larson, Joyce Benoit, Frances Robichaux, Ellen Hardeman, and all book-loving pals. I thank son-in-law Charles Caillouet for his goodness, and always my dear, dear daughter Gretchen for being her wonderful self.

A New Orleans Author in Mark Twain's Court

PROLOGUE

Acquaintances Made, Mentors Gained

Your letters are nearly as good as your stories.
—NINA TO GRACE, JULY 14, 1891

At the age of thirty-three, Grace King had little reason to expect to begin a literary career or to be welcomed into a circle of famous writers and respected publishers. In 1885, she was simply a disgruntled eldest sister with an urge for freedom but few prospects to achieve it, a relative drudge who spent her energies managing the house for an eccentric family and yearning to escape their incessant rebellions.

The center of the seven Kings was their mother, Mimi, whom Grace publicly called "a charming raconteuse, witty, and inexhaustible in speech" who "turned every episode of her life into a good and colorful story"[1] but privately termed her "an ambitious woman, determined to surpass every one, & succeeding." Grace most often bemoaned her life *en famille* in uninhibited letters to her *intime* May, the only sister who escaped the erratic household when she married in early 1884 and moved to North Carolina.[2] She labeled older brothers Fred and Branch unsympathetic, demanding, and disagreeable; and unmarried sisters Nan and Nina, lackadaisical and argumentative, "like unreliable watches, always running down or stopping and never giving the correct time of day."

1. Grace King, *Memories of a Southern Woman of Letters* (New York: Macmillan, 1932), 1, 183. Hereafter, *Memories.*

2. Grace to May Flora King McDowell, February 28?, 1885. Hereafter, May. All emotion was fair game when Grace wrote her confidante May. Small pleasures were often overshadowed by fear, trepidation, and physical issues that were laid bare, the latter often with proposed remedies for their shared experience of unruly hair, freckles, sunburn, nerves, menstrual cramps, or the more serious fibroid tumor from which May suffered, as did Warner's wife, Susan.

Nan she pictured as "utterly ignoring any social or domestic duties," and Nina as "lying in bed with malaria—half the day—doing fancy work the other half." Lastly, she saw her youngest brother, Will, as unrealistic and grandiose rather than responsible and contributing. Exacerbating the turmoil, money was always scarce and penny-pinching was commonplace as the older brothers tried to provide for the genteel family, as expected (their father had died in 1881). Grace craved a life apart.[3]

Providence arrived in the forms of the spectacular World's Industrial and Cotton Centennial Exposition, in the famous activist Julia Ward Howe, and in visiting editors Charles Dudley Warner and Richard Watson Gilder, who came to New Orleans to write up the fair and seek new writers. The exposition ran from December 16, 1884, to May 31, 1885, and the Bostonian Howe led its Woman's Department, where jobs, education, opportunity, and suffrage were regularly deliberated by women from all over the country. She was a leading suffragist and *littérateur,* having written poetry, travel books, essays, and sermons, but her greatest fame rested in her iconic northern anthem "Battle Hymn of the Republic." Although southern ladies resented Howe's appointment and her rather haughty style of leadership, she made significant contributions and managed a successful department that featured women's work and their increasing opportunities.[4] She also opened doors for Grace King.

Grace did not participate in the Woman's Department or its exhibits at the Cotton Centennial Exposition. Instead, she nattered from the sidelines

3. Mimi was Sarah Ann Miller King (1820–1903), New Orleans native of Huguenot heritage and second wife of prominent attorney William Woodson King (1813–1881). Nan was Annie Ragan King (1856–1933), younger sister, willing reader of Grace King's stories, helpful researcher, and companion on European trips. Nina Ansley King (1861–1942) was the youngest, sickliest, unmarried sister who outlived all her siblings. Fred was eldest brother Frederic D. King (1850–1922), attorney and later judge. Branch Miller King (1850–1905) was a lifelong bachelor who, after his father's death, supported the family as a banker in the factoring business of his maternal uncle, Thomas DePasseau Miller (1824–1888), and then in his own such business, Flowers and King. Will was William Augustus King (1859–1901), the youngest and most troubled brother. May Flora King (1854–1920) married Franklin Brevard McDowell (1849–1927) on January 9, 1884, and moved to Charlotte, North Carolina, for the rest of her life. Grace King was born on November 29, 1852 (although her tombstone reads 1851), and died January 14, 1932.

4. Julia Ward Howe's first volume of poetry brought her attention: *Passion-Flowers* (1853). For struggles and triumphs in the Woman's Department, see Miki Pfeffer, *Southern Ladies and Suffragists: Julia Ward Howe and Women's Rights at the 1884 New Orleans World's Fair* (Jackson: University of Mississippi Press, 2014).

about what people were doing, saying, eating, and wearing. These were subjects of immense interest to the women in her family. Food, settings, and manners signified gentility. Clothing was so much a marker of status that the King women concentrated much effort on appearing *au courant,* often by remaking and retrimming old garments, and Grace was jealous when the finery of others underscored her own lack: "It seems almost strange to me now, that any one can have a season for getting new things—instead of a pocket-book—& that there are people in the world, who really go out & have pleasures, instead of duties."[5] She wanted more.

Howe was a conduit for King's ambitions. She and her glitzy daughter, Maud, who led the Woman's Department's literary section, first boarded in a house nearby and then moved to one proffered by the "Lottery King," John A. Morris, at 21 South Rampart Street, next to the Kings' rented house at 23.[6] In addition to her responsibilities in the Woman's Department, Howe chose to revive the Pan Gnostics, a lagging literary club. There, participants read aloud their essays on serious subjects and edited them for possible publication, as northern hopefuls had done before them. King eagerly joined, awakening a long-held ambition to write.

The dynamic Howes were intermittent darlings of the social set in New Orleans and likewise arranged soirées of their own. At one of the latter, Grace met Charles Dudley Warner, editor at the *Hartford Courant,* coauthor of *The Gilded Age* with his friend and neighbor Mark Twain, and literary critic for *Harper's Magazine.* He had come to the exposition to assess changes in the post-Reconstruction South as he found them; Grace would steer him to see things through her lens, and she found a mentor in the process.

5. Grace to May, February 28?, 1885.

6. John Albert Morris (1836–1895), the "Lottery King," owned the corrupt Louisiana Lottery and was prominent in thoroughbred horse racing. His estimated worth at his death was $25 to $30 million. He had known Howe's brother, Francis Marion Ward, who died in New Orleans of yellow fever while setting up a branch of the Howe family's New York investment banking firm, Prime, Ward, and King (no relation to Grace King). In 1876, King had traveled with Morris and his wife, Cora Hennen Morris (1838–1922), to the Centennial Exposition in Philadelphia and to their home in Throg's Neck, New York. Their early New Orleans home and one of the Kings' many rented houses were in the first square off of Canal Street, now a commercial block. The families were close while neighbors but were later estranged, especially when the Kings became fervently anti-Lottery. A seven-alarm fire in 2019 burned most of the later Morris home at 2525 St. Charles Avenue.

She was prepared to practice the guile of belles on the glamorous traveling man who regularly encouraged young women writers. At the second "stupid" soirée at the Howes', Grace wrote May, she watched for an opportunity to seize Warner's interest and "snatched it when it came." He was "about fifty—grey haired & bearded & married—but so clever, refined & original—Of course we are affinities & of course the fashionables are racing after him."[7] Warner wanted to interview the respected Creole historian Charles Gayarré, by chance Grace's early advisor and a family friend. The three spent part of a day together.[8] Warner accompanied Grace to a meeting of the "Pans" and squired her home, the two creating "quite an excitement. He is very much run after—& people imagine I am with him far more than I am; so I was the envied," a condition she relished.[9]

Under Warner's immediate influence, Grace became obsessed with understanding the act of writing, and she began to read with more purpose. She wrote May that she was "deep in 'George Eliot,'" probably *George Eliot's Life as Related in Her Letters and Journals,* three volumes edited by her husband, J. W. Cross. Grace admired how "quietly & coolly she separates herself from her family & writes" and how completely Eliot was "buoyed up by her confidence in her own powers [. . .] expressing her thoughts fluently & elegantly," qualities Grace sought for herself. "Of course I am limp, crazy now on the subject of books & am reading all the time trying to learn what the greatest woman of England knew at eighteen" that Grace did not know at thirty-plus. This study was pertinent to a work of criticism she was researching to deliver to the "Pans," and she confided to May: "Next week, I am going to devote myself to it—& if I can only manage to steady my voice enough to read it—am determined to make a tremendous effort. After all Warner's encouragement, I am as bold as a lion & if I make a failure it will be an audacious one."[10] That "Heroines of Novels" became her first published piece, printed in the *New Orleans Times-Democrat* on May 31, 1885, and Grace glimpsed autonomy in the mere five dollars she was promised for it.[11]

7. Grace to May, April 17, 1885.

8. Judge Charles-Étienne Arthur Gayarré (1805–1895) was the celebrated Creole historian of Louisiana; King was his protégée. His wife, Sarah Anne Sullivan Gayarré (1820–1914), lived with the King family for years after his death.

9. Grace to May, April 26, 1885.

10. Grace to May, May 7?, 1885.

11. The *Times-Democrat* ran King's critique but made her wait for her five dollars, a practice of publishers that exasperated her throughout her career.

In addition to Warner's presence in New Orleans, editor Richard Watson Gilder of *Century Magazine* had come to the exposition seeking writers to fictionalize the Old South before it disappeared. Or to describe its confrontation with the "New South" that this World's Fair trumpeted.[12] Gilder hoped to piggyback on his success with George Washington Cable's early stories of exotic local color, later published as *Old Creole Days* (Scribner's, 1883). Grace wrote May that she also had "got quite thick" with Gilder[13] and, in her memoir, reported that he goaded her to write her first story when she complained of Cable's portrayal of the Creoles.[14] Perhaps Gilder did not know that Cable was persona non grata in New Orleans because of that fictional treatment, especially in *The Grandissimes: A Story of Creole Life* (1880) and, more so, for the liberal views expressed in his essay "The Freedman's Case in Equity."[15] He had already moved to Northampton, Massachusetts, in fear of physical reprisal and, during the period of the Cotton Centennial, was sharing stages with Mark Twain across the Northeast. Their antics on tour were reported in newspapers and would later be a source of entertainment for Grace when Twain satirized Cable's nonsmoking, nondrinking, non-billiard-playing, Sabbatarian ways.

Neither Cable nor King was Catholic or Creole (descendant of Spanish or French and born in the New World, sometimes with the addition of African or Native American parentage as a Creole of Color),[16] but Grace, like her Huguenot mother and many elite girls in New Orleans, had received a solid French education. Three Instituts: St. Louis, Sylvester-Larned, and Cenas plus private tutors predisposed her to identify with the Creole community, which

12. Promoters of a "New South" advertised the region's readiness to rejoin the Union after Reconstruction, its desire to partake of the burgeoning industrial age, and its observance of the Amendments that assured black citizens their civil rights. These declarations were more aspirational than actual, layered as they were atop persistent sentiments of the Old South.

13. Grace to May, April 26, 1885.

14. *Memories,* 60.

15. The loudest criticism was that Cable had betrayed his home people to appease northern editors. "The Freedman's Case in Equity" and the second episode from Twain's *Huckleberry Finn* ran in the same issue of *Century Magazine,* January 1885.

16. This is an oversimplification of complex and contested terms. New Orleans was home to people with a spectrum of skin tones and origins who shared overlapping families and activities at least until the political dominance of the Americans (who arrived after 1803) and the 1896 decision of the Supreme Court in *Plessy v. Ferguson* ("separate but equal"). The city became a de jure binary place yet retained the lingering emotional ties that King wrote into her stories.

was still separated from *les Américains* by language and culture. Like Cable, Grace attended Presbyterian churches, but where he was devout, she was skeptical. On the other hand, she did believe in southern mythology; the memory of the Civil War was burned into her mind at an impressionable age. Although her prejudice favored the superiority of whites, her view of people of color was complicated by behavior-cum-class or the physical proximity or service to the King family.[17] Grace claimed to better understand the spectrum of the city's populace and the constancy and respect among the communities well enough to write it into her "Monsieur Motte," in which a formerly enslaved woman secretly finances the schooling of the child of her previous owners but hides the fact by creating an absent benefactor. King insisted that the source of the story was in the experience of people she knew or observed, and she wrote it contra Cable.

Her end-of-life memoir seems to suggest that first story came in one sitting following Gilder's dare, but she also claimed that at age ten she had asserted, "I want to be a writer!"[18] Were the latter so, Grace would have been deciding to write herself into history the year Union troops took New Orleans, 1862. When the path did appear, her head was already full of stories, "all ready to be written out," she later recollected. Grace King could now pursue her "inward hopes and dreams, the secret wish" of becoming a writer that she had previously kept for herself alone.[19]

By the time "Monsieur Motte" was completed, Charles Dudley Warner and Richard Watson Gilder had left the city, but Warner stayed in touch and was to return often to New Orleans to enjoy the hospitality of the "dear family at No 23."[20] He also knew how to make a woman feel special. Soon after leaving, he sent Grace "an engraving of myself that is to appear in Harper's next fall. It is against the rules of the house to let such things go out in advance of publication. I send it therefore on the understanding that you are not to show it—but keep it to yourself—until it appears in the magazine."[21]

17. The Kings had an easy familiarity with skilled, French-speaking plantation workers and "an affable way" with house servants (*Memories,* 86) but used the epithet "nigger" (in quotations) for profligate men and women who committed obvious breaches of propriety and morality.

18. *Memories,* 48.

19. Ibid., 66.

20. Charles Dudley Warner to Grace, May 2, 1885. Hereafter, Warner.

21. Warner to Grace, May 7, 1885.

Thus began a flirtatious correspondence between a man-about-town and an admiring novitiate. Grace had had one long-past eager young suitor in New Orleans whose ardor her mother had cooled,[22] but Warner was a sophisticated man of her own choosing whose tales of travel lifted Grace right out of her tedious life. She wrote May: "When I see how beautifully he writes, I am quite aghast at my great familiarity with him. In one respect, I was more intimate with him than with any man in my life before—& he declared, that he never would believe that in three weeks he could have become so attached to a stranger as to grieve for days over the prospect of a separation."[23] When Warner began to sign his letters "your affectionate friend," Grace was enthralled. His encouragement gave her confidence; his books and articles inspired her.

The writing did not come easily, however, and Grace was not buoyed by her own talent. But fellow "Pans," club members Henry Austin and George C. Préot,[24] recognized the promise in her prose. Austin, a newspaperman from Boston, spent nearly all day going over "Heroines of Novels" with Grace. She wrote May that they went "page by page—a most fatiguing process—I assure you—but he was so friendly & nice that I bore up and actually got accustomed to hear my sentences read over five or six times with different intonations in order to fix the punctuation—which with me is you know a matter of mere guess-work." She used the pseudonym "P. G." on the piece, presumably for the Pan Gnostics. It would be a while yet before she used her own name, a bold move for her time, but her desire for fame and her business sense were already evident. She was thrilled that Austin told her she "ought easily to make from \$300–\$450 a year writing—& for me to keep right on,"[25] but she was distressed when he "mutilated" her first piece by compressing it for publication in the *Times-Democrat.* Tampering with her work would be a common complaint for Grace throughout her writing life, but her sponsors were generous with

22. Garret Walker had wanted to marry nineteen-year-old Grace King, but her mother urged them to wait two years. He knew that her mind was already divided between accommodating societal expectations and following her own star (Garret to Grace, n.d., 1871). His last letter to King was near his forty-first birthday, in which he congratulates himself that fifteen years earlier he knew she would gain public acclaim (Garret to Grace, January 3, 1887).

23. Grace to May, May 7?, 1885.

24. Information on Henry Austin is limited to King's comments; George Covington Préot (1855–1901) was a New Orleans writer and notary.

25. Grace to May, May 24, 1885.

assistance. Judge Gayarré had imbued her with his love of Louisiana history, but George Préot, a local writer and a notary in Civil Court, was a hands-on supporter of her early career.

GRACE TO MAY

New Orleans, June 13, 1885

[. . .] I wrote a thing for the paper last week. I don't know whether they will accept it or not. I was in doubts about it—& then I enclosed it to Preot—begging his candid opinion. He came and spent a nice long evening, pointing out the faults & telling me how to get rid of them—faults in style & expression; & told me to be sure & send it to the T D. He says he wants to see my style in a story, because he has a beautiful plot, & is looking for a collaborator—& may-be I will do. We had a great deal of fun about it—I am grinding away for dear life—but it is the hardest work I ever undertook—Of course it is fascinating—& I almost fall on my desk with weariness—& I get so discouraged that I could commit suicide—but still, as long as I see the prospect of a dollar at the end—I shall keep on [. . .] kiss yourself in the glass for me—

Your ever loving & devoted Sis.

My piece is called "Grown folks' playthings" syn. G. Bane—in today's paper. The title I don't like but it was Preot's choosing.

When Grace finished the "little Creole story I commenced last winter," she also submitted that to Préot.[26] Letters show her path was more fraught than her memoir suggested. Her courage lagged, so she studied French novels—she couldn't stand American ones—"to see if I can't win some of their charm of style without their naughtiness."[27] Préot suggested she send the story to Gilder at *Century Magazine,* but she did so "under a most elaborately contrived incognita,"[28] and it was rejected. Then he encouraged her to send it to Warner, who had taken her ambition seriously.

26. Ibid.
27. Grace to May, July 14, 1885.
28. Grace to May, August 14, 1885.

The letters between Grace and Warner had already become increasingly familiar and audacious. She liked his portrayals of her South. She called him "the good Warner" for his favorable writings about the region and for his attentiveness to her. He sent her articles and seven books "all beautifully bound." His continuous travel fanned her desire to flee. "Not that I think it is so indispensable to travel," Grace wrote her touchstone, May, but "I can tell you there's a very thin thread holding me in New Orleans." She was "resigned as a Turk"[29] to make a success of writing but was often in "utter despair," fearing that her "brilliant career should be cut off so short but had resigned myself—to a future as nurse in a hospital. But last night I took a good drink of brandy which made me sleep deliciously sound; so today I am all OK, except my hand-writing which is still in a depraved dissolute condition."[30] She gave herself a deadline.

GRACE TO MAY

New Orleans, September 1, 1885

> [. . .] My little story was returned most promptly—and now I have it under consideration—in odd moments I wonder what I shall do with it—If it were not for the money, I would just keep it by me—and work on quietly—until some day I should strike the public fancy, and then the rejected article would find a value—I have about made up my mind that this was not a taking subject—[. . .] This morning, instead of polishing up another one I had on hand—I put it by and started out on a third I had thought of, quite different in tone and style—I have fixed the 1st of November as the term of my experiment—

Sitting idly by was not Grace King's style; like other members of her family, she was keenly aware of which friendships were worth cultivating. Details gathered in one moment might be useful later; kindnesses expended would be repaid. Grace combined flattery with a request that Warner critique her first story. Her boasts of their closeness might worry her youngest sister, Nina, who objected "to the words love and affection from a married man to an unmarried woman,"[31] but he could offer personal and career enhancement. That was no small thing.

29. Grace to May, July 26, 1885.

30. Grace to May, August 21, 1885.

31. Grace to May, September 8, 1885.

☙ GRACE TO CHARLES DUDLEY WARNER

New Orleans, September 9, 1885
23 Rampart Street, South

You see, I lose no time in answering your letter although I wrote to you only Saturday. As usual you are most kind, too kind to me; and I feel that I can tell you freely all that you want to know, not that it is worth knowing but to show you, that I trust in your affection. [. . .] I tried my hand at a little story[32]—an incident of my own school life—but one that is common in almost every one here. My Mentor kept it some time; made a few corrections and then coolly proposed my sending it to you—for your opinion. This, I felt would be a great humiliation; a kind of stripping. I eluded my engagement until very nearly the last evening—when I read a very rude composition "Heroines of Novels"—The young men were kind enough to make a fuss over me and playfully seized my manuscript and carried it away—Most of them contributed to the Times Democrat—They asked if they might publish it. I refused. I dislike "newspaper" women so much. One of them—our only married member, a good friend of my family—a notary public whose relations with us gave him the knowledge and right to advise; came to me and said I had better perhaps not lose any opportunity of the kind; that I might in the future need some such opening etc etc—

Now my dear friend, you see my confidence to you, has to break through the reserve which we have rigidly maintained towards the people here about our private affairs. The notary is only too correct, I cannot afford to miss any opportunity which may throw any light on my present prospectless future. [. . .]

Flare-ups in the family intensified Grace's immediate "prospectless future," and her youngest brother drove "the very last impulse I needed to my desire to be independent," she wrote May. Only Warner's favorable "verdict" would "extricate" her from the "horribly embarrassing position" that Will's irresponsibility and drinking imposed. "As far as I personally am concerned I would be willing to go out with out speaking to or meeting my family for the rest of my life, if thereby they would only be goaded into working and improving themselves,"

32. The story was "Monsieur Motte."

she added. "Who knows! perhaps, one of these days, I shall wear pretty dresses, and be able to play on the piano (of course music is out of the question in these mental excitements) and read, and write and lead a harmonious life, according to my own ethics."[33] And then there was hope.

GRACE TO WARNER

New Orleans, September 17, 1885

> I felt like a young lady in a novel when your letter came to day and *almost* hesitated to open it. Confessions of poverty, both of pocket and intellect, are not pleasant food for recollection—[. . .] You see, I wanted you to know frankly all I had done in the way of writing—bad, as well or more particularly than good.—I am thankful the exposé is over. Now, don't you worry about Monsieur Motte—if no one else finds it good I shall be satisfied with your opinion and my own endeavor to call attention at least to some of those relations brought on by slavery, honorable to all concerned. It seems to me, white as well as black women have a sad showing in what some people call romance. I am very tired, and I should think others are too, of these local stories, but as I recollect little things, I think I shall try and write them—if no one else does it better, one of these days they may prove a pleasant record and serve to bring us all nearer together blacks and whites.[34]

Grace's stories about postbellum struggles and close ties among women became her literary niche. Before long she would glimpse the life she sought, and Warner was the key.

33. Grace to May, September 13?, 1885.

34. King thought she was giving an accurate, realistic picture, and that is how her stories were first received, especially in the South. Local color stories eventually fell out of favor, and her own southern biases also later damaged her reputation.

CHAPTER I

THE PATH, 1885–1886

[Y]ou have at last found the path of life you have looked for so long.

—MAY TO GRACE, NOVEMBER 8, 1886

WARNER TO GRACE

New York, September 29, 1885, 11 PM

UNIVERSITY CLUB

MADISON SQUARE

I'm going to throw myself on your mercy, my dear friend, for I've taken a great liberty with your genius and your prospects in life. You must know that I took your Monsieur Motte down to the Harpers over a week ago. Mr Alden was absent. [. . .][1] On Saturday Prof Sloane of Princeton came to see me.[2] He is one of my dearest friends, a delightful man of the world and one of the most accomplished scholars in the country. [. . .] [I]n July it was decided, with capital behind it to start in January the "New Princeton Review." [. . .] Every number is to have a strong political paper, a good book review, a philosophical article, [. . .] a short story (or a novel not to run more than two or three months) and crisp editorial comments. [. . .] He wanted a paper on "Society in the New South", [. . .] he said that he was in a search for a story, [. . .] I told him that I had a story of such and such a character which might answer, but that I had left it at Harper's. I went down, [. . .] and as Alden had not yet returned I took the story away. Sloane had it that afternoon and liked it, [. . .] asked if he would be

1. Warner's handwriting is almost indecipherable, thus the abundance of ellipses. Henry Mills Alden (1836–1919) became King's editor at *Harper's.*

2. William Mulligan Sloane (1850–1928), educator and historian and editor of the *New Princeton Review,* published King's first story.

at liberty to make slight changes—I told him that he might do any thing he pleased that did not affect the substance and effect. He took it home yesterday afternoon but I have just received this telegram from him: "Will keep story and make necessary changes especially shorten introduction"

I shall have to apologize to Alden for having taken it away without telling him. [. . .]

Ever yours affectionately
C. D. W.

GRACE TO WARNER

23 Rampart Street, South
New Orleans, October 4, 1885

My dear Friend,
Your letter which came yesterday was an overwhelming surprise to me. I never dared hope that you would find others to reiterate your good opinion of Monsieur Motte. Undoubtedly it is a great honor to get in the new review, one which counterbalances for any pecuniary advantage possible elsewhere. You have indeed acted, not as a friend but a loving relation—and I hope to prove, for I cannot write it, my faithful love and gratitude to you—I am too much of a woman not to dwell more on the sentiment that you cared enough for me to take so much trouble—than on the immense practical advantage your intermediation has been to me.—I should on the contrary be better pleased if a critical hand should prune away any faults—such correctives would be of immense service to me; I am afraid of my English—and general criticisms are hard to apply with effect. I would not like any changes which would alter the pure disinterestedness of Marcelite's devotion—The friend I showed it to here wanted me to give a cause such as saving her from the auction block—but I feel this was gross and untrue to my own conception—Great instances of devotion were found among even the worst treated slaves. I love to dwell on this, which I would call, holy passion of the negro women, for it serves to cancel those other grosser ones, with which they are really victimized by their blood. And besides, I think it highly honorable to the Southern women that they could be so served and loved by slaves. Do you

> recollect how finely Goethe puts it? "Fidelity in this case is the effort of a noble soul struggling to become equal with one exalted above it." I hope the closing sentence will come under the knife—I wanted to end it with a "bel phrase"—but it seemed impossible to think of one that suited me; it sounds sectional to me.

And then, in the same letter, Grace complicated matters with a blunt stance:

> Your Republican party has such an aggravating way of grabbing for political capital any recognition on the part of us Southerners of even the humanity of the negroes, that one fears to speak his heart about such things—This is all I am afraid of in your "Society" article. If one could only write of our social customs without dragging in those everlasting colored teachers—and negro grievances. But you have an excellent foil in Cable's venomous articles—Oh! such gossip as I could tell you of George Washington C—if you were a woman, but men are so peculiar they do not like to hear things about their friends.[3]

She expressed her yearning and issued a challenge to Warner that perhaps prompted the later invitation to Hartford:

> May I tell you that your last "Drawer" was exquisite?[4] "The sweet invitations of companionship, congenial tastes and orange blossoms" is so delicious and so like you. I enjoyed the description of Hartford immensely—What a delightful abode it must be—for Hartford people—all clean and nice and rich and good. I looked at your house with a sigh, and a feeling that I never would be "correct" enough for your good Puritan townspeople. What great friends Mrs Stowe and the Gatling

3. This gossip about Cable implies a possible involvement with a woman of color, as was acknowledged of Charles Gayarré. (About Gayarré, see Rien Fertel, *Imagining the Creole City: The Rise of Literary Culture in Nineteenth-Century New Orleans* [Baton Rouge: Louisiana State University Press, 2014], 92–93.)

4. "Editor's Drawer" was Warner's regular column in *Harper's Magazine.*

gun folks ought to be![5] It was a great relief to me that it was Mark Twain not you who indulged in a bust.[6] I long for you so, well, about once a week—there are so many little things being said not worth the writing, but so amusing, the listening. [. . .]

Your's affectionately
G. E. K.

WARNER TO GRACE
Hartford, October 9, 1885

Your long, lovely, most entertaining letter, my friend, would repay any one for a little service. I have found out something and it has made me a very selfish person. Won't you know there is no pleasure in life equal to that of doing something, however little, for those we are fond of? [. . .] [Y]our paper made its own way when it fell into hands that paid attention to it—and it was wise luck that Prof. Sloane wanted a story of about that length. [. . .] He will have to shorten the introduction a good deal and trim it in other places. [. . .] I think it will be published anonymously—it will excite more interest. [. . .] [I]f you do another, we will see what the Harper's say to it.

A second one also should be a southern story, Warner postulated, with as good a motif as "Monsieur Motte," for such stories were "hard to find." Grace took direction well, but the actual writing was difficult. She wrote May that she was "still shut up pegging away at my writing—I have just finished the last line—and in an hour or two, when my hand gets rested will commence the copy for Préot. I haven't read any thing since Sunday, except my own story—which I am sure I know by heart, having copied it over at least six times."[7] Although

5. The Colt family of Hartford had bought the patents for the machine gun from Richard Gatling. King seems to suggest that both the gun-makers and Harriet Beecher Stowe were killers of a culture.

6. Apparently, King considered it unseemly to sit for a bust, but in this case, Twain might simply have been encouraging the career of his protégé Karl Gerhardt. A photo of the bust is the frontispiece of *Huckleberry Finn* (1885).

7. Grace to May, October 5, 1885.

changes would be necessary, Warner had reminded Grace to "keep your own peculiarities of style."

WARNER TO GRACE

Hartford, November 12, 1885

Prof. Sloane said the other day in New York, that he got your address to forward the proofs. He said "you didn't know and I didn't know how good that story was it is much, much better than we thought. I like it immensely, and you will. I have had to cut it down in order to get it in a magazine, & I am very sorry. [. . .] But it had to be done." [. . .] Sloane really felt very badly to sacrifice any of it, but in making up the first number, variety had to be insisted on. [. . .] And now I must tell you another thing to bring down your ride. Sloane did say, and I repeat it honestly for your benefit, that it was strange that a woman of your genius did not write better English.[8]

In addition, Grace had a lot to learn about the business of publishing. When proofs of her story arrived, she did not know what they were or what to do with them. Warner also guided her into that world of her profession.

GRACE TO WARNER

New Orleans, November 14, 1885
23 Rampart Street, South

I had not the slightest idea of writing you a letter—but just now, when I was at my busiest (a white silk dress) a bundle of stuff was handed me labeled "Proof Sheets and Copy"—It nearly frightened me to death. And now I am puzzled to know if there are any responsive duties connected with it. I would not for the world ask you to write me, but if you have got a clerk about who could tell me if I am expected to do or say anything about this queer looking bundle. Any little old mean cheap kind of clerk would do.

8. Perhaps King's syntax was the problem, ensuing from her French education.

Literature is a very complicated affair evidently. Is there any work published on the subject which I could get and read?

Yours in great haste,
Grace E King.

I don't think it's at all nice to have one's servant initiated into one's affairs this way. You literary people have no sort of modesty.

WARNER TO GRACE

Hartford, November 16, 1885

Why you dear innocent little thing. You are to read this "proof" of your story and *correct it* and send it right back to the address given you *immediately*. The printers are waiting for it. The "copy" (your own MS.) you can keep. Prof. Sloane telegraphed me for your address in order to send you this "proof," so that you can see if it is all right and as you wish to have it appear in the magazine. As I suppose you do not know how to read and correct proof, go at once to some printer or proof reader—some person you know in one of the newspapers and have him show you how. You will have to learn how to correct proof yourself. In Webster's unabridged, I think, is a form for correcting proof.

It makes me laff, to know how nice and uninitiated you are. Don't delay an hour in "correcting" the proof and returning it. You have the printer's address on the cover. If you want to write or make any suggestions about it, write to Prof. Wm. M. Sloane, Princeton, New Jersey.

You are a dear child, all the same, and I am so far from being proof against you that I am Yours affectionately

C. D. W.

GRACE TO WARNER

New Orleans, Sunday Night, November 22, 1885[9]
23 Rampart Street, South

9. A short excerpt of this letter appears in Robert Bush, *Grace King of New Orleans: A Selection of Her Writings* (Baton Rouge: Louisiana State University Press, 1973), 379. Hereafter, *GK of NO.*

Did I appear like a very great simpleton? But I assure you they were the first proof sheets I ever saw in my life. If you only knew how much trouble I have over little trifles that you could explain away in five minutes! However, after my note to you I thought of my friend who had read the story in MS; he came to my assistance a little, but I did not venture to return it until I got your note. I write any suggestions to the high and mighty Sloane!

You must think me brave,—no sir! If he likes to cut a story in two at such a sentence as: "My God! I never thought of that," he can. It seems to me a notice promising new and startling developments in the next would have answered his purpose better. No denouement in the wide world will satisfy the expectations raised by that sensational exclamation. It was a martyrdom for me to read it over, it is so wretchedly inferior to my idea, I begin to think it is not good enough for the Magazine. Sloane is perfectly right about my English, I am ashamed of some of the corrections made. I am not sanguine about ever writing better, but you were right to stand up for me as you did. You are a good, good, friend and I love you very dearly for all your kindness. The only vocation I feel, is the desire to show you that a Southerner and a white person is not ashamed to acknowledge a dependence on negroes—nor to proclaim the love that exists between the two races, a love, which in the end will destroy all differences in color; or rather—I had better say—that that love, is the only thing which can do it.—Wouldn't Sloane squirm at my letters?

May I send you another little one, when you have time to read it, and I to copy it?

GRACE TO WARNER

New Orleans, December 6, 1885
23 Rampart Street, South

Now I want simply to ask you how I was to know that the editorial mind had changed and that I was not to be brutally divided asunder. The second installment of proof conveyed no such meaning to my unpractised eye and it was not corrected and sent back as you fondly hoped, until after the arrival of your note. I try to do every thing you tell me. You said:

"learn to correct proof yourself," I thought, with two months ahead of me, I could do it nicely; but I tell you I got it off in a hurry when your inspired epistle came to me. Thank you so much for writing that particular time. I see I shall have to employ a clairvoyante to help me penetrate the occult mysteries that envelop the literary world. My unaided faculties are useless.

The *New Princeton Review* published "Monsieur Motte" in its first issue, January 1886, in which Warner's "Society in the New South" was the lead essay. King's story ran without attribution; her "anonymity was strictly guarded" for a year, she wrote later in *Memories.*[10] However, New Orleanians were too excited to keep her secret, and when her first check arrived, King was also smitten with the possibility of a career in literature. Her family placed no demands for her to contribute to the household, but she proudly paid some lingering bills with her first money and bought souvenirs all around to celebrate her newfound independence. The Kings' favorite store, D. H. Holmes, had recently demanded payment of the family's debt, so the check arrived at a good time.

☙ GRACE TO MAY

New Orleans, Tuesday, December 22, 1885

My dear old Partner,

[. . .] $150.! isnt' it grand.[11] In moments of great exultation, I dared hope that it might be $100, but generally I fell down from $75. to $50 and would have sold out for $30. I was dressed to go out when the letter came—from Lathrop & Son—the publishers of the review—I tore it open with real excitement, and when I read out the check, payable to Grace King for $150, for "Monsieur Motte"—a great calm seemed to fall on us all. Nan & I of course got weak, Nina maintained her equilibrium and commenced immediately to advise me how to spend it. Nan's first exclamation was "And they say that literature doesn't pay!"

10. *Memories,* 65.

11. This amount, $150 in 1885, would be worth almost $3,800 today, according to the Inflation Calculator from the Bureau of Labor Statistics, the source of all calculations herein.

A path to autonomy began to appear.

The enthusiastic response to "Monsieur Motte" brought intimations of fame for its anonymous author. For Grace King, the story's publication promised financial autonomy, fanning her aspirations and igniting her business savvy. "Now that I see how long it takes to get money for a story—I want to try and get one off every three or four months," she wrote May.[12] She noted that a second tale could bring "another $150. in the Spring."[13] Grace had not been satisfied with the first story's ending, but Warner quoted positive reviews from five papers, including the *New York Times, Tribune, and Post* (which attributed the story to Cable). He assured her that "Monsieur Motte" had pleased his friends, including Olivia Clemens.

☙ GRACE TO MAY

New Orleans, January 9, 1886
[quoting from Warner to Grace, January 5, 1886]

All of my friends who have read it are thoroughly charmed with it, think it very strong, vigorous, pathetic and wonderful in giving pictures with a few strokes of the pen. Mrs Warner thinks this, and Miss Fanny Baylor[14] and Mrs Clemens (Mark Twain's wife) and they are all good judges of this sort of thing. I am more than satisfied with it—it only needs to be read to give you instant recognition.

☙ GRACE TO WARNER

New Orleans, January 10, 1886[15]
23 Rampart Street, South

The "Courant" came on Friday and—well, I can't tell you *all* my feelings only the principal ones which rushed straight to Hartford in search of you—and they are still there for you won't give me time to bring them

12. Grace to May, January 11?, 1886.
13. Grace to May, January 6, 1886.
14. Pseudonym of the American writer Fanny Courtnay Baylor.
15. The letter was erroneously dated 1885.

home again—You are so constantly kind to me.—Your letter yesterday frightened me into a long forgotten trick of shyness. I don't know what to say or how much to believe. I would be afraid that you were laughing at me, if I did not feel so sure of your good heart. [. . .]

Do you remember, I wrote to you that I hoped Sloane would strike out that last sentence. I didn't like it, only put it in temporarily until the thing that could be said would come to me, but Mr Preot didn't understand my objections to it—You didn't notice it—and the critical Sloane let it pass, so I ceased to think about it—but whenever I did, I winced over it. I should have had self confidence enough to trust my own judgment; [. . .] I am only so sorry that it comes too late to do this story any good. The truth is, that I am naturally timid and have been found fault with a good deal—and so have little confidence in my own opinions.

GRACE TO WARNER

New Orleans, January 14, 1886[16]

[. . .] It is presumptuous for me to give you my opinion of your work—but you must remember that you were only born, for me, last year and I can't help ignoring your long brilliant reputation made before I knew you.

I admire so many writers, but so few men—and its to the man in you, that my heart goes out when I read such articles. I suppose you get thousands of letters just like this.—

[. . .] I send you my little story.[17] I am not at all sure you or any one will like it, but you must read it, all the same for it is as true a circumstance as the other. It was a twin idea with the other, to do feeble justice to another form of devotion that almost every one of us has experienced from negro women. [. . .]

You are so good to me.
Affectionately G E K

16. The letter was erroneously dated January 14, 1885.

17. "Bonne Maman."

☙ GRACE TO WARNER

New Orleans, January 20, 1886[18]
23 Rampart Street, South

My dear friend—
[. . .] Every letter you write me, converts me from a scoffing skeptic into a very grateful touched little body indeed—However—I see self consciousness yawning like a gulf before me—so I beg you (in all seriousness) not to tell me any more nice things any body says—They only say them to please you any how—I am in great hopes about your finding proper fault since you did criticize the last line in Monsieur Motte—The publicity of the thing is what I most dread. If you really knew how much I hated it you would really know how much I have to be grateful for to you. The little thing I sent yesterday was written so entirely for you (because I think you sympathize with our dreadful struggles after the war) that if you think proper for it never to go out of your hands except into the fire I would not care. I am beginning already to forget the vexation I had over it. [. . .]

G E K.

Warner's response to Grace's new story, "Bonne Maman," was: "Story received, read, like, but not quite as well as other." Sloane liked it but did not want anything until fall, so Warner promised to offer it to *Harper's Magazine.* "He criticized it a good deal and said that the first part must be reworked," Grace wrote May about Warner's response.[19] Perhaps he referred to the atmospheric, mythical, sensory, and ambiguous qualities: "He keeps warning me about—indistinctness, and what he calls 'a glamourous use of words'"—the truth of the matter is I work too hard in the dark, and my mind is too seldom fine to apply it wholly to my work. I allow my attention to stray off from my subject."[20]

Nevertheless, acclaim for the writer of "Monsieur Motte" kept her "in a whirl." She received a check from *Harper's* for $150 for "Bonne Maman," yet to be published. Also, a letter arrived "from Armstrong & Son asking to be my

18. The letter was erroneously dated 1885.

19. Grace to May, January 31, 1886.

20. Grace to May, n.d., perhaps late January 1886.

publisher in case I wanted to print in book form," and Warner made a welcome visit to New Orleans. This was heady matter for a neophyte.

☙ GRACE TO MAY

New Orleans, February 10, 1886

> [. . .] He came about ten OC and after the first effusive greetings began to talk business. Alden had never read M: Motte but took "Bonne Maman" on its own merits. He was pleased with it, but insisted on certain corrections which he would facilitate by sending a printed copy; a great favor, one not usually accorded—he wishes to secure me entirely for Harper, but Warner told me not to bother about it at all—but fix my attention on my stories—and the rest would come along quite naturally. He also is to take upon himself the selecting of a Pseudonym—which the Harper's want—they will not publish it "by the author of M: Motte" as the Princeton would—and I decidedly will not allow the "Grace King" which Warner persists is an ideal name for a writer. He mentioned that I must quietly resolve the possibility of continuing—M: Motte making say four more numbers—each one containing the exact duration of time as the first one—forty eight hours—I think it's a splendid suggestion, the Princeton would take them—at the end they would form quite a nice volume which if it were successful would be immensely profitable. Doesn't it sound fine? I think it is very feasible. To day I received a letter from Sloane about it—I enclose it to you: This is to be kept a profound secret—Warner pointed out on my rough copy today, the obscurities which Alden told him about, and showed me the proper way of correcting them.[21]

The second check allowed Grace to treat her mother to a trip to visit May in North Carolina instead of Mimi having to ask older brother Branch for money: "Now I can give it to her—It gives me the greatest of all pleasures to be able to do this." Grace stayed behind, agreeing with Warner "that for the present I must remain in this one locality."[22]

21. King did write three more stories, later published in book form as *Monsieur Motte* (Macmillan, 1888).

22. Grace to May, February 10, 1886.

In April 1886, Warner returned to New Orleans again. He took daily lunch with the Kings. He supplied the mint juleps—"a piece of dissipation that has proved very beneficial to us all, physically & mentally"—smoked his cigars, and "discovered a passion for Cherry-bounce." He went carefully over the proofs of the story "Bonne Maman" with Grace, and she helped him "look over a huge pile of contributions to the 'Drawer' and arrange his mass of correspondence. I am going to answer a good many letters for him," an intimate act that she confided to May.[23]

GRACE TO MIMI
New Orleans, April 17, 1886

I have at last got my little story off. It was very trying, going over it with Warner. He was so determined to root out any and all faults or danger of faults. I wrote a great deal of it over again. He doesn't like it because it's different from the first, but he says it has great merit. It won't come out for five or six months and that's a comfort, if people are going, like W, to compare it unfavorably with M Motte.

[. . .] [F]rom what Warner says, I can make plenty of money as soon as I get to work again, and all this is really a preparation for work, and a preparation of the best kind.

And then Warner was gone.

GRACE TO MAY
New Orleans, May 3, 1886

Warner got me so screwed up with advice and admonition that I started to work bright and early Saturday morning with reading and writing. [. . .] He has little doubt that I can sell every thing I write—if only I take care to write it well—[. . .] Yes, Warner is a love of a man it's a great mistake that he is married—but he would have been a Bluebeard for wives if they had died of[f] in time, his fascinations are quite innumerable.

23. Grace to May, April 6, 1886.

Grace regularly used May as a sounding board as she fashioned her writing self, refined her themes, and bemoaned the uncertainties of her literary life. She took grammar lessons; she thrashed about for models and, given her education, was instinctively drawn to the French.

GRACE TO MAY

New Orleans, May 28, 1886

[. . .] As French stories are my modes—I must restrict myself to them—I have been working at the continuation of Monsieur—just to see what I could do with the old material. As usual I am very confident about it—I have always too much confidence at first—and too little afterwards. If I finish it by August I shall be satisfied; but I see lots of work at it.

GRACE TO MAY

New Orleans, June 10, 1886

[. . .] I shall finish it by the 1st of July and then lay it by a week or so before copying it—I am in a terrible panic about the Harper story. I am afraid that people will misunderstand it—It is another view of the same everlasting darkey character, but I wanted to describe the situation of whites and blacks after the war—and give a hint as to the position of Cable's beautiful quadroons here. People at the North generally made so much money by the war that they never understood how the people at the South, the women particularly suffered—[. . .]

Lovingly *Sis*

GRACE TO MAY

New Orleans, Sunday Morning [June? 1886]

[. . .] I have been plodding away at my reading—but somehow, I don't feel as if it were doing me any good; perhaps I am too impatient. I am going to commence the continuation of M Motte, right off, and "May the Lord have mercy on my soul"—I feel confident that my fate will be to disappoint every one with my second performances—My essay last night I am sure was not considered as good as Heroines—"Bonne Maman," Warner does not like as well as Motte—& the second chapter of Motte will be inferior to the 1st and so on. You ought to thank Heaven that you were made to marry instead of to write. [. . .]

Your own loving Sis.

WARNER TO GRACE

Hartford, June 23, 1886

[. . .] Every body whom I have seen who has read it likes it exceedingly, and good judges, also they are. You have a style of your own, a real Grace King flavor, and that is a rare and immense distinction, no body who read this and did not know your name before, will think this was a story by the author of M. Motte. So you see that you are recognized and have something of your own. [. . .]

Warner was complimenting Grace's distinct style and subject matter, and he would continue to do so. She wrote May that "Mr Warner was afraid I would get vain from compliments—but I honestly think I need all the encouragement I can get."[24] As if to confirm the mounting interest in her stories, additional publishers began to court her, including McClure, Henry Holt, and editors of a "Literary Encyclopedia." *Harper's* wanted to include her in a "short notice of ten of the new Southern writers." Noting the value of inclusion, Grace declared to May: "Of course I don't believe in advertising & I consider this advertising but I couldn't afford to be left out such a list, so I will only go in after they have got permission of the others."[25] Her business reflexes were good even as she strove to retain a veneer of gentility by standing back. She accepted some offers and refused others.

Despite praise, King struggled for confidence and sought guidance from

24. Grace to May, July 1, 1886.

25. Grace to May, August 25, 1886. King was featured second after George Washington Cable in *Harper's Magazine* 74 (May 1887): 837–55. Others included with portraits were R. M. Johnston, Joel Chandler Harris, Thomas N. Page, Charles Egbert Craddock (Mary Noailles Murphree), M. G. McClelland, Frances Courtnay Baylor, Julia Magruder, Amélie Rives, Lafcadio Hearn, and Robert Burns Wilson. Other writers received brief mentions.

literature and her trusted friends. She pledged to herself to study all of Tolstoy for his "perfect knowledge of human nature and his perfect art in representing it—the real and the ideal sides of it" and to "go through the whole Russian repertoire—and train my eyes as much as possible after their manner of looking at things."[26] She was grateful to Madame Marie D. Girard, her former French teacher, who pointed out some faulty French phrases in "Monsieur Motte."[27] However, the writing life was lonely, she discovered, while wrestling to get that "vexatious 'Madame Lareveillère' off my hands," the protagonist in the second part of *Monsieur Motte*.[28] May, however, was "perfectly delighted & charmed" with the story, noting its "steady improvement" over the first and thinking "the refinement & polish" wonderful.[29]

☙ GRACE TO MAY

New Orleans, September 27, 1886

My poor old Darling,

[...] Sometimes I think life is harder to me now than it ever was, it certainly has more self denial in it. I haven't heard from Warner yet about my last story, and while I am waiting I find it almost impossible to concentrate my mind on the next—I got another communication from a publisher asking for my terms—If I only felt more inspiration, & could write more, I wouldn't need to be such a stay at home. [...]

I am your same loving old Sis

☙ GRACE TO MAY

New Orleans, Thursday, November 4, 1886

[...] When I came up stairs I found letters from you and Warner—and at last I have got Sloane's opinion about my last. He, according to W is enthusiastic over it, says it is "literature" and an exquisite "genre" picture. I

26. Grace to May, August 25, 1886.

27. Grace to May, August 11, 1886. King later honored her in *Madame Girard: An Old French Teacher of New Orleans* (1922).

28. Grace to May, September 8, 1886.

29. May to Grace, November 8, 1886.

am so relieved the suspense about it almost killed me, and discouraged me from the thing I am on. Warner said that the Harper article on the Southern writers was taking shape—he says that I cannot prevent them putting me in if they want, that what I have written is public property—that the only question is about the picture, and for his part he is not ashamed of my "lovely" photograph—[. . .]

Ever devotedly Sis

Publishers might label her stories "genre," but King apparently considered them realistic. She insisted that she wrote from her own experience and her observation of people and scenes around her. She declared in her memoir that the Commencement Day scene in "Monsieur Motte" came straight from her school days at the old St. Louis Institut, where its head, Madame Lavillebeuvre, was the model for Madame Lareveillière and that she had taken the quadroon woman Marcelite from life.[30] One thing was sure: whether told from within the sensual walls of a convent school or in the steamy shed of sugar production, as in the second part of "Monsieur Motte," this writer knew her territory. Her strong sense of place was incontestable. Therefore, King's neighbors and friends trusted her to write the Creole life more justly than Cable had done, and they graced her with their own precious sources. One Eloche T. Proctor wrote a letter of introduction to Madame St. Michel at the old Ursuline Convent to help Grace in the "search of very interesting subjects for your 'petites nouvelles.'"

☙ ELOCHE T. PROCTOR TO MADAME ST. MICHEL

New Orleans, December 26, 1886

[. . .] Miss King is one of our elegant writers, and will, I know appreciate your establishment,—as we creoles think of it, and like to hear its praises by writers of her ability and popularity.

I would like her to be able to write the whole history of a school,[31] where so many of our creole ladies who are now, the ornaments of many

30. *Memories,* 61.

31. The convent was near Poland Avenue from the 1820s to 1912, when the nuns moved to State Street in New Orleans. The old convent was destroyed to make way for construction of the Industrial Canal that was dedicated in 1923.

homes in Europe were educated in arts, science, and deportment, I am too ill to write all I would like to say about this Lady, but I know you will appreciate her immediately.

With much love and affectionate remembrance to all the ladies.
I am truly yours
Eloche T. Proctor
359 St Charles Avenue

In the accompanying letter to Grace about the convent, Proctor advised that she should also seek out the daughter of Marie Laveau, the renowned queen of voodoo:

PROCTOR TO GRACE
New Orleans, December 26, 1886

[. . .] The Convent is some 118 years old, the ladies are all very aristocratic in their ideas of refinement, and arts, and when you tell them in your sweet way your wishes I am sure they will tell you little interesting items of passed days. [. . .] I must beg of you, that my name should never be mentioned [. . .] we are a very retired people, [. . .] anti diluvian set—[. . .] Do try and see Marie Lavau's [*sic*] daughter on St Ann st. she is a very intelligent woman, and would say all she knows to try to defend her mother, she calls herself now, Madame Legendre. I expect she can tell you very very interesting things of old times, when these coloured ladies ruled the country, with their grace, and their dangerous proximity to the white ladies.[32]

Proctor's letters confirm Grace King's claim that her stories were taken from the life she knew around her, however biased was her lens.

32. Eloche T. Proctor refers to Marie Laveau, the queen of voodoo whom the Ursulines educated. Her daughter Madame Philomel Legendre was the only surviving child of fifteen children of Laveau and her second husband, Captain Christophe Dominique Glapion, as the *New York Times* told it on June 23, 1881. Glapion died on June 26, 1855; Laveau on June 21, 1881 (https://www.nola.com/haunted/index.ssf/2000/10/the_dead_voodoo_queen_the_new.html). Legendre was possibly the second woman known as "Marie Laveau." No evidence suggests whether or not King acted on the suggestion.

CHAPTER 2

TRAVELING NORTH, 1887

You will meet my favorite Mark Twain—
—MIMI TO GRACE, MAY 21?, 1887

Forces were now aligned to widen Grace King's world. In April 1887, Charles Dudley Warner passed through New Orleans once more, and King began to make plans to go to New York for business. Or to escape.[1] She claimed to be worn out by work and her brother Will's inexplicable actions. He was off on what he called "Mark Twain's Miss River" and wrote that a new friend claimed that Twain was "pretty tough to run with Bixby," but had then asserted that the author had not been a river pilot.[2] Will had borrowed money that the family had to repay, and he upset Mimi by threatening to go to sea. To help Grace's flight from her burdens, May and her husband, Brevard, offered to pay for a one-way ticket to Charlotte (about twenty-five dollars including sleeper) as a comfort stop on Grace's way to New York.[3] Then a splendid letter arrived.

SUSAN L. WARNER TO GRACE

New York, April 22, 1887

My dear Miss King,

My husband tells me that you are coming north before long. Now, when may we expect you to come to us for a good long visit? I am so delighted

1. King had never traveled alone, but she had visited Throg's Neck, New York, in 1876 and again in 1880 with the John Morris family.

2. Will to Grace, April [?], 1887.

3. May to Grace, April 16, 1887. Calculated in today's money, the twenty-five-dollar fare would be $663.17.

at the prospect of seeing you.—for I have known you so long. It is hardly spring here yet—and we had a big snow storm a week ago today. There is no dependence on our climate, so you must prepare to be disgusted on that point and you will leave your oasis behind you also. We have literally nothing but a few tolerable times. You will not wonder that my run-away, stay-away husband is so bewitched with your Garden city. I have been on a three day shopping expedition to town and am just this moment starting for the train.—So please forgive this hasty note and confusion.

my most cordially
yours
Susan L Warner

I haven't time now to thank you for your great loveliness to my Beloved but I appreciate it I assure you. S. L. W.

GRACE TO SUSAN L. WARNER

New Orleans. April 25, 1887
23 Rampart Street, South

My dear Mrs Warner,
Thank you so much for your cordial invitation to me. I wish that you knew something of our life "among the roses" here so that you could appreciate the full value of such an opportunity to change to a brisk, fresh climate.

I have gone through a week of such great anxiety and distress that I declared over and over again that the mere idea of going away was an impossibility; but your kind husband who is quite one of us in our family affairs insists that I must take a change of air or stop work. This is evident even to me, and so in thanking you, by letter, I am only anticipating thanking you in person for your ready cooperation in Mr Warner's charitable designs.

I hope to be able to tell you of the great good he has done our people here and of the love we all bear to him and though I fancy you must be tired of welcoming all the literary waifs he recruits in his travels, I beg that to me, your hospitality may be extended not as to a stranger, or literary foundling, but to one sincerely attached to you and yours by the dearest ties of gratitude.

Believe me Your's Sincerely and gratefully.
Grace King

Although Grace was usually fastidious about chaperones, apparently she and Warner traveled on the same train as far as Atlanta or perhaps to Charlotte arguing Yankee and southern positions. Her sister Nan wrote that "you & Mr Warner must have had one good long talk & settled finally the colored question. And by now you are in Charlotte."[4] Nan also announced that fan mail had dwindled since Grace departed but that "Bonne Maman" should reignite interest in her.[5] Grace had already observed the fluctuations of elation and disappointment in celebrity. "Fame is very evanescent," she had written Mimi.[6] Yet, Grace had also adopted her mother's code of "perseverance and determination," so she was not easily deterred.

MIMI TO GRACE

New Orleans, May 26, 1887

Dear Sissie—
[. . .] I cannot understand your self reproaches about your work—my dear child, could any one work harder, and attain better results—to be successful, you must have time to deliberate to think, and as the preachers say inwardly digest what you read, and above all, have health and strength—all this you are gaining. this summer the benefits of the quiet month you have passed with May, the pleasurable excitement, freedom from care—will be of the greatest advantage and in the winter, you will be in better spirits I hope—why you feel discouraged is a mystery to me. [. . .]

4. Nan to Grace, May 4?, 1887.

5. Nan to Grace, May 18, 1887.

6. Grace to Mimi, May 22, 1884. King was more prescient than she knew, given her shifting reputation over time.

I suppose you are busy preparing for your Hartford trip—and you are brave to start off into a nal terra icognita[7]—but then you know Mr Warner so well—it seems to me that I have known him all my life—he is so kind, so thoughtful so considerate I am sure that there could not be a man in all the wide world more true in his friendship—you have proved that. Mrs Warner from her face, I should think equally good—there can be no doubt of her sincerity—certainly no reason exists for her affecting an interest she does not feel—they can not fail to like you—so my dear child go with a light heart, be yourself, I know no more charming character—enjoy as much as you can the pleasure your own energy and talent has procured you—and come home to us, well in body and refreshed in mind—you will meet my favorite Mark Twain—do you remember how much your father enjoyed his Innocents—Branch says be sure & mention to Mark his acquaintance with his Cossett relations [. . .][8]

Lovingly
Mimi

And then Grace actually met the literary lion.

☙ GRACE TO NAN

Hartford, Sunday, June 5th 1887[9]

My own dear Nan,
I was so glad to get your letter yesterday—I have felt better ever since. I do not feel so much like a wanderer when correspondence is established and the letters come and go between me and home. I have been to church. Mr Twitchell, the great friend of the family here did not preach in his church,

7. Mimi probably means "into the unknown land," but she adds "nal," which is superfluous in the phrase.

8. Perhaps Branch refers to Henry La Cossitt, the proprietor of the *Hannibal Gazette,* where Twain was first apprenticed as a printer's devil.

9. A portion of this letter was previously published in Robert Bush, "Grace King and Mark Twain," *American Literature* 44, no. 1 (March 1972): 31–51. Hereafter, "GK and MT."

so Mr Warner took me to hear Mr or Dr. Edwin Parker—quite a celebrated Congregationalist preacher. The Congregationalists it seems have a great liberty of service and Mr Parker has adopted a very beautiful ritual containing the best things of the Episcopal and Presbyterian Churches. The music was grand and thoroughly religious. The church is not handsome, but massive, large and in good taste. The sermon was excellent in every respect. There were one or two very good things in it. "Every man believes something—there is no man with[out] a certain measure of belief—then let him confess that. He may not be able to accept all the creed, or all the thirty nine articles—but let him confess what he does and say simply 'Lord help thou our unbelief[']"—"Men are actually as much ashamed of confessing a belief as confessing sin"—They sang "Lead kindly light" beautifully.—The walk to church lay through the most rural part of Town—I am constantly coming on bits that remind me of nooks and corners in the park at Roncal.[10] Mr W showed me his old residence where he wrote "My Summer in the Garden"—& there was the garden too[11]—coming home we met Mark Twain—he walked along with us—and of course kept me giggling all the time. He talks just as he writes. He was animadverting on Sunday. "The most horrible detestable abominable day that ever was invented. All his life he had been trying to get rid of the Sundays. He was so glad to get to Chicago that time on Sunday—Cable went round Psalm singing in three churches & he played billiards till midnight in a saloon winning his agents money from him." He "pulls" his words just as Bixbey says and if you will drawl this ought ending to sample you will get the effect exactly.[12] His anecdotes are always a little risqué—Talking of some conceited person, he said that he felt like apply-

10. Roncal was the country home of Judge Charles Gayarré and wife near Osaka, Mississippi, where the King girls visited when young.

11. The house was at 133 Hawthorn Street, later the girlhood home of actress Katharine Hepburn from 1908 to 1917.

12. Will M. Clemens (apparently no relation) in *Mark Twain, the Story of His Life and Work* (San Francisco: [Will M.] Clemens Publishing Co., 1892), 34. He tells what must have been known: that steamboat captain Horace Ezra Bixby (1826–1912) asked Twain upon first meeting, "What makes you pull your words that way?" and Twain answered "I don't know, mister; you'll have to ask my ma. She pulls hern too. Ain't there some way that we can fix it, so that you'll teach me how to be er pilot?" (https://archive.org/stream/marklifeworkooclemrich/marklifework-ooclemrich_djvu.txt).

ing to him what Clapp said of Osgood the preacher. "He was waiting for a vacancy in the Trinity to apply for it"[13]—We came home and there was Mrs Warner in a beautiful new white flannel dress waiting lunch for us. We had cold roast beef, lobster salad,—tea chocolate & milk for lunch—all so exquisitely served! To night we take tea at the Clemens—Tuesday start on the visit to the Church's—Do exchange all letters with May, for I cant recollect whom I have told which—(Isn't that neat?) I am writing in my pretty room—You can almost see me if you look at the picture in the views of Hartford in the Insurance advertisement book—it is the room on the right side of the house—an octagon. From my window I can look out on a lovely little round pond, surrounded by magnificent trees in the centre of which a fountain is playing.—

Yesterday Mr Warner took me all over the magnificent white marble capitol. He is a commissioner to put up a statue to a "Hale" some revolutionary hero—who was hanged as a spy by the English. His last words were "I regret that I have only one life to give for my country."[14] This is engraved on the pedestal.—So Mr Warner had to go and it was quite convenient for him to take me. Carl Gerhart[15] the sculptor (a protégé of Mark Twain's) was standing by superintending the erection of the pedestal. I was introduced to him, as Mr Warner thinks he is going to be very celebrated some day. He is very small, slight, Creolish looking—not a promising face for genius I don't think—he winks and blinks his eyes continually, which set me off immediately to try and find out whom he looks like in N.O.—I saw the original charter which was hidden in the Charter Oak[16]—[. . .] The Capitol is situated in the centre of a beautiful park on the descent of a little hill—We walked home, and I installed myself in the hammock with a book to read; only of course I did not

13. This anecdote was apparently part of Twain's lexicon, telling about Henry Clapp, a witty New York Bohemian, who said this of Rev. Dr. Samuel Osgood, a pompous Park Avenue minister (*Mark Twain's Travels with Mr. Brown* [New York: Knopf, 1940], 276).

14. Nathan Hale (1755–1776) was a spy for the Continental Army during the Revolutionary War whom the British captured and hanged. Surprisingly, Grace King seems unfamiliar with this historic figure and his famous declaration.

15. Karl Gerhardt (1853–1940). Twain commissioned him in 1884 to make a medallion of himself and George Washington Cable for their tour.

16. According to tradition, the Royal Charter of 1662 was hidden in a hollow in Connecticut's largest oak for safekeeping and away from England's governor-general.

read, only lay back and looked at the trees and thought and thought. Mr Warner brought down a very pretty letter from Placide Canonge for me to translate for him.[17] I was deep in it, when I heard a sort of half-scream, half ejaculation. "Who! Who! Who is that?" I believe I would have been frightened to death if Mr Warner hadn't been there. Of course he knew it was Mrs Stowe. She is always wandering around under the trees, picking wild flowers—She thought of course I was Mrs Warner. She left a bunch of wild flowers for her and hurried away without stopping—repeating "I must go, I must go!" Her mind is so feeble that at times she is idiotic.[18] Her face is really beautiful—more spiritual than her pictures. Her short grey curls flutter as she walks from under the frills of velvet. I have seen her several times, with her hands full of flowers, or tightly clasped looking straight up at the heavens, walking on very fast. Her figure is slight, erect and graceful—she walks like a girl—in a short black dress—without veil or bonnet. [. . .]

I think of you all every minute of the day—and oh long so much for some of you to be enjoying all this with me—it will come some day—so keep up, and prepare yourself against that time. Don't study too hard, read and enjoy yourself and learn Spanish and French poetry—and keep well—[. . .]

If I send this now it will catch this evening's mail—

Ever lovingly
Sis

King recorded a "First Impression" of Twain in her journal as a "disappointment to the eyes until he begins to talk," with an air and manner that was "the unconscious carelessness of the preoccupied," and as "a man of genius" with a humor "fleshy—course grained—but solid and generally wholesome."[19] To

17. Louis Placide Canonge (1822–1893) was a New Orleans–born Creole, French-language playwright for the Theatre d'Orleans. He also wrote for the city's French newspaper, *L'Abeille.*

18. By 1887, Harriet Beecher Stowe must have been suffering from early dementia.

19. For the complete entry of June 4, 1887, see Melissa Heidari, ed., *To Find My Own Peace: Grace King in Her Journals, 1886–1910* (Athens: University of Georgia Press, 2004), 22–23. Hereafter, *To Find My Own Peace.*

family members, she penned wide-eyed remarks on all manner of people, places, fashion, and food and included some shorthand references that they could grasp, such as describing someone as "creolish."[20] Although knowing that her family considered *Uncle Tom's Cabin* a "hideous, black, dragon-like book that hovered on the horizon of every Southern child,"[21] she nevertheless applied a sympathetic tone toward its author, a then-failing Harriet Beecher Stowe.

King's hosts, the Warners, seemed eager to introduce her to the rest of their world. After just a few days in Hartford, she embarked with them and the Clemenses and their minister Joe Twichell for the "magnificent house" of Frederic Edwin Church, the famous American landscape artist and major figure in the Hudson River school of painting. The house and the people prompted one of Grace's most effusive letters.

GRACE TO MAY

Hartford, Tuesday, June 7, [1887][22]

Dear Dear May! Just think of it! Here I am sitting in the beautiful house of the Church's[23] looking out of my window on the loveliest scene imaginable—the Hudson winding in and out between its hilly banks—sail boats dotting the water here and there with the Catskills—off in the distance like great clouds—we are on a hill seven hundred feet high—The road wound and twisted its way up through a magnificent forest—then all of a sudden—a sprint of the horses brought us in an open space where is this magnificent house—set in a magnificent scene. The house, planned & decorated by Church himself is Byzantine—made of stone & painted on the outside in bands and mosaics of the richest colors. They were waiting for us—on a terrace and we were instantly taken into the hall where lem-

20. With "creolish," King seems to suggest a person a bit bronzed, with somewhat hardened features and the air of other nations, wearing clothes naturally but a little negligently rather than for style or cut; an insular person devoted more to family and the arts than to money or ambition yet, if male, having a penchant for gambling.

21. *Memories,* 77.

22. Portions of this letter were published in "GK and MT," 33.

23. "Olana," a Moorish-styled Victorian mansion near Hudson, New York. They would have traveled through Connecticut, Massachusetts (not Maine, as King indicates), and New York to reach it.

onade, tea, and sponge cake were served. I sipped and looked around—of course there are more gorgeous homes, more wonderful rooms in the world, but surely there is none other arranged as this is—& now possessed by an American artist—I am not going to pretend to describe it—the hall is square—(that is my impression. I have only been here an hour & now should be dressing for dinner) a carved wood stair-way is broken by a landing in which is a huge window in gold colored glass all interlaced & embroidered—like an old Venetian wine glass—under the stair way is a kind of little temple in which are brass gods & ornaments brought from the East—After our tea we were brought to our rooms—The Warners are in the Church's own bed chamber—It is hung with the most magnificent pictures—from the bed one can look through a window framed in heavy oak with an interstice filled with small diamonds of gold glass on the scene that my window commands—Such a picture! Heavens! and all this has been in this world so long & I have never seen it before! The Clemens, Warners & I left at 9 this morning—traveled through Connecticut, Maine [Massachusetts] & New York to get here. You know the country—all like Saratoga—Mark Twain sat off and read in a corner of the car. He was rather disgusted because we all exclaimed on entering the car how hot it was & begged to have the windows put up—"If a lot of women were sent to hell the first thing they would want to do would be to open the windows" he grumbled to CDW—I suppose I had better dress now for dinner—I was going to wear my long black—saving the white until to morrow.

After dinner—
The dining room is a great square space—with heavily framed oil paintings hanging on the walls—The only light comes through high gothic arched windows at one end—the soft northern light—I noticed a magnificent carved Florentine chest on one side—A carved settee against the wall—a table inlaid with mother-of-pearl—gorgeous old Persian rugs every where.—The dinner was very elaborate, beautifully served. Mrs Clemens wore a picturesque toilette of white crepe with a satin stripe in it, if you can conceive of such a thing, over a heavy corded white silk—trimmed with pearl passimenterie. Mrs W—a black lace dress—"Mark"

started in very correctly in full evening dress—but soon after dinner was over he shuffled in amongst us in slippers with a big pipe in his mouth—After dinner I saw that the house was built around the square hall, whose four immense arches opened into parlors, libraries, sitting room & dining room—The walls are decorated in Moorish style—the great pictures a mass of color. Two huge brass cranes stand on turtles on each side of the stair case—holding vases or lamps in their mouths—Mrs Church took us up into the Tower to see the sunset—a regular tower—with arched openings painted & decorated with Mexican tiles—Of course I am not going to describe the sunset to you—but I felt all through it that we ought to be looking at it on our knees. We were called down for coffee served on one of the piazzas—Tiring of the talk I wandered around & got into a kind of verandah which commanded another beautiful view. I propped myself on the bannisters and looked until it disappeared in darkness. Turning my head I was caught by a mass of color—It was the lamp in a window burning just in front of one of Church's pictures—a sunset he had painted from nature on the Island of Jamaica—I came through the library after a while to meet up the others & found Clemens reading some antique book—I showed him the beautiful picture—Then found the others—we conv*arse*d (as old Adis used to say) until 10 OC—when of course the married women proposed retiring—of course I couldn't sit up with the men so here I have been in my room—hanging out of the window—writing this, and thinking, thinking volumes.—It is nearly midnight—I shall commence to undress—Good night—How much I think of you—of them all at home too!

After Breakfast, Wednesday—
Have just come in from the loveliest drive imaginable—The first thing after breakfast was to admire the pictures, the arum, the flowers & rugs—then there was a whisper that Mr Church was waiting for prayers; so in we marched into a little sitting room—where Bibles were placed every where—Mrs Church gave the place the 15th Chapter of St. John—& read the verses then requested Mr Church to "follow suit"—He evidently had not counted on his personal assistance, & could not find the place—but his wife read & then we all in turn. It was pretty trying—Mrs Warner &

Mrs Clemens are so English in their pronunciation & intonation that I feel like a squeaking Manatee[24]—However my verses were short and it only came to me twice—Clemens found his place and read along with the rest—Then Mr Church read a prayer—It was a very touching little ceremony and chimed in well with the beautiful surroundings in the house and the scenery outside—and I should think even Ingersoll would feel devotional here.[25] The drive was round and round the hill. Mr Church has taken advantage of every accident of ground. In a hollow where once was a cornfield, he has constructed a lake of about 20 acres surrounding it with trees of his own planting—Every time we came to the Hudson—it was a new revelation, a complete surprise—Mrs Church and Mrs Clemens were in the small dog cart driven by Mr Church's most elegant young valet—we were in a six seated one—driven by the most dignified stylish white coachman that it is possible to conceive. Gladstone himself could not be more English.[26] I sat with Mr Church, Mrs W with Clemens—Mr Church is a terrible invalid. Rheumatism I suppose is what has doubled him up in this painful manner, but he has the sweetest manners imaginable—Southern in cordiality—I really feel more at home here than at the Warners—

I must tell you that I used your fan yesterday—It was greeted with rapturous admiration. Every one declared it was the handsomest he or she had ever seen. I was so delighted & am thankful to you. Today I have on Nan's flannel dress—Some how I enjoy things more when I have on borrowed finery—Will you be able to make any thing out of this? Will you think me utterly silly—or will you take it as I mean it—silly or not, just a witness of how much I think of you & how much I love you all. Sis

In the Northeast, Grace King sharpened her objectives. She cultivated every person who could forward her career and social standing, including peripheral figures who might offer useful insights. She was prudent; she took no liberties with

24. Manatees communicate in squeaking noises.

25. Robert G. Ingersoll (1833–1899) was the leading agnostic orator of the American Secular Union.

26. William Ewart Gladstone (1809–1898), prime minister of the United Kingdom, 1868–1894.

famous husbands and instead befriended their wives, thus creating a safe space for friendships to grow. She was a grateful guest with good manners, an intelligent conversationalist with a quick wit, and a willing if imperfect card player. Grace was extraordinarily observant and resourceful, a blend of naiveté and worldliness. When alone in the Gilded Age houses of her hosts, she freely explored them and speculated on their northern lifestyles. Then she described her discoveries in long and gossipy letters that were common among mother, sisters, and brother Will. Older brother Branch's letters were more pragmatic; oldest Fred's were all business, even to his formal closing, "Your brother, Fred D. King."

GRACE TO NINA

Hartford, June 10, 1887

Dear Nina,

As you see I am back again "home"—The West Point trip had to be given up after all—The Warners received a telegram yesterday morning that Mrs Warner's intimate friend and cousin, the wife of Professor White of Cornell University, had died suddenly. They were both begged to come to the funeral which takes place to morrow at 3 OC. They were very much cut up about it. She had been a bridesmaid at their wedding, at all that sort of thing—So this morning I returned with the Clemens and Mr Twitchell while they waited at Hudson for a train to Ithaca—It was very doleful leaving them there. They will have to travel until late to night, if it does not take them until tomorrow morning—to reach their destination—and then after all our pleasure, for them to wind up at a funeral!—I waited to write you from the Church's yesterday, for Miss Meta's friends the Osborne's spent the day and took dinner there.[27] They are such nice sensible people and so thoroughly cordial to me—"Joe Twitchell" the pastor of

27. Meta Kemble de Forest (1852–1933) in 1880 married Lockwood de Forest II, painter, interior designer, and amateur architect, who, with Louis Comfort Tiffany, formed Associated Artists. The de Forests were considered American Orientalists. Isabel Church was related to Lockwood de Forest; Meta Kemble was related to the du Ponts and transcribed many of de Forest's letters (see Robin S. Karson, *A Genius for Place: American Landscapes of the Country Place Era* [Amherst: University of Massachusetts Press, 2007], 270). William Henry Osborn (1820–1894), a friend and collector of Church's work, shared the artist's fascination with nature.

the whole crowd came Wednesday evening. A splendid looking man of about forty genial and warm hearted and sympathetic as a Southerner. He made the party complete, and that evening we had a fine time. He told stories, Clemens read Browning,[28] Mrs W played on the piano. With all the gorgeous surroundings I wondered if I ever could forget it. Yesterday was the busiest kind of pleasant day. In the distribution of the crowd I was put down to walk with Clemens and Twitchell. We were at it for about two hours, just meandering through the winding roads up and down the hill, under the grand forest trees, and all around the little lake. When we returned the Osbornes were there and we sat on the "Ombra" as they call a large square piazza overlooking the river, and talked—then an early dinner at 2 OC. Then a long drive to Hudson to see the Osbornes to the train. Such a charming drive in the evening—and Hudson is a beautiful quaint old town—with lots of fine buildings in it. When we got back Mr Warner was waiting to take me to a bend on a high cliff overlooking the river to read his Cazenovia address to me.[29] He had been busily writing the two days we were enjoying ourselves so much. If I could only describe that scene in the beautiful sunset—I am afraid that many sentences of the Cazenovia address fell on deaf ears. In the evening Mark Twain just let himself out. He is the greatest circus I was ever at. One of his funniest hits was an imitation of the sermon Cable took him to hear in the little Prytania St. Church[30] when he was in N O—more music—more conversation and then a very lingering good night; for we all knew that it was an eventfully pleasant day in our lives. Having walked about three miles I was too tired to pack my things; but this morning I was up at 5 OC, to see the light break on the Catskills and then I packed and wished that I had brought writing paper enough to have commenced a letter at least to you.

The road to Hartford was over the New York and Boston RR between a succession of soft green hills and rocky brooks—Most of the road lies through Mass: passing Chatham, Chester, Pittsfield, and Springfield.

28. Poet Robert Browning (1812–1899).

29. Cazenovia College, a small liberal arts college in Cazenovia, New York, founded in 1824.

30. Prytania Street Presbyterian Church, corner Prytania and Josephine Streets in New Orleans; later, Fellowship Missionary Baptist Church; it was destroyed by fire in 2011. Twain was in New Orleans in 1882.

We rode some time along the Connecticut river. It is a beautiful stream flowing between rich meadows, covered with fruit trees—miles in the distance—I was reminded of the time Dickens came up the river to Hartford on a boat which was so many feet "short"[31]—Going on we were over an hour in Springfield. After going on a shopping tour with Mrs Warner, Mark Twain put us in an open car and we had a charming drive through the old Town—saw the Armory which is very celebrated,[32] and more pretty stores & churches than I thought could have been crowded into one little city.—The Clemens and Mr Twitchell were ever so nice—I really begin to feel intimate with them. Mrs Clemens looks like your friend Mrs Forsyth[33]—She is very wealthy in her own right and dresses in the handsomest style—She is very prim and precise but an unaffected little woman the very essence of refinement, while her husband is simply a Joaquin Miller in leading strays[34]—One can soon discover however, that under his great shock of grey hair lies a very profound vigorous intellect. He is not at all refined,—wore slippers all the time at the Church's and smoked a pipe, and ate like a corn-field darkey. Their carriage was waiting for us. They have the most stylish vehicles and teams here. I wouldn't let them drive me home, but ran over in the little private path that leads from one house to the other.—he accompanied me to see that I got a good warm welcome. Little Annie Price was so nice and glad to receive me—Did I ever describe her to you all? She is small, as small as a child of twelve—with a large head and hair almost perfectly white—large sad eyes, and a sad but angelically good homely face. She is lame—I thought she was about thirty five but she told me she was forty two—A little buggy was at the door, Ward Foote[35] was about taking her on a drive. I

31. King refers to the 1842 trip of Charles Dickens as part of his tour for *American Notes.* He remarked that the steamer was Lilliputian.

32. The Springfield Armory was the primary center for the manufacture of military firearms, 1777–1968.

33. New Orleans matron Theresa (Mrs Lucius) Treadway Forsyth (1852–1901).

34. Joaquin Miller (1837–1913), "Poet of the Sierras," whose celebrity came as much from his frontier garb and extravagant style as from his poetry. He was often a guest in the King household during the 1884 Cotton Centennial Exposition and encouraged King to write.

35. Andrew Ward Foote (1865–1925) of the seafaring family was also related to the famous Beechers.

insisted on her going—she made me promise to lie down and rest—but Lord! as if I could rest with all this mealy[?] mind wanting to come out and take a journey to N O. I have eaten my lunch, drunk two cups of tea—You ought to see what a tea drinker I have become—have read three good letters waiting for me—hung up my dresses, put away all my things—and am only now beginning to be tired and sleepy. It is nearly 5 OC and I must be dressing for dinner. The weather is superb—bright and cool. The green is of the vividest—the fountain is playing its best sending out silver sprays half the time instead of water—the sky is perfectly blue—

By the bye—The most persistent questioning has not revealed to me an item about Thurlow Weed Barnes[36] No one here, has ever seen him or heard a word about him. As for the Morris's I haven't dared own up to the friendship yet—for there have been some very bitter denunciations against the "Lot[tery]" in my presence several times. I have written my congratulations epistle to the Foster however.[37] Well I shall write to May now—In comparison with the great display at the Church's things look simple and home-like here. The Warners won't be back until Monday night. In their absence I am going to try and write something.—

Dear Nina—Ever your loving
Sis

GRACE TO MAY

Hartford, June 10, 1887

How glad I was to get your letter to day! I was a hungering for home news all the time I was at the Church's and I was consoled a little for the disappointment about not going to West Point, by the idea that I would find letters waiting for me here. Of course you got my erratic, incoherent,

36. Thurlow Weed Barnes (1853–1918), publisher in Boston, was at the time engaged to Frances Isabel ("Belle") Morris, daughter of John A. Morris, the Kings' neighbor. The engagement details helped tumble her father's Lottery business when Belle's million-dollar dowry was published, exposing the staggering wealth of the monopoly's owner.

37. May and Grace referred to Cora Morris, wife of the" Lottery King," as the "Foster," signifying foster mother because of her generosity. They were later estranged over snubbing and the anti-Lottery activism of all the Kings.

rhapsodical scrawl—I am determined not to travel again without elaborate writing accoutrements.—The reason I did not go to West Point was that one of the oldest and dearest of the Warner's friends died suddenly, a kind of connection in fact—and they were telegraphed to come to the funeral. She was a Mrs White, wife of Professor White of Cornell.[38] They were both very much distressed about it, but determined to keep up and not spoil the pleasure of the party, so we had the gayest sort of a time and the gayest kind of a trip here to Hartford—We left the Warners at Hudson. Mrs Clemens and I got quite intimate on the homeward journey. She is a good hearted little woman.—it is very curious to be sitting up in this charming room (library) writing to you—To tell you the truth, it is quite a relief the absence of my elegant hostess. I feel as if I were on vacation. This is her paper pen and ink I am writing with—I could have taken much handsomer paper—for her little writing table is filled with all sorts sizes and qualities of writing material. On the staircase landing there is a handsome carved Florentine chest just filled with boxes of paper. That is the way we live! Annie Price has been talking to me all the evening—She is such a nice sensible little body, she gives me lots of news about my friends—the W's and some very valuable for my guidance. Ward Foote the young man who stays here is talking too. He is a nice handsome New England boy full of pluck and energy; has apprenticed himself in a foundry and expects soon to get an appointment in Columbia College.—These people are all so good, so genuinely good—They are the most practically Christian people I know of—When I left the Church's this morning, they were so nice and cordial; I can't help thinking of them. They said they hoped it would not be my last visit to them—I am sure I echoed the wish in my heart—I thought of Mrs McD,[39] when I eat the green peas, snap beans, and strawberries. As I predicted I am still liking early strawberries—I must confess that they equaled those in Charlotte, but I am sure that they did not surpass them. I am so glad that you have not weakened out of the book-club. Do keep it up "Culture's" the thing—But you must not suppose that the people here read much. They seem to

38. Andrew Dickson White (1832–1918), historian and educator, cofounder and first president of Cornell University. He was ambassador to Germany and to Russia in other years.

39. May's mother-in-law, Rebecca Rowena Brevard McDowell (1823–1904).

know all about literary people and the names of books, but they have not a "connaissance approfondie"[40] of any thing in particular. The Clemens run to German. I have given her the name of several books that she had never heard of.—

Saturday Morning—You can appreciate how very sleepy I was at this point I just could get up stairs and to bed. I felt as I did in Charlotte, when undressing seemed absolutely beyond the extent of my powers. This morning it is as cool as an Autumn day. I am really chilly, I have on my traveling dress and an undersacque. I have adopted Mr Warner's proposition of using his office while he is away. It is up in the third story of the house a long narrow room, with a big table in the centre covered with the usual literary litter. A litter supposed to be artistic but which I find confusing only. He has shelves of books all around the walls and pigeon holes for letters, and engravings every where and his wife's photograph dutifully enshrined on the mantel piece. When I finish this I am going to try and write some thing else—but it does seem to me when I take up a pen, an impossibility to use it otherwise than for a letter. I don't think I shall need any more clothes, not even a bonnet. The Warners will be going away constantly on short trips, and when they are not here, I don't care how I dress—and I have plenty when they are here. I wish you could hear Mrs Warner play—it is an extraordinary performance for an amateur and an invalid. She is a "femme maitrisse"[41] a little too "picky" and fond of correcting her husband, who is just a little afraid of her. I don't wonder I am as afraid as death of her, although I conceal it perfectly and am as cool and dignified and self-possessed as with Mrs. Orr.[42] I see that this is the way to impress her. Mr Warner talks a great deal of Charlotte, and compliments you every chance he gets. What a nice restful time that was! What would I have done here without that month of preparation? [. . .]

When I am in all these pretty rooms, I compare in my own mind of course our possessions with these; Your rooms come out in the most gratifying way, as do our parlors. I wouldn't be at all ashamed for either the

40. Deep or thorough knowledge of something.

41. A forceful woman.

42. Wife of Henry B. Orr, professor of biology at Tulane University. Why Grace King might have feared her is unclear.

Warners or Clemens to see them—in fact I think even they might pick up some ideas from us as I do from them. You see I am beginning to recover my equilibrium.—I was so glad to get the Charlotte papers yesterday. I am going to write home for them to send me the Sunday papers. I never see anything here but the Courant, and there is not much to interest in that except Mr Warner's editorial.—These people here do not seem to know or care much about politics religion or the South. They are as easy going as it is possible for people to be. They have the contented expression of face and speech of souls assured of salvation in the next life and prosperity in this. Having both soul and body in sight of damnation, I do not feel so much at my ease, and in fact a little dé classeé.—This is a very quiet, nice place to write in. There are so many birds singing; the great big "eelum" trees[43] stand all round outside the window, a window garden of Nasturtiums are glistening in the sun. Every now and then I see a squirrel frisking along a trunk, or branch, and way off in the sky are the green hills.

Well—a bientot—Lovingly
Lovingly—Sis.

Grace had stumbled into a world that would vastly expand her horizons.

43. Someone at home must have pronounced "elm" as "eelum."

CHAPTER 3

AFFECTIONS FORMED

❧

Mr Clemens is so good natured and good hearted.
—GRACE TO NINA, JUNE 18, 1887

Leisurely days overlooking the Hudson, and the return trip from Frederic Church's "Olana" had allowed Grace King to enter the private domain of Sam and Olivia Clemens. She discovered that the three of them shared opinions on literature, food, family, and nondoctrinaire churchgoing. As the daughter of a Catholic city, Grace had a predilection for ritual but, like Olivia, judged preachers, sermons, and churches by the axioms of their narrow creeds.[1] Once back in Hartford, she became friends with all members of the Clemens family on their own terms, including daughters fifteen-year-old Susy, thirteen-year-old Clara, and seven-year-old Jean. She brought her polite southern deportment with her to the North, but also her prejudices and guile.

❧ GRACE TO MIMI

Hartford, Sunday, June 12, 1887

Dear Mimi,
I have to write a little letter of thanks to Mrs. Church, but perhaps I can work myself up to it better by a few lines home first. It is the quietest of Sundays. I miss the Warners dreadfully, the house is so quiet, and the meals so staid and somber. Mrs Clemens sent over this morning to apologise for not being able to take me to church in her carriage but one of

1. Harold K. Bush, Steve Courtney, and Peter Messent, eds., *The Letters of Mark Twain and Joseph Hopkins Twichell* (Athens: University of Georgia Press, 2017), 31. Hereafter, *MT and Twichell.*

the horses was sick. Her daughters however, very nicely suggested that I should walk down with them. They are pretty bright girls of thirteen and fifteen, perfectly unaffected and simple in their manners, dressing in cheap little toilettes, quite different from the gorgeousness of their mother. They came to me at half past ten; with Koto House, a Japanese young lady, the adopted daughter of a Mr House—some literary character spending a vacation with the Clemens.[2] The walk was delightful. You can't imagine lovelier weather—like our warm winter days. The trees and grass are so green, the sun so bright, and the sky so blue[3]—The houses are all handsome sitting back from the street on large undulating lawns. I was almost sorry when we came to the church. Mr Twitchell is the "Joe" of the Clemens and Warners, and he calls them all "Susy and Livvy, and Charlie and Sammie"[4]—He seems to be a very lovable character, strong frank brave and handsome. His sermon was direct and to the point; not as polished nor as original as Dr Parker's of last Sunday. He adheres too nine strictly [?] to the regular Presbyterian Service. Parker has borrowed every thing possible from the Episcopalian liturgy. The Choir is composed entirely of young men—The organ is directly in front and under the pulpit. The Collection too is taken up by young men. I squared up with my conscience for all past stinginess by putting fifty cents in the plate—or rather wooden box at the end of a long pole. I must say that I do not approve of simply bowing the head in prayer—it is neither reverential nor appropriate. I wonder why the Congregationalists—who seem to be made from the scraps of other denominations—do not boldly adopt the position of kneeling.[5] Coming home with the little Japanese—she told me that she had been studying "Art" in N Y—whereupon I immediately risked an inquiry about our friend Lilly Mott.[6] Her ugly little broad face brightened

2. Edward H. House (1836–1901), a critic on the *New York Tribune,* spent ten years in Japan and returned with an adopted daughter, Koto. He was a friend of Twain's, but later they were estranged over conflicting claims about the production of *The Prince and the Pauper.*

3. They walked through the Nook Farm neighborhood toward the Asylum Hill Congregational Church of Joseph Twichell.

4. Twichell's letters are addressed not to Sammie but to Mark (*MT and Twichell).*

5. This seems a surprising complaint. King was not a "believer," as was her mother, Mimi, but apparently she appreciated ritual.

6. Lilly Mott was the daughter of Mimi's friends. King encountered her later in Paris.

into a smile and her narrow slit of eyes beamed and she told me that she knew Lilly quite well. They had been very much together, and Lilly had told her that if she ever came to N O, she must hunt her up. She confirmed all the compliments we had heard of Lilly; said she worked very hard, and attained splendid results. Church was over and done by half past twelve—at one we had luncheon—scalloped lobster—tea, brown bread and white bread with butter and raspberry preserves, all served with the quaintest nicety in the artistic bric-a brac china of the house. I am going to get some nice recipes for you from the cook here. She is Swedish and a perfect cordon-bleu. But I must say I am constantly reminded of the remark of the little Ygnaga to Uncle Henry after her dinner at his house. "Nice—but small."[7] The Church's live entirely in the Southern fashion—great abundance of every thing on the table. How I did enjoy some curried chicken they had! I noticed that instead of cutting their snap beans the length way—they cut them across, making little squares of them. You all must try it, it is a great improvement on our plan. The Warners will return to night or to morrow. Mr Warner is going to deliver the address upon this unveiling of the Hale Monument Tuesday. I am anxious to hear him, but I am a little afraid that Mrs. Warner will take me with her to Farmington to a concert there (where we are invited). By the way—In a moment of lunacy I mentioned that carved Mahogany bedstead I saw in N O for $12—and I have been persecuted ever since by Mrs Clemens about it. She is crazy to obtain a four-posted carved bedstead—will you go to the place—that little old house next to where Anna Ogden used to live on Royal St—see if the bed is there—When I was there it was kept in a room on the side lying down on the dirt floor—examine it yourself, if it is worth transportation and if the man will still take $12—or less for it—finally let me know—Mrs Clemens persists that it ought to be sent at once, the price being so small she would not consider the loss if it didn't suit. If there is any doubt about it—just write me that you couldn't find it or any excuse. I am not very particular about obliging the Clemens any way. The people here are simply silly about old furniture, rugs, bric a brac, etc. I am sure I can gladden Mrs Warner's heart with many a pretty piece

7. Ygnaga is a Cuban name; the young woman has not been identified. Henry Carlton Miller was King's maternal uncle.

after I get home. Do tell Emma that she must write to me, and Pat too if he is good.[8] I would write to Emma but I know she gets all the news from you all and I think of her whenever I write home. I wish she could come up here and see how things are done. I am sure she could do any thing that any of the maids here do. Mr Warner is always talking about how nice we have things—how nicely they are served—just as I do about all here. How curious it is about Will. I wish I could see him and remind him how hard it is for Branch to get money and how unworthy it is for him to black-mail the family in that way. Perhaps however, he is beginning to hope more for himself—and thinks that he is at liberty to borrow in the prospect of some work.[9] I am trying a little to work. Only, in my beautiful little room, the very artistic three legged table is rickety—and it wobbles so when I write, as to make me despair—if I only could write on my lap as all the other women do here! When Mr Warner is away, I can use his room as I am doing now; this is simply perfect. Oh my!

I do wish some of you all were with me or could change places with me. I am convinced the more I see of the place, that Nina was a little baby intended for Hartford—the Warners perhaps—but she mistook the road and wandered down to us and New Orleans. Miss Foote[10] the sister of Ward Foote who stays here, was sitting out under the trees all day yesterday sketching—It did remind me so much of scenes in novels—and I fancied how Nina would love to do it—I wonder if Eucloux could make me a red petticoat—Cheap silk satine—or any other nice material. My white petticoats are entirely too long—and they get so soiled out walking that it will ruin me to keep them washed. Eucloux could wait on her pay until I get back—& it could be sent by mail. I would like nothing but a small plissé around the bottom, and a belt with draw strings on the top. I enjoy my nice clothes very much—and I do not object to being dressed a little differently from the people here, for their dressing is rather formal and stiff—not Mrs Warner. She dresses like a French woman.

8. Emma was the Kings' steadfast servant; Pat, their sometimes unruly errand-boy.

9. Will contracted a two-hundred-dollar debt that the family had to pay. His letters are filled with grandiose plans that rarely materialized. Strong drink was his bête noir.

10. Lilly Gillette Foote (1874–1948) was the sister of (Andrew) Ward Foote and governess to Susy and Clara; they were cousins of painter Mary Foote (1872–1968), who also lived with the Clemenses for a time. Nina and May also liked to paint.

> Did I tell you that I went to a musical reception at a Mrs Bunce's—to welcome home a Miss Nellie Bunce "sweet friend" of the Ws—She sings delightfully, had been studying in Italy for a year. Her brother "Will Bunce" is quite a celebrated young artist[11]—of course I thought of our "Buras" all the time[12]—but dear me! these people were the quintessence of elegance—Well, I cant go on forever
>
> Ever devotedly—Sis

King's lengthy letters home told of Hartford's toney set into which she was invited. The Warners guided her into the sophisticated life of famous neighbors and literary friends. One day, Grace and Warner walked through Nook Farm and along Woodland Street toward the Twichell home in Asylum Hill, passing the fine houses of Lucy Perkins and James Goodwin on the way.[13] On another day, Susan Warner invited Grace to a "very select concert" where Miss Porter was to attend, she of "*the* select school" to which "none but the elite are admitted."[14] The manufacturer Frank Cheney invited Grace and her hosts to a "Rose party" in South Manchester and gave her a personal tour of his beguiling silk factory from which she yearned to tuck glimmering samples into her bag. The Thomas Lounsburys at Yale University invited her to spend a day and night.[15] She wrote Nan with a twinkle: "We live in a very exalted sphere here; our feelings and emotions are as refined and cultured as our minds."[16] Such courtesies lifted Grace's self-esteem.

11. Nellie Bunce (1853–1922). Later, she and her husband, Archibald Ashley Welsh, founded the Hartford School of Music, later renamed the Conservatory. William Gedney Bunce (1840–1916) trained in Europe and was known for palette-knife paintings of Venice.

12. Unidentified reference.

13. Grace to Nan, June 26, 1887. Lucy Maria Perkins (1833–1893) was the wife of Charles Enoch Perkins (1832–1917), Twain's lawyer during the Hartford years. The Perkins house was on Woodward at Niles Street. The granite mansion of Lucy Morgan Goodwin (1811–1890) and James Goodwin (1803–1878), president of Connecticut Mutual Life Insurance Company, stood at the intersection of Woodland Street and Asylum Street and Avenue. It was demolished in 1940.

14. Grace to Nan, [June 14?], 1887. Sarah Porter, education reformer, filled her college preparatory private school (founded 1843) with debutantes and daughters of men of note.

15. Professor Thomas Raynesford Lounsbury (1838–1915), Chaucer scholar, biographer of James Fenimore Cooper, and friend of Charles Dudley Warner.

16. Grace to Nan, [June 14?], 1887.

GRACE TO NAN
Hartford, Tuesday Morning [June 14?], 1887
Before Breakfast

[...] In all these invitations I am invited by name not merely as the guest of the Warners. I do not as yet know what I am going to do—I leave of course the arranging of it all to the Warners who seem determined that I shall see every thing to be seen hereabouts. The Clemens all came over yesterday evening to tea with Koto House. Mrs Clemens had on such a pretty dress of white Albanot[?] trimmed with striped surah silk—Yellow, green, red and gold. She is exceedingly polite to me—has been to see me twice. I wanted to go over this morning and see her but there is to be a musical in a few moments which I must not miss. [...]

I don't think I have yet told you of the Geoge[17] Warners; He is a younger brother of "Charlie" resembles him very much in appearance but totally different in manner and temperament. He is the president of the American Emigration Society, lives during the week in New York, coming home only Saturday nights. His wife was a Gillette—she is a tall handsome blonde with lovely manners. Her mother is a prim old Quak-eress, dresses in light grey with white little cap and kerchief—and sits as if her bones were knitting needles. Frank Gillette, the actor—is her son. He must be very amusing and clever although it was a great scandal to the family that he should take to "play-acting." Then there is Annie [Lilly?] Foote—the sister of Ward Foote[18]—a typical New England girl—She teaches the Clemens and [George] Warner children—a sweet nice face and girlish manners—but is innocent looking and simple—I can't tell whether she looks old or really is so. Every body here is so much older than he or she looks—that I get very much confused.

[...] I am afraid that I may have overdrawn the picture of things here from the overawed tone of your letters. I do not believe they are as wealthy after all—only exceedingly nice. I am picking up lots of ideas that will be of service to us at home. If they go to Casanovia & leave me here, which I hope they will I am going to interview the cook about some of her dishes—

17. Perhaps from the French, King regularly spelled George without the *r,* as Geoge.
18. The name of Ward Foote's only sister was Lilly. Perhaps King misidentifies this person.

—Well, the musical was very delightful. [. . .] I had a good opportunity of studying the character of the Hartfordians; and I must say they are a hard-featured set and illy dressed. I looked in vain for any evidences of culture on their faces and persons, and yet some of them as I afterwards learned were wealthy, traveled and artistic. Miss Cheney I like very much and her friend Miss Ferguson because she asked me if I knew the Dicksons and Bohns in N.O. Miss Belle, & Miss Janey educated her, and she knew Harry and Daisy[19] and was delighted to talk about them. It is so good to meet people who know home people. I doubt if most of the people I meet know there is such a place as N.O. Mrs Warner gave them all strawberries and after they left we raced up stairs to dress for the address—took lunch and started off. Mr Warner was so nervous about it that I sympathetically got into quite a state of fright before we reached the Capitol. There was a good crowd there, we got nice places and began to look around for our friends. There were only two or three that she had ever see[n] before. None of Mr Warner's friends had paid him the compliment to come and listen to him except our immediate coterie. She says it is always that way, that the people here have very little inclination or public spirit. Mr Twichell made the "Invocation" as they call the prayer. We pray here sitting down and closing our eyes except when we are peeping around. Mr W's address was very pretty, simple and touching—if he had had more voice to deliver it, it would have been very effective. Lounsbury the governor[20] replied—The statue at first glance is exceedingly beautiful. He is represented with outstretched hands, just before mounting the scaffold saying the memorable words "I am sorry that I have but one life to give to my country"—He stands on one foot, the other just rising from the ground—His eyes looking upwards where the flags were withdrawn. I thought it was ideally beautiful but after a while I tortured myself by fancying that was just the way he must have looked dangling at the end of the rope. Gen Hawley,[21] Gerhalt the sculptor Mark Twain and Twitchell all came and spoke to us and we would have had a very gay time if Mrs

19. Unidentified New Orleans people.

20. Phineas Chapman Lounsbury (1841–1925), fifty-third governor of Connecticut, 1887–1889.

21. Gen. Joseph R. Hawley (1826–1905), co-owner of the *Hartford Courant,* Civil War general, governor, U.S. representative, U.S. senator.

> Warner had not to hurry off to catch the stage for Farmington. [. . .] This seems a very bad narration—but—I do so think to tell all the facts that I do not leave room for the fancies. Dear love to all. Ever devotedly
>
> Sis
>
> Mr Warner sends his love to you all. Howdy to Pat & Emma.
>
> Dear child. Mrs Clemens is persecuting me for a nice list of books proper for her girls to read—French books—Now you see I can't remember any such books—but I don't want to confess ignorance. Can't you get some of the Cenas tribe to send me the names. I am sure Frances would do it.[22] The girls are always acting little plays. I mentioned Marie Augustin's & she is crazy to get the MS & have some copies printed. What is the name of that little comedy Nina or an other idea?[23]

A short time later Grace wrote to Mimi about her trip with Warner to Yale University. The campus overwhelmed her with its spectacular grounds and richly appointed buildings. She was especially enthralled with its abundant library, which wealthy alumni had donated. "I believe if I could move a bed in one of the corners of it I would not leave it for the rest of my life. Such rows and rows of books! And it seemed to me I wanted to read every single one of them," she wrote Mimi. "I am sure that whenever the Almighty hears that these people up North want anything he just gets it ready and sends it down to them all made. I suppose I feel it more from the contrast at home."[24]

She wrote to twenty-six-year-old Nina about the Clemens girls and the "Browning" readings at the Clemenses. As usual, she had strong opinions to convey, this time about female colleges and their students, a surprising attitude given her parents' insistence on educating their daughters as thoroughly as their sons. Given that training, Grace seems to have had no regret about choosing a life of defiant self-sufficiency as a hardworking writer rather than one as a

22. Heloise Cenas and her sister, Frances, had tutored the King daughters in French in their mother's Cenas Institute.

23. Pierre Marie Augustin Filon, French playwright. The play mentioned here is unidentified; perhaps the postscript is intended for Nina.

24. Grace to Mimi, June 17, 1887.

submissive wife. Her professional choice was again validated at this time by the positive reception of her latest story, "Bayou l'Ombre."[25]

GRACE TO NINA

Hartford, June 18, 1887

Dear Nina,

So you are at Evan Hall![26] I am so anxious to hear what you are doing there, how you like it, and if you are not stronger than when you were there last year. [. . .] Yesterday I was pretty tired all day from my New Haven exertions. I put on my blue wrapper in the morning and thought I would stay quiet and write letters. The blue wrapper by-the-bye is so extravagantly admired whenever I put it on that I am ashamed to wear it—it always looks as if I am fishing for compliments. I shut myself in my room but first Mrs Clemens came to invite us all to dinner Sunday at her house; then the "Browning" met at 11 OC there and she said I must come to that too. I began to write a long letter to Preot—when Mrs Gay, the lady who invited us to the concert at Farmington came in—of course I had to see her, she was very pleasant that is as much as she could be to me—reminding me every minute as she did of Cousin Susan Jones.[27] Eleven OC came, they would not hear of my dressing, said the ladies went in wrappers or any thing they had on, so over I trotted to the "Browning" holding a parasol over my head and a fan in my hand and a vol: of Browning under my arm. I found pretty nearly all the ladies I had met in Hartford. They are very sensible; they all sit and follow in their books while Mr Clemens reads. He has a great talent for it, and his voice is simply grand. They were reading "The Ring and the Book." I got so deeply interested in it that I am determined to finish it "right away." Mr

25. Grace to Nan, June 26, 1887. "Bayou l'Ombre: An Incident of the War" ran in *Harper's New Monthly Magazine* 75 (July 1887): 446.

26. Evan Hall was one of the plantations of Thomas DePasseau Miller, King's maternal uncle, who employed her brother Branch as a banker in his cotton and sugar factoring business. It was northwest of New Orleans not far from Baton Rouge. Grace thought their Uncle Tom should be more generous to her needy family.

27. According to editor Melissa Heidari, Susan Jones (d. October 18, 1933) was the daughter of Charles Jones and Louisa Catherine Griner (see *To Find My Own Peace,* 223n5).

Clemens is so good natured and good hearted he seems never to churl of doing any thing but what his wife wants for the amusement of people. They have the nicest children I ever saw, three girls, they and Daisy Warner and Hattie Foote (Ward's sister)[28] are always to be seen under the trees every where reading, studying, or playing Tennis—the eldest is named for Mrs Warner and their Aunt Susie and Uncle George—the people here in true mealy style. Mary Barton is staying a few days here on her way home from school. She is a typical College girl, pale and thin from over study—shy, sensitive, awkward with not the slightest eruption of chest development—and though eighteen looks fourteen. She enters Smith College as freshman next year—has gone through higher mathematics—a good Latin scholar, reading Lives and Virgil[29] and seems to have mastered all the hard things possible for a school to invent; or either they have mastered her; a more dried up uninteresting specimen it would be hard to find. I compared her with the ignorant coquettishness of the Bohn girls and determined if ever I had daughters to educate they should be educated not to make a living, but to make a man make a living for them.—

My visit to Lounsbury woke up a great interest in Chaucer in me. You know he is a great Chaucer scholar. Yesterday I read "The Parliament of Fowls," an exquisite little thing, which much to my relief I could understand perfectly in spite of the old style spelling which after all is only bad spelling. To day I shall begin the Canterbury Tales—I manage to do a good deal of reading in spite of interruptions. I am trying to write a little but that is harder—to concentrate the mind in the midst of such diversions—

After Breakfast.—I do believe I am running out of news. At first I thought I could write a half dozen letters a day and now I find that one letter exhausts my topics. I don't think I have told you enough about Annie Price. She is just the personification of self abnegation that we read of in works where the old Maid Aunt and Cousin does all the disagreeable work and gets no reward for it, than the drones do for their selfishness. If

28. Margaret "Daisy" Warner (1872–1931) was the daughter of George H. Warner (1833–1919) and Elizabeth "Lilly" Hooker Gillette Warner (1838–1915) and the niece of Charles Dudley Warner. King might have misidentified Lilly Foote as Hattie here.

29. *Plutarch's Lives,* one of King's favorites, and Virgil's *Aeneid.*

I can be axiomatic, I should say that every woman is brilliant or accomplished at the expense of some other woman—and Annie Price is what enables Mrs Warner to play so well, and Mr Warner to write. She dresses very plainly—and although the intimes of the house are all devoted to her, to outsiders she is merely a kind of little housekeeper, that is all. I am fond of her and do all I can to give her a little pleasure, and I really think she is getting fond of me. She does all the mending for the Warners, and is unceasing in her efforts to serve them. Mrs W, like all invalids, is a little selfish in practice, although in theory she is volubly effusive, kissing petting and complimenting Annie—making her lie down or worrying her about walking so much, but when there are pleasure parties or excursions I find all plans made with out reference to her. Mr Warner adores her; and her little withered wrinkled faded face beams with delight whenever he is about. Her hair is almost perfectly white—she is not taller than a child, and has one leg much shorter than the other. It is only too sadly true that the good in this life have very little fun. [. . .]

I know you are having lots of fun talking with Lilly—If she tells you any thing remarkable about the Creoles do make a note of it for me. This is a poor letter—but it will do to swell your heart there.

Ever your loving
Sis

The gracious Clemenses soon arranged a dinner to honor Grace. As was her habit, she related every detail to family about the food, table settings, guests, and mode of dress.

GRACE TO NAN

Hartford, Sunday, June 19, 1887[30]

My dearest Nan,

Here I am sitting up in your cherished blue silk writing a letter to you. I half expect it to cry out and protest, but you see even the dresses get "to the Manor born" in this cultured atmosphere. It is a rainy cold Sunday,

30. A portion of this letter was previously published in "GK and MT," 37.

but it is the day the Clemens have selected to give me a dinner. The Warners leave this evening for Cazanovia where C D is to deliver an address; so the repast will no doubt be curtailed to enable them to reach the train. I was not fully aware of the compliment until I suggested that I was not feeling well enough to attend when there was the greatest out cry imaginable. The choice lay between the white chemise silk & this, vanity decided the day and I think wisely. Poor Mrs Warner has a sick headache—She is going in her traveling dress and intends lying on a sofa and watching but she has kept this house in hot water with this headache now for two days—so it will be a great relief for her to go away. I was waked up this morning by that old pain in my stomach—attempted to go to church, had to get up and go out and have the same little spell that you had at the Porcelaine factory so you know exactly how I feel. Annie Foote [Price?] came home with me, we slipped in the house without Mrs Warner seeing us and I was undressed and put into May's Mother Hubbard[31] before I knew what I was about—was made to lie on the bed, drink a glass of water—have a handkerchief wet with cologne on my head and a flannel with lineament on my stomach and then left to go asleep. Of course I could not sleep. I pitched and turned. My little prayer book was the only literature within reach, I read the hymns from beginning to end and then began to repine[?] at my waters[?] when Annie Price came in with sad accounts of Mrs Warner and said "Charlie" too she found drinking soda and water in the pantry: indigestion—Then I concluded I had better get up and select a freer day for my sickness & that is the way I have recovered for the dinner. Mrs W has just come in & admired my pretty dress. It is so hard to keep from telling that it is not mine. I wonder what they do think of me with all these pretty clothes—I am afraid I impose the same idea of wealth on them that they do on me.

The white dress came yesterday. You precious thing! I have an abundance of clothes and now you'll see I'll put on then one of yours every time instead of my own.

At Night.—Well, my dear, if that wasn't a dinner! Talk about style. Pshaw you've never seen style, you don't know what it is. What a Jubilee

31. A loose dress worn generally for lounging. It was probably Annie Price who came home to the Warners' with King.

I sang to myself that I wore the blue silk—Oh it had a great effect. When we got there all the guests were assembled; at the last moment Mrs W concluded not to attempt it, so Annie Price, Mary Barton (her niece), Mr Warner and I went over with our waterproofs and umbrellas, for it was raining hard. The Geoge Warners were there. Mr House and Koto in full Japanese costume; gorgeous blue and gold brocade—straw slippers & her hair coifed as if she were a picture on a fan; and my abomination and detestation, the man I've been railing at like every thing for a week—Gen. Fairchild. He is a very good looking, sleek faced one arm rascal—Hypocrite is written all over his face and drops from his tongue whenever he opens his mouth.—The table was beautiful—round with an exquisite cut glass bowl in the centre filled with daisies, ferns, and grasses. A bunch of white roses was at each one's plate. Of course Clemens took me in, Mrs Clemens Gen Fairchild!—The candelabra were of twisted silver with yellow candles and shades. Olives, salted almonds, and bonbons in curious dishes were on the table and decanters of quaint shape and color held the wine. The soup was "Claire"—the Clairest you ever saw, delicious flavor—sherry—Then fresh salmon in white wine sauce, Apollinaris water—sweet breads in cream served I vow, in what looked like pomatum pots[32]—with covers (little flat round ones, exquisitely painted in blue) Claret Broiled Chicken, Green peas & new potatoes (they are very rare here) Tomato Salad—I really cannot write a description of this—The salad dish is an immense deep plate of Hungarian ware on the lettuce leaves were placed the Tomatoes, sliced but still in shape—over it all was poured the Mayonnaise and such condiments for serving—gold & silver and carving. The dessert was a most magnificent dish—Charlotte Russe and wine jelly with candied cherries in it, with whipped cream—eaten of course with forks—and last and prettiest of all—plates of strawberries with the stems still on—strawberries the size of walnuts, laid around what I took for a form of whipped cream (a kind of rosette). It turned out to be powdered sugar—we of course dipped the strawberries in it and eat them with our fingers. The butler in full evening dress served from the side table, and I assure you each plate was simply a chef-d'oeuve of artistic porcelaine. Their cook must be a French one, never in N O have I seen

32. Pomatum was a pomade, a greasy substance used to keep the hair in place.

such beautiful dishes & such exquisite flavorings. At intervals I looked around the dining room. Their latest acquisition is an old fashion spinet with the strings all taken out and top and bottom filled with shelves which contained a gorgeous display of cut glass. Fairchild launched out about his G A R and how he shed tears as big as chestnuts when he heard of Cleveland's design—that he did not at all regret his "palsy" speech,[33] extravagant as it was and that he thought God—would have interfered to prevent it—etc etc—I was immensely amused, and the Clemens never thought of it until afterwards when they came up & made profuse apologies—but I told Mr Clemens I didn't mind it at all, if he would only come out and let me privately give him my opinion of the G A R. They wanted to tell Fairchild—but I of course would not let them. After coffee, Mr Clark, one of the editors of the Courant, a Mr Dunham[34]—whose sisters have been very polite to me, and Karl Gerhardt, the sculptor came in and we had a very gay time. Mr Clemens repeated two of Joe Twichell's jokes, which were witty of him, Mark—Joe is a temperance minister visiting an old woman of his congregation, she offered him some splendid home made wine—He replied—"You know I'm a tee totaler"—"So am I" said she, "but I'm not a fool"—A gentleman returning after a long absence inquired after the Baxter boys—twins so much alike you couldn't tell them apart. "They went out as missionaries I believe"—"Oh yes the savages eat them a long while ago for Philopoens"[35]—The guests were all very nice thanking me for "my dinner"—and Mrs Clemens kept repeating that she was so sorry that the brilliancy of Miss King's dinner had been diminished by the absence of the Warners. They leave on Wednesday, but we are

33. Grand Army of the Republic. Fairchild's arm was crushed at Gettysburg. He was ridiculed as "Fairchild of the Three Palsies" for railing about Cleveland's order to return Confederate battle flags: "May God *palsy* the hand that wrote the order! May God *palsy* the brain that conceived it! May God *palsy* the tongue that dictated it!" (Thomas J. McCrory, *Grand Army of the Republic, Department of Wisconsin* [Madison: Prairie Oak Press, 2005], 32).

34. Charles Hopkins Clark (1848–1926), staunch Republican, anti–woman suffrage, anti–park systems. Austin Cornelius Dunham (1833–1918), businessman and philanthropist, the subject of one of Twain's letters to the editor, *Hartford Courant,* September 29, 1875 (see Gary Scharnhorst, ed., *Mark Twain on Potholes and Politics: Letters to the Editor* [Columbia: University of Missouri Press, 2015], 88).

35. Philopena, a game in which if one player finds a nut with a double kernel, he shares it with a fellow player and then can call in a forfeit, a philopena.

to see each other every day—I am quite in love with them now, naturally. Well—good night—time for me to go to bed.—

Your devoted
Sis

Even her co-honoree, former Union general Lucius Fairchild, could not mar the pleasure of the occasion or dim her budding friendship with Sam and Olivia Clemens. But this antagonist's presence did loosen her sectional tongue after the fact. At dinner, Fairchild had railed not only at President Grover Cleveland's return of Confederate battle flags to southern states but also at the South's treatment of Union prisoners. He was as passionate a Republican as Grace was a flaming Democrat. Livy Clemens was mortified when she realized her faux pas, but her genuine dismay made Grace King love her all the more. A few days later, Livy again repeated her mortification over Fairchild's outburst, and Sam Clemens had shared his wife's upset, for as long as he could stand it. A wry Mark Twain, however, could have made something of the hapless seating of two rival generals at one elegant table.

When Grace wrote May about the dinner, she had more to tell about Fairchild and more gossip about northern tastes and female students. Perhaps the latter stemmed more from Grace's jealousy of the privileged few unappreciative of their privileges than from a blanket disapproval of women's higher education. Self-governance and success were matters of the individual for Grace King; she joined no movement for the advancement of all women as had Julia Ward Howe and her ilk.

GRACE TO MAY

Hartford, June 22, 1887[36]

My dear May,

If they send you the letters from home you will see why I do not write to you oftener. Whenever I get a letter from you I want to run straight off and write and then I remember I owe a line to some one else and I dare not of course duplicate—I have been wearing the blue matineé you em-

36. A portion of this letter was published in "GK and MT," 37.

broidered for me and I do wish you could hear all the compliments paid it—Between you and Nan I shall get so stuck up about my clothes that I shall never be contented with a wardrobe provided by and for any single person. Of course the people up here have too little "fancy" in dress as in every thing else. The aim of life seems to be a respectable uniformity and I must say they hit the mark exactly—I can understand now why the literature of the North is so devoid of colouring and poetry. Annie Price with her niece Mary Barton are making an effort to get away this morning—They want to go somewhere in Pa where the Bartons live. They have missed the train, poor things. The carriage came too late—and they returned in perfect despair. They are going in a later train but are in a stew at missing their connections every where. It seems so strange to me that Ward Foote or some other connection or dependent does not come to see them off, buy their tickets and check their trunks. Women have not as much attention as with us, that's a fact. I shall be now entirely alone until Thursday or Friday night when the Warners return. Of course Ward Foote stays at night. And the two nice servants are very kind and attentive so I really think I am going to enjoy it, particularly as I have got a fairly good start at my story and am beginning to be so interested in it that I prefer working at it to anything else. I am to dine at the Geoge Warners—or they are to dine with me every day. The Clemens leave to day too at 2 OC. I am to go over and see them off. I payed them a nice visit last night. They are so mortified and distressed at Fairchild's talk at the dinner Sunday. It was not very pleasant for a southerner to hear, but of course I did not mind it, seeing what sort of man Fairchild was. Mr Clemens said that he was so mortified and disgusted with himself for not being able to think of something to turn the conversation with that he did not know what to do—that he felt horribly all the time. Mrs. Clemens said she could not go to sleep at night thinking of it, and talked about it until her husband had to tell her for Heaven's sake to "let up." They admire Fairchild immensely and only object to the sentiment being expressed before me. "Blatherskite"[37] I imagine must have been invented to apply to the sort of man the general in chief of the G A R is. Of course don't mention any of this where it will get publicity on account of the Clemens. They are im-

37. A person who talks at great length without making much sense.

mensely kind and polite to me and it is a great advantage to be "in" with them. Mrs Isabella Beecher Hooker came to see Annie Price yesterday & she begged me to come to her room and be introduced to her. Mr. Warner had laid down his orders that I was not to be taken to see Mrs. Hooker or have anything to do with her; She is one of his aversions. I was very glad to see what sort of person she was. I found her remarkably handsome, tall with grey hair and really beautiful features. She is the great friend of Victoria Woodhull, the step sister of Henry Ward Beecher, a spiritualist and every other kind of "ist" that a woman ought not to be. She believes Henry Ward to have been guilty[38]—and his family won't have any thing to do with her. Her son in law will not let her see any of her grandchildren, and the Daughter is only allowed occasionally the privilege of an interview. But she does'nt seem to mind it at all. Mrs. Day the daughter has been here several times. She is a sad, lovely woman—who I hear lives unhappily with her husband etc etc—You never heard in all your life such curious histories as these men and women have—not scandals but divergencies of religious, political and social opinions. I enjoy supremely seeing and studying them. I have not been able to interview Mrs. Sue about Kreuznach.[39] I am biding my time. She is as you might suppose very high and mighty but only "in spots"—I rather dread being left alone with her, but very likely Mrs Cabell[40] will be along soon to pay a short visit which will relieve the tension; Annie Price told me that she "Sue" was fifty-two—I could hardly believe it—she looks and talks so young. The crowning cause of her ill health was crawling on her hands and knees into the Pyramids of Egypt to please Mr. Warner when she should have been in bed. Annie says that she just dragged herself all over Europe until she

38. Victoria Claflin Woodhull (1838–1927), suffragist leader, clairvoyant, presidential candidate. With help from Cornelius Vanderbilt, she and her sister, Tennessee Celeste Claflin (1844–1923), were stockbrokers, publishers, and lobbyists. She also peddled to newspapers the story of Henry Ward Beecher's alleged adultery with the wife of his assistant, Theodore Tilton.

39. Bad Kreuznach, a German city of mineral baths where Susan Warner went for treatment of a fibroid tumor, an ailment that also plagued May McDowell.

40. Isaetta Read Carrington Cabell (1855–1923), widow of Edward Carrington Cabell, of Richmond (died 1883), was a writer for newspapers since 1880. "Isa" attached herself to the Warners, particularly Charles Dudley Warner. She served as literature editor at his *Hartford Courant* from 1889 to 1892, traveled with them, and often stayed in their house. Although she died in New York, her body was buried a few feet from the Warners.

broke down completely and had to go to Kreuznach and stay six months all by herself—She has paid one visit since—She used to stay in bed exactly one third of every month. At one time she went over everything Mr. Warner wrote correcting and polishing it. I don't think she could have been a very lenient critic, for she told me the first time she heard Mr. Warner lecture she was so mortified that she did not think she could live through it, and she could hardly wait until she got in the street before she began "Well Charlie, if you can't do better than that I think you had better give up. I never heard such reading in my life—You were a perfect stick—the people paid no attention to you in fact they were bored—etc etc"—She has gone to Cazenovia all primed to find fault. He would not let her read the paper; he begged her to wait until he delivered it and then give her opinion—She was very anxious to know what I thought of it. I said that I was no critic of mere style and form but that I knew the ideas were fine, and the address a noble one. She began again to complain of "Charlie's" voice—I told her that of course he was not an orator, but that people liked his earnest unaffected manner—that he spoke from the heart and what he said actually went to the heart etc etc . . .—

I wonder how Brevard would like such a "super-fine" wife. [. . .] I am so glad that I did not bother about that other bonnet in Charlotte. I haven't needed it at all; but I could not have got on without the "Mother Hubbard." The people here I see are a little astonished at my clothes—and no wonder—they would be more so if they knew the secret of it.[41] I am reading Numa Roumillian by Daudet (splendid) The Ring and the Book—Browning and skimming through The Masters Hist. of the U S—the last would interest Brevard very much I am sure. Well Honey, I've got to write a short letter to Mimi—so no more today from your "tonier" half.

Sis—

No matter how lofty her life was becoming, no matter how far she wandered from her home base, Grace never escaped the tangled web of family. However reserved she might be in polite company, her biases were freely expressed in

41. King was wearing the best items from all of her sisters' wardrobes.

letters home. She wrote Mimi that Koto, the daughter that Colonel House adopted in Tokyo, was a "very nice little 'colored person' I don't think she is as light as Emma, her hair of course is straight, but her eyes and mouth are the queerest things in the world. She and I are quite intimate, but I do not think years would ever accustom me to kissing her as the ladies here do."[42] On the other hand, Grace did seem to have had good relations with individual servants upon whom her household depended, especially with Emma Nixon, whose devotion and allegiance seem straight out of King's stories. Emma defamed *Uncle Tom's Cabin* as much as did the King family and applauded Charles Dudley Warner's favorable view of the South.[43]

EMMA NIXON TO GRACE

New Orleans, June 20, 1887

My good Miss Grace,

I thought you had forgotten me and I am so glad you think I can do as good as Annie and Mr Warner maid. I thought you would not like me anymore now I want to ask you how you are and are you resting your self. frome your letters I know you are having a nice time I know there is not more dignified looking Lady then you up there and when you put on your long trail you you ~~a~~ look some prety pictur I have seen. Mr Branh has taken Mrs King and Miss anna [Nan] to the Lake and Miss Nina has gone to brounty to Mrs Macall and I am all alone with pat and he has gone to bed now so I thought would write to you we have such a nice cook and you will lik her and cooking and her name is ant Chraty [Charity] and her tins shine just lik sliver [silver]. I read your stroy [story] in arts and letters[44] and I it is Buetfuly this Sunday so I thought I try and finish my letter I just givren pinaple surip I all way think of you bring it up don't you think is a good iead [idea] Miss Grace to have my teeth fix now I got time am losing my farnt [front] one Miss Grace when you write will you

42. Grace to Mimi, June 22, 1887.

43. King probably felt she had influenced Warner's views for his "The South Revisited" in *Harper's,* March 1887.

44. *Arts and Letters* was a short-lived literary journal in New Orleans, which poet Mary Ashley Townsend edited.

give me the Discripion of Mr warner house and Mr Mark twain and Mrs stow it will be so nice to keep and you to write it

pat is doing some of his fine cuting up want to go in the street he is very Bad Boy Miss Lottie Miller has just came to tell Mrs king good By alwy has ben well sence you Left and just the same as left me I have to go and set dinner table now & will Close, have a good time for you need it

June the 19
your searvent
Emma Nixon

Despite Grace King's desire to be thoroughly "intimate" with people like the Warners and Clemenses, she remained more diffident and formal than the brazen Isa Cabell, who soon invaded Warner's household and Grace's head.

GRACE TO MIMI

Hartford, June 22, 1887

Dear Mimi,

[. . .] Tell Nan that if she can't know the Clemens, her clothes can. I couldn't resist wearing her dress to the Clemens yesterday evening. I never really appreciated how pretty it was before—[. . .] And it's so comfortable too—I love to dress up when I go to the Clemens. It seems to me the better I dress—the more polite they become. It is a good thing that they leave today to stop the competition. I have written a nice note to Mrs. Steers though of course I could not tell her exactly when to expect me.[45] Mr Warner won't ever let me mention the possibility of going away. There's plenty of time I am sure ahead of me to satisfy every one. I haven't seen the Harper yet. They don't seem to get the magazines any earlier here than in New Orleans. [. . .]

Don't worry to hunt up old furniture for any one—in fact the responsibility is too great at such a distance. Mrs Clemens only asked about that

45. Kate Clarke and Schuyler Bliss Steers, whom King knew in New Orleans, invited her to their mansion "Lakelands" in Cooperstown, New York.

one bedstead—and as for Mrs Warner when I get home there's many a nice thing I can send her now I know her taste.

Thursday Morning—it has been raining ever since yesterday morning and all my plans about walking and riding in the horse-cart are frustrated. I am entirely alone now in the house, Annie Price and Mary Barton having left yesterday. The Warners return either this evening or tomorrow. I rather enjoy it, and amuse myself going around and looking at things. Removed from the glamour of the brilliant hostess—I am very much surprised to find things really as ordinary as other people have—and the furniture not nearly so handsome as ours—Their servants give me the tastiest meals and I simply stuff, for I have a very good appetite and do not satisfy it completely when Mrs Warner is here. She of course does not eat much—By the way—you must not picture us as indulging in a puritan Sabbath. Congregationalists do not let religion interfere with their pleasure or comfort. We always get back from church by 12, have hot lunch at 1. Dinner at 6. Mrs Warner plays the piano all day long if she wishes. The minister Joe Twitchell gets through his services [with] time enough to visit on Sunday evenings and have a good time generally. I have just received the Picayune with the announcement of Belle's engagement. There is a life of Thurston Weed down stairs & I propose to read him up completely. Is'nt it funny that Mrs Morris has never answered my letter informing her I was at Hartford. I wonder if they are really afraid I am expecting an invitation from them. To night I am invited to a large reception given by one of the fashionables. I am going if the rain stops with Mrs Geoge Warner. Saturday night I am going to a whist party at the "Dunhams" very nice people here. I went over yesterday to see the Clemens off. All the neighborhood was there. They insisted that I would be here when they returned in Sept, so would not tell me good-bye.[46] Tell Nan to be sure & get the Lippincott and read Amélie Rives' story & tell me what she thinks of it and all the other southern productions.[47] I am

46. The Clemenses were off to Quarry Farm in Elmira, New York, where they spent summers, as Livy had done as a girl, where the daughters were born, and where Twain wrote much. It is now the Center for Mark Twain Studies. King never visited there.

47. Amélie Louise Rives (1863–1945) was a novelist, poet, and playwright from Virginia who gained prominence with her first novel, *The Quick or the Dead?* (1888), which caused King to view her as a competitor.

trying very hard to get at work. I am getting to feel so well and strong—and I can see by the looking glass how much better I am looking.—I am afraid the year will never be long enough to allow Uncle Tom to take any of us to his plantations—there are so many to come before us. I suppose we are at the very bottom of the list. I sent Nan the Century yesterday, the one I bought on the cars coming on. [. . .]—Love to all

Ever your devoted—
Sis

CHAPTER 4

EXPANDING VISTAS

They are good people to know.
—GRACE TO NAN, OCTOBER 6, 1887

After another short time with the Warners and a quick sighting of Sam Clemens, Grace was off on her very own journey. She went first to Cooperstown, New York, but remembered her manners as she left Hartford.

GRACE TO MIMI

Springfield, Friday 10 1/2 OC a.m. [July 29, 1887]

Dear Mimi—
Here I am en route for the Steers—I must wait an hour for the Albany Express which takes me to Cooperstown, I drew a draft yesterday on T.D.M & Co[1] for $50. which I hope Branch will see properly greeted. The Warners were as always as kind as possible—this last week that I have been alone with them has been perfectly delightful—Music all the morning and books and talk all the evening.

Mark Twain came Wednesday for a business trip home—It was like seeing an old friend again, he is so cordial and nice and funnier than ever. Yesterday Mrs Warner took a coupé and made me pay up all my duty visits—I was so tired from packing & it was as hot as it could be and I hadn't slept the night before from excitement but I did my duty and really felt repaid when we got tea at Mrs Colt's[2]—You know they are the rich

1. Thomas D. Miller & Co., the firm of King's uncle, where Branch deposited Grace's money. As a single woman, she was able to sign checks at will.

2. Elizabeth Hart Colt (1826–1905), wife of Samuel Colt, firearms manufacturer. The house is on Wethersfield Avenue, Hartford.

people of Hartford and their grounds and house are simply palatial—She was as kind as every body to me, we walk[ed] around on the lawn and she gathered me a bouquet of flowers. Her grounds are a triumph of prospect gardening—with the ponds, statues, and flowers and trees—they looked like another Central Park—I gave all the servants presents, and left a 2 lb box of candy (from Haylers[?]) on Mrs Warner's desk—and a pretty blue flannel sacque all basted with lace & ribbon trimmings for Annie Price, in her bureau drawer. They persisted that I was only leaving them for a short time—but I explained to Mr Warner in the carriage that I really could not think after so long a visit, of staying with them more than a day or two merely to say good-bye on my way home.—That if I got to working I would like to go to some cheap little farm house for a month. He promised to arrange for me—and overwhelmed me with directions what to do here and in Albany—& not to stay at the Steers if I did not like them, & not to be sensitive—& to try & like them—& to be a good girl in regular avuncular style—So write your prettiest to them—you can't say too much to them—for they couldn't do too much for me—Be sure & tell her to consider *your* house her house for any visit to N O—She is dying to come there—

Lovingly
Sis

Grace King had left Hartford at the end of July 1887, for her trip alone to "Lakelands," the mansion of philanthropists Schuyler Bliss Steers and Kate Clarke Steers in Cooperstown, New York. Like many of Grace's acquaintances from home who had come to Louisiana in the boom years from the 1830s to the 1850s, the Steers had residences in the North and in New Orleans. About the people of Cooperstown, Grace complained to her reading partner May that people there "as far as I can judge have read but one book 'Deerslayer.'"[3] But she was "in a state of idiocy over a new and beautiful scene," the "transcendently lovely" Lake Otsego.[4] Nature invariably captivated Grace; men less so. She ig-

3. Grace to May, August 6, 1887. *The Deerslayer, or The First War-path* (1841) was the last of James Fenimore Cooper's *Leatherstocking Tales* but chronologically the first of hero Natty Bumppo. It was set on Otsego Lake near where the Steers mansion was located.

4. Grace to Susan Warner, August 5, 1887.

nored the widower the Steers couple threw in her way, going no farther than to accompany his mediocre singing on the piano and take turns rowing on the lake.[5] Unlike in her early twenties when she did have a serious suitor, King's focus now was clearly on fostering a career rather than a romance, although she regularly noticed when *beaux* were absent from the scene at hand.

She was three weeks in Cooperstown but did not unpack her trunk. She missed "Nook farm, and its 'farmers'" and was eager to get back to writing. She wrote Susy Warner to help find her a boarding place nearby. They settled on the Elm Tree Inn in Farmington, Connecticut, about ten miles from Hartford.[6] During her brief stop with the Warners on the way back, she wrote May.

GRACE TO MAY

Hartford, August 19, 1887

My beloved May,

[. . .] I got here Wednesday night at nine OC after a long and trying journey. A wreck on the track ahead of us delayed my train, until all connections seemed hopelessly missed. However—there was an accommodation train from Springfield to Hartford; which saved me from staying in Springfield all night entirely alone. I leave here tomorrow for Farmington. A friend of Mrs Warner's is going to drive me over in her carriage and see me fairly installed. My address will be simply Farmington, Conn. I really anticipate a very nice time there. I am so tired of being entertained and having to "dress up"—There I am determined to keep my mornings entirely to myself and give only my evenings to visits & visiting. My visit to the Steers wound up nicely and with a great many pleasant speeches on all sides. Mr Savile[7]—gave me a Lake dinner at the fashionable place the evening before I left & they all came down in the morning to see me off. On Tuesday quite a New Orleans deputation came over to see us; the Walmsley's, the Bowlings and the Mays—It was so nice to be with them all again. They were all particularly polite to me, in fact I would be quite

5. Grace to May, Cooperstown, August 12, 1887.

6. Ibid. The building still stands.

7. Henry T. Saville of Nottingham, England, was the widower the Steers pushed toward King and brother of the Steers' son-in-law F. Saville.

spoiled by the kindness of people if I didn't think they were trying to make up for the long past.[8] The lovely Warners insist upon calling this my *home* and received me with open arms. The last trace of hauteur has disappeared from Mrs Susy, and she is just as "sweet and lovely" as anybody. She and "Charlie," leave today for Lake Minnewaska a charming Summer resort. I shall be in the house alone tonight. I am invited to the Geoge Warner's for dinner. The House's dined here yesterday we had a very jolly (English you know!) time. I took the liberty of abusing John Brown a little, and found that Mr House was an ardent admirer of his—was with him when he was executed. Mr H was a reporter for the Tribune in young days and went through a great many hairbreadth escapes during the war. He has promised to relate some to me. I shall write you a long letter from Farmington. I have to dress now [. . .]

Ever devotedly
Sis

If there is anything particularly good in Critic & Nation send—if not don't waste stamps.

Grace was happy at the Elm Tree Inn, boarding for the first time in her life and for a reasonable eight dollars a week. She became "quite sociable with the ladies at my table," who were "intelligent, travelled, neither over nor under refined," but she had no need to cultivate them. While there, she discovered the appeal of the small village and visited the "queer little" two-thousand-volume library in its tiny cottage. She noted that the "ladies here walk around the streets at all hours of the night quite alone. There is no such thing in Farmington as street lanterns so they have the curiousest little lamps imaginable—which they carry. They look too funny and cute—like fire-flies darting across the gullies, and coming around the corners." She saw the famous Miss Porter—"the ugliest woman I ever saw"—whose high-toned school in Farmington "costs at least $1200 a year. The girls are all very rich and dress a great deal, studying as little as they can. They ride, drive, and go out pretty much as they like." They were

8. King harbored perceived snubs deeply and long. The people mentioned lived most of the year in New Orleans as members of the elite set.

not allowed to drive to Hartford, she wrote Nina, but of course they did, and they all had to attend the Congregational Church.[9] Later, Grace viewed the "sumptuous" studio at Miss Porter's School. "Every thing that one can require in the way of externals. From what I hear however study is the last thing these young ladies care about."[10]

Grace missed her educated sisters, who acted as first readers of her work. "I feel so funny writing a story without the prospect of you or Nan seeing it [. . .] before it gets in print," she wrote Nina. She would "submit it to Mr Warner however." She also missed home: "I can see you all at home—sitting on the gallery—If I could only catch a real glimpse of you."[11] From that spot, the Kings gossiped and watched the weather and the passing parade of New Orleanians.

Soon, Grace left the Elm Tree Inn for two weeks to join a former teacher from home who was visiting unmarried friends in Watch Hill, Rhode Island. *Comme d'habitude,* Grace braved a morning stage alone. "I don't care so much about going," she wrote May, "but I think I ought to see as much as possible of the country and view the little outing beneficial before I get to the horrible task of copying my MS for the Magazine." While in Watch Hill, however, she gained an important insight for one who would remain single all her life. The small circle of friends was "the jolliest set of old maids I ever came across. I did not know such jollification could meet in the state of single blessedness." The women danced and sang, drank and talked art and literature well into the night. Grace also experienced the freedom of a lone bathing venture "down to try the surf, as there are no men about."[12]

After her cavort in Watch Hill, Grace expected to return to work, even if "the first part is always the hardest to get over." However, Warner telegraphed her to come to Hartford to meet William Sloane of the *New Princeton Review,* who had published two of her three stories to date. "There now! grand excitement! grand terror! grand quivers and shakes and shivers all up & down my back bone," Grace wrote Nan.[13] It was the first of several jaunts she would make between Farmington and Hartford, either by train or in a "wheezing & creaking and lumbering" old stage—"not rapid under the best of circum-

9. Grace to Nina, August 28, 1887.

10. Grace to Nan, September 16, 1887.

11. Grace to Nina, August 28, 1887.

12. Grace to Mimi, September 8, 1887.

13. Grace to Nan, September 16, 1887.

stances."[14] Sloane had already impacted Grace's life and career; now they cemented friendly ties.

GRACE TO MIMI

Farmington, September 19, 1887

Dear Mimi—Here I am again, after oh such a delightful time in Hartford! I wrote to May yesterday,[15] telling her all about Sloane, how nice he was, the beautiful ring the Warners gave me. The delicious dinners—the cordial meeting with the Clemens—and all about my enjoyment of the whole thing. [. . .] This morning after breakfast Mr Warner Mr Sloane, & I started off on our excursion to Wordsworth's Tower[16] at the top of Talcott mountain—Mrs Warner at the last moment felt too unwell to go so I had to be the only woman to these two beaux—I must confess I think I shall never have had distinguished and devoted attendance again. [. . .]

Goodnight—Sis.

Every trip to Hartford seemed eventful. During one, Grace heard a piano concert at the Warners by fellow New Orleanian Bertha Pemberton, a young Creole. Grace was relieved that Susan Warner was "delighted with her playing; really amazed at her technique and memory," for she feared that should Bertha disappoint, it would reflect badly on Grace and their city. The next evening she was at the Clemenses: "When the talk ran down Mr Clemens read Browning's "In the Villa" & "Ben Ezra."[17] Browning was already a favorite with Grace, who had sat "just gorging on the two volumes" in 1885,[18] one of which included "In a Balcony," which might have inspired the title of her later collection of stories. Sam Clemens also took his Browning seriously, notating in his book where to

14. Grace to May, October 1, 1887.

15. The letter is missing.

16. Also known as Bartlett's Tower.

17. Grace to May, October 1, 1887. The full titles of the poems are the satirical "Up at a Villa—Down in the City" and "Rabbi Ben Ezra." King mentions for the first time, in this letter, that her right hand "gets too stiff to write and the words do not come easy."

18. Grace to May, August 25, 1885.

breathe, what to emphasize, and where he left off at the end of each session.[19] Grace's trips from Farmington to consult Warner and Sloane also brought two stunning invitations: to write book notices in the offices of the *Hartford Courant* and to spend a night in the magnificent suite at the Clemenses, where George Washington Cable, William Dean Howells, and other famous guests had slept.

GRACE TO NAN

Farmington, October 6, 1887
Elm Tree Inn

Dearest Nan,

[...] Well sir! I had a fine time in Hartford. There was the usual gush of greetings on both sides—And the usual demand on me that I should not return to the Inn. I had hardly kissed Bertha, or been presented to Miss Lee,[20] before Mr Warner pulled me into the hall with a new and brilliant project. It seems that the books in the Courant office have accumulated beyond all room, the editors have been so lax in writing up the notices. It is work they all hate to do. Every year about this time they have to hire some one to take the job off their hands. The brilliant project was for me to do it this year. I wrote a good many during the Summer which Mr Warner liked and he says I can do it perfectly well. I know I can do. I don't know what the pay is. Whatever is offered at the end of the job I shall return, the half—& this way I can circumvent too much generosity in case the W's push their kindness too far. Of course it is a kindness to Mr Warner to do them but at the same time I shall be in his house which ought to offset it. They wanted me to stay straight along, & when I said I would have to return to pack they made me promise for Thursday—But since I got here Mr Cowles[21] has sent me word that he has arranged a

19. Examples of Clemens's markings and marginalia are in the Mark Twain Library in Redding, Connecticut, and online at https://www.nytimes.com/interactive/projects/documents/twain-books#document/p1.

20. Aline Lee, Susan Warner's cousin, "an aristocratic, elegant, refined high toned, supercilious New York lady of a certain age" (Grace to May, October 1, 1887).

21. King refers either to Samuel Wallace Cowles (1826–1900) or his son Walter Goodman Cowles (1857–1929).

party to Northampton and Amherst for Friday—so after all it will be the 8th before I return to Hartford. I am crazy to visit Amherst. They say it's a beautiful place. Northampton you know is the place where Cable lives & the seat of the famous Smith College.—[. . .]

Sunday night at the Warners, we had quite a concert; the Clemens came in, & the Twichells, and Gen Hawley, and I was very proud of New Orleans when I saw how completely carried away they were with Bertha—She is so little, and "cute" as they say, they find her creole English fascinating—and as for her dress, and "little ways," that I trembled over—they did not notice them at all. So I said nothing. The people here are the most uncritical in the world about appearance, dress, or social manners. Things that drive us wild, they do not see at all. Mrs Warner says she is convinced that New Orleans is the most cosmopolitan in America, she can see it by Bertha & me—that we have never been to Europe & yet by our manners no one would suspect it, & yet the people here who go to Europe so much are still provincial in every respect. The Hugers have been so kind to Bertha, making her stay with them and interesting themselves to get her letters.[22] They were very much shocked Bertha says to hear I had passed through N Y without coming to see them. I sent them all kinds of polite messages. Their school is larger than ever before, every room taken. I will have to pay them a visit as soon as I get to N Y.

Saturday I go to the Clemens to stay over Sunday—They have taken a great fancy to me—They are good people to know, other wise, I could not stay in Hartford away from the Warners. [. . .] I have not heard from Sloane yet. If he defers accepting the MS, or refuses it, I shall want Branch to send me the $35 he has of mine—So you can explain if he gets a sudden check from me.

It is so good to hear the news from home—& to know that the Summer is at last over and people are coming back.[23] [. . .] Now, I am going to pitch into a big pile of books I brought over with me.—I was such a fool

22. Col. John Middleton Huger (1809–1894) and Elizabeth "Meta" Huger (1811–1890) had residences in South Carolina, New Orleans, and New York. They would have provided Pemberton with letters of introduction.

23. Elite families and any others who were able to leave New Orleans did so from May to October or November to escape heat and diseases.

yesterday—I left my toothbrush & rose water & glycerine at the Warners, so I must get out before dinner & buy some more.

Ever devotedly
Sis

Soon, Grace would enter a world not previously imagined.

GRACE TO MIMI

Hartford, [Saturday] October 8, 1887

My dearest Mimi,
I certainly cannot go to sleep to night without giving you a little account of my gorgeous surroundings. You must know that I am at the Clemens; came over for dinner to day. I have a large bed-room, a large dressing room, & a bath room with every accomplishment in the way of toilet and bath. The maid has hung up the dresses and placed all my things for the night on the dressing tables. There are lights lighted every where, and I do feel very much like Beauty did when the Beast left her alone in the palace.[24] The Clemens are very nice and kind. I wore my white India silk to dinner—The Geoge Warners & the Houses were the other guests. We had the same exquisite menu as before when I dined here—different china but as beautiful—and the style is simply perfect. Mr Clemens is of course at his best at table and he just talked along as if he were writing another "Innocents Abroad"[25]—I've got over my timidity with him, and so can "talk back" & have lots of fun. The country here is all wild about the American board of Missions,[26] which recently had a meeting to determine whether to preach to the savages probation or not; I don't know whether you have kept up with it or not. Well after a long contest, they decided by a vote of 80, against 53 that there should be no probation after death, & that the ancestors of the savages had to burn, nolens volens. So

24. This line from King is quoted during tours at the Mark Twain House in Hartford.

25. *The Innocents Abroad* was dear to Mimi; it had been her husband's favorite. He bought it even while in dire financial straits.

26. Created in 1810, the organization was the largest and most important missionary organization in 1887.

Clemens came in with the paper this morning and "News! News! Hell's elected by thirty majority"—The Charles Warners came in to tea. "Mark" got down in his usual position on the rug in front of the fire place & we all had a mighty nice time.—

The Warners take it as a great compliment that the Clemens have invited me here, they seem delighted at any attention I receive. Yesterday I left Farmington at 8 OC, went in the cars to Northampton with Mrs Gay, Mrs Hardy, (a very nice woman) & the Cowles—It was a beautiful day and I could enjoy to the utmost the wonderful autumn foliage. No description I ever heard does it justice. Northampton is one of the handsome New England towns; Smith College for girls, makes it one of the most noted ones here. It is almost a University for girls, the course is so high. They have great big recitation buildings, Art galleries, chapels & gymnasiums exactly like the boys. Miss Hess the Warner's friend has use of the buildings where the girls stay, she has twenty six under her charge. We went to see her, she showed us all over the sleeping rooms of the girls. Dainty tiny little rooms with nick nacks, & bows & Japanese fixings every where, but somehow I didn't like the appearance of the things. Three hundred girls off from home, given over to a college life this way. It seemed unnatural. They didn't look pretty and girlish a bit, and the mathematics seems to have just cut all imagination from their eyes and coquetry from their dresses.

We got a vehicle and drove to Amherst, passing through Hadley, which, as you seem to know more of American history than I, you may recollect as being famous in its day: an indian massacre or two I believe; and one of the Regicide judges—Whaley, lived concealed there.[27] The site of Amherst is the most beautiful of any college I have seen. It is on an elevation surrounded by a lovely valley—in the near distance the Holyoke mountains; you must imagine what it is, with the trees all yellow and red, a blue sky, a bright sun and the faint autumnal mist like a veil over its face, softening every thing. The chapel is very beautiful, and the buildings massive and grand. I had heard so much of Amherst I could not really believe that I were here.—When we got back to Northampton we drove through the town again and I took the cars for Springfield—where I had to change

27. During Cromwell's time, Theophus Whaley is thought to have hidden at Judges Cave near New Haven, Connecticut.

for Hartford. It was a two hours ride and quite dark when I arrived. I would not let the Warners know by telegraph as I did not want to give Mr W the trouble of coming for me; so I got in a carriage and drove there all by myself. Mrs Warner was busy typing up tickets for the Aus der Ohe concert; next Saturday.[28] She was as cordial as if she had been one of you all—I felt as if I were nearer home than I had been since I left Nook Farm. To day was the anniversary of their wedding day—and Mrs Warner has been quite sentimental over it all day long. She is terribly in love with her husband still. Mr Warners friend Wm C Prime[29] came in quite unexpectedly for a visit, he is spending a week here with his sister-in-law, Annie Slosson. (a widow) He is a most fascinating old gentleman who looks just like Schwartz.[30] He is a traveler, literateur, and a millionaire, a trustee of the Metropolitan Museum & Princeton College, & I don't know what all besides. After lunch, we wanted to take a drive, but Mr W, couldn't get a carriage so we contented ourselves with a horse car, & rode over to Weathersfield (another historical place) & back. [. . .]
I am sleepy so goodnight

Ever lovingly Sis

After two nights at the Clemenses, Grace gave May an account of her stay. She also began to use quotation marks around "Mark" to distinguish the performing persona from the beloved homebody to whom she was becoming ever more attached. He was now Mr. Clemens, and Olivia (Livy), even as a confidante, was Mrs. Clemens.

GRACE TO MAY

Hartford, [Monday] October 10, 1887
FARMINGTON AVENUE, HARTFORD, CONN.
At the Clemens.

28. Adele aus der Ohe (1861–1937), German concert pianist and composer.

29. William Cowper Prime (1825–1905), journalist, art historian, and the travel writer whom Mark Twain ridiculed as Mr. Grimes in *The Innocents Abroad.*

30. Unidentified New Orleans person.

My darling May,
I have a few minutes before breakfast—just to tell you that I am here, have had such a lovely time, and am going to return to the Warner's after breakfast. The Clemens are the loveliest people here, after the Warners. Yesterday was an ideal day. After a nine OClock breakfast we talked until church time, after church, a drive, then lunch, then a long talk in the "Ombra" a big circular gallery at the end of the house over looking the little stream of water & overshadowed by the trees. Here we intercepted the Charles Warners on their return from church, and had a fight over the sermon; which was "mighty poor" to me. "Mark" read aloud the "Bee-man of Orn" from Stockton's new volume.[31] It is too killing funny. We had Gen Hawley & the Warners to dinner & the Twitchells after. I laughed so much at the jokes & stories that this morning I am really tired. I have to go back to make my MS a little shorter. Armstrong[32] says he will have all the rest of the Magazine printed and put me in just as soon as I can alter—I am too long for the space allowed. It is all so beautiful here—a regular grand establishment. Mrs Clemens is a perfect housekeeper, ordering her servants & family marvelously for such a delicate little thing. I am in a great big bed room—a dressing room, and bath room. I parade through all these admiring all the exquisite details wondering how it would be to live here. It is before breakfast & my time is up. I shall finish at the Warners.

~~Tuesday.~~ Wednesday—You see how time flies, and events fill it up; this letter has been on my mind—and if my thoughts could only have photographed themselves on paper you would have had a voluminous budget before this. Mrs Clemens is coming in a few minutes to take me driving. She is so kind. I will have to tell you all about it, writing can't do it all justice! Not the kindness but the affection that people bestow upon me. I came over here Monday morning, went right to work on my MS. shortened it and got it off yesterday at noon. Since then I've paid a visite de digestion to the Clemens and noticed sight books.[33] Mrs Warner is all alive about a concert she wants Bertha Pemberton to give for the "Union

31. Frank R. Stockton (1834–1902), popular writer of children's fairy tales.

32. Andrew C. Armstrong with his son, the New York publishers of the *New Princeton Review*.

33. Sight books teach children how to recognize written or printed words. King is here reviewing them for the *Hartford Courant*.

for Home work"[34]—Bertha will get $50 for it—Louise, who is also in New York now will sing—all expenses to be paid.[35]

Thursday, Before Breakfast.

After a nice drive with Mrs Clemens, I went into town and did a little shopping—some ruffling for Mimi that they had sent for, & a pair of gloves—& some gloves for myself to wear to the Colt Tea, to day; (the rich and beautiful Mrs Colt) I shall go with Mrs Clemens—we are to take up Mr Warner at his office. Of course black silk, & Dolman, as it is pretty cold. Got your letter yesterday morning—have kept the letter to the Dr to mail today[36]—as you left it open I thought I would read it—I have really not had a moment of privacy to do it in. It will go to that address, only you have forgotten that there is no more Prussia, all "Germany"—What a splendid idea for the old ladies book club. I felt quite hungry to read those books myself. Last night Mrs Warner's music teacher was here and we had duets of classical music until 9 OC at night. All the neighbors came in. It was very pleasant, but I get very tired of so much classical music at once. I think two or three pieces are sufficient at one time. When I came up stairs to bed I was so cold and sleepy—I wanted to write to you but had to go to bed. To day I hope to get through lots of notices. I am so anxious to finish up every thing & start home wards. I could easily live in Hartford I believe the people are all so nice. They know you all by name now, and are constantly wondering when they will meet some of my family. Breakfast time! I am ashamed to send such a letter, but you know how it is. Dear love to you and Brevard—

Your devoted
Sis

Hartford's elite continued to embrace King. In October, she wrote Nina that she was going to a whist party at Mrs. Colt's, wife of the famous gun manufac-

34. A social settlement in Hartford, founded in 1872.

35. Louise Pemberton Hincks, acclaimed singer in New York and London, sister of Creole pianist Bertha Pemberton of New Orleans.

36. May McDowell was considering going to Bad Kreuznach for treatment, as Susan Warner had done.

turer. For a second time, "Mrs Clemens is to take me, & I am to spend the night there. Last night we took tea with them as usual—I went over before the others & we had such a nice conversation the Clemens, Houses & I."[37]

And then, as suddenly as it had begun, her stay in Hartford and Farmington was over in mid-November. Grace wrote a note of thanks to Susan Warner from May's house in Charlotte, North Carolina, for "what you have done for me in the past Summer, what you have been to me can never, never pass out of my heart," she gushed. If I had only met you earlier in life I believe I would have been much more satisfactory to myself and my friends."[38]

Thereafter, letters from Hartford informed Grace about events in Nook Farm. Susy Warner wrote of "luncheons, dinners, teas," of the "Browning" on Wednesday mornings, whist classes, a "Who do you call it" Club for anything, including charades. Mrs. General Custer had spent Sunday with the Clemenses, as had the Twichells and Houses. The Clemenses had held a Dickens day for Charles Dickens Jr., his wife, and daughter (they had six other children at home), had a "tea" for them, and a dinner. Everyone wore Dickens outfits except Mr. Dickens.[39] Susy Warner told of a lovely chrysanthemum dinner preceding a reading from *David Copperfield* at Trinity Hall, "the perfection of reading—naturalness itself."[40]

Annie Price also wrote from the Warner household. Their dear Olivia Clemens was in New York, and Annie had promised to "look in on her mother," Olivia Lewis Langdon, who was visiting from Elmira. She "set awhile" with her playing whist, Mrs. Langdon's favorite game. Another day, Annie reported, they had all dined at the Clemenses, where "there were all ages there from Mrs Langdon to Clara Clemens" having a good time with charades. Then she gossiped about the coziness of Isa Cabell and Charles Dudley Warner: "This is very private but I can't resist telling you that Susy has had to acknowledge since Isa's last visit that some of my remarks are only too true. They are *just as good* friends, but a woman as charming as Susy cannot become blind to peculiarities." On the other hand, "Mrs. Cabell was very sweet and has completely captured the hearts of the Clemens family. My thoughts are as they were, though I feel

37. Grace to Nina, October 16, 1887.

38. Grace to Susan Warner, November 12, 1887.

39. Charles Dickens Jr. (1837–1896) compiled dictionaries and edited his father's magazine, *All the Year Round.*

40. Susan Warner to Grace, November 15[?], 1887.

so disloyal to Mr Warner by harboring such feelings."[41] Grace would later speak this gossip and cause herself trouble, but like fellow New Orleanians, she recognized sexual straying, corruption, decadence, and political shenanigans as easily as goodness, romance, devotion, and religious piety. Her city's Mardi Gras was the epitome of abandon, satire, and caricature but was also a season deadly serious for wealthy fathers and their daughters who made débuts as maids and queens of old-line krewes. The King girls might have had such opportunities had the family kept its money and status, but instead Grace had to make a name for herself apart from society columns and Carnival balls and had to accept kindnesses gratefully.

Like others in Hartford, Charles Dudley Warner assured Grace in his usual Christmas letter that she was "always spoken of with real affection" and that the Clemens children were "delighted" to receive her letter and picture. The Warners and Clemenses "had our Christmas table and exchange of gifts Monday morning—such a lot of little things, and all for love."[42] Lilly Warner, wife of George, sent thanks to Grace for a "*most acceptable* Christmas greeting" that delighted her; she treasured "each one of the words in your own hand—right from your warm heart." She told "what a warm place you left in the hearts of this household as well as in those of the other: and still the other, for I mustn't leave out the Clemens by any means! We all missed you for a long time, and talk of you together very often." She also mentioned Mimi's "beautiful letter" of gratitude to Susan Warner and wished that "there come to us more of your beautiful fine stories to add to the happiness of ours." They accepted Grace for herself alone and without family attachments, a gratifying compliment. Even minister Joe Twichell wrote that "we shall talk about you surely—for we always do—nice talk too."[43] Lastly, the Clemens daughters sent their own notes of thanks to their friend Grace King.

CLARA CLEMENS TO GRACE

Hartford, n.d. [between Christmas and New Year], 1887

Dear Miss King,

We were *so* delighted to receive your letter and photographs. I think

41. Annie Price to Grace, November 18, 1887.

42. Warner to Grace, Hartford, December 27, 1887.

43. Lilly G. Warner to Grace, n.d. [January 1888?]; Twichell to Grace, December 20, 1887.

the photograph is very good of your hair, but I don't think it flatters you otherwise.

Miss King I have meant to write you before, but I didn't get to it someway. I have thought of you a great deal and wished very much that you were here, but I hope that you will come soon again. There has been a little skating, and we have taken one or two slay-rides.

It is raining now, so everything will be spoiled. I have seen "Tannhäuser," part of "Siegfried," and the Merchant of Venice this winter. Irving and Ellen Terry took the parts of Portia and the Jew.[44] Miss Terry was beautiful and charming and everything else. We went in behind afterwards (Irving asked us to) and she hugged me, kissed me, and gave me some violets.

Mrs. Cabell has been here a good deal of late and I am perfectly charmed with her. We had a lovely Xmas. I hope you did too. Mary Foote[45] spent it with us and most of the holidays too, oh we are having such fun! Mamma received cards from Mrs. Hinx and Miss Pemberton. I am so crazy to see them again.

I wonder if you couldn't remember me to Mrs Hinx when you see her. If it is not proper why then of course don't do it.

Miss King I don't seem to have much to say except that I am reading Margaret Fuller's life and don't practice much now, but I don't suppose any of this is very interesting so I will say farewell, wishing you a happy New Year and thanking you very much for your photo.

I remain yours lovingly Clara

P.S. I want you to know Miss King that I love you very much and think of you a great deal.

SUSY CLEMENS TO GRACE

Hartford, January 1, 1888

Dear Miss King,

Clara and I were so glad when we came into the school room Christmas

44. Henry Irving (1838–1905), English stage actor and innovative manager. Alice Ellen Terry (1847–1928), leading Shakespearean actress in partnership with Irving.

45. Cousin of Ward Foote and friend of the Clemens girls, later a painter of note.

morning, & saw your photograph on the centre table (the presents were arranged on three tables) and your lovely note underneath.

We thank you very very much for both.

I should enjoy the picture without the slightest drawback, but that it always makes me want to see you so much.

Ah! I hope we can soon come back to the Northwest Spring!—if you only could[,] know how be-you—tiful it would be!

Yes indeed, I hope we will be able to see your house some day. But I am afraid this castle in the air is too ideal to ever come to pass.

The "South" sounds so perfectly enchanting, and all Southern people seem so nice, that is if there all like Mrs. Hinks, Miss Pemberton & you.

Dear Miss King *this* is only a short note with lots of love and thanks in it but next Sunday when I have not so many Christmas letters to write, I will dedicate a long epistle to you, because I want to say things to you about my lessons and reading, and I want to write some day as you do, perhaps you can tell me how to work for this end.

But now dear Miss King I must say good-bye, oh! I wish you were coming in this evening to sit by the fire with us & Cousin Charlie Warner!

Wishing you a very happy New Year, I am
With much love
your own
Susy Clemens

From New Orleans, Grace wrote to Susan Warner, "I received such nice letters from Mrs Clemens, Susy and Clara. What warm hearted genuine people they are! And Mrs Lilly Warner has thanked me for my photograph so sweetly. What would my life be now without that trip!"[46]

46. Grace to Susan Warner, January 7, 1888. The letter from Olivia Clemens is missing.

CHAPTER 5

CLEMENS VOICES, 1888

You have a very tender spot in the hearts of this Clemens household.

—OLIVIA CLEMENS TO GRACE, JUNE 17, 1888

Grace's intimacy with northern friends continued into 1888. Annie Price regularly shared what she was reading, seeing, and hearing. She wrote that "Mrs. Clemens is well and busy as usual, French and German lessons, housekeeping, and society fill up her time—We see her every day nearly you know the continual running from house to house between these three," the George Warners, Charles Dudley Warners, and the Clemenses. She hinted there was gossip about the Warner household, but "I cannot write to you freely for there are things I would talk about to you which I don't think prudent to commit to paper."[1] May McDowell encouraged Grace to "keep up with your northern friends, they will be very useful in the future!"[2] Indeed, they were.

Clara Clemens wrote her in the spring begging her to visit again.

CLARA CLEMENS TO GRACE

Hartford, n.d. [March 23, 1888?]

Dear Miss King,

I thought I would write you again in hopes I would receive an answer.

Miss King don't you suppose you may come up here again soon? I should *thank* my stars if you could. What a snow-storm we *did* have I suppose you have heard all about it. It is *very* cold now, but there is no wind & the days are beautiful longer, & very sunshiny days. I have to go to New

1. Annie Price to Grace, Hartford, January 8, 1888.

2. May to Grace, February 22, 1888.

York (have gone & am going very often. I have seen Miss Terry twice (*oh* she *is so* beautiful bewitching & everything else I think). I saw her in Portia & after the play met her, she gave me some violets (perhaps I told you all about it & afterwards sent me her picture.)

Then a week or two ago I saw her in "Olivia." Dos'ent she do marvelously in that? Then among other things I have seen Ada Rehan twice in the "Railroad of Love," & three times in "Midsummer Night's Dream" & I am perfectly charmed with her.

I enjoy going to New York very much I have great fun. I just a little while ago read "Barnaby Rudge" & I think it is *delightful.* I am now reading "Great Expectations" and "Old Curiosity"[3] I always have two or three books at a time on hand.

Now dear Miss King I have really no more to say except that I love you *very* much & hope some time to hear from you. I am studying Roman History, latin & algebra now I will close with more love

Yours lovingly
Clara.

By this time, March 1888, Grace was waiting for proofs from A. C. Armstrong & Son, publisher of her first book, *Monsieur Motte.* Warner had suggested three more interrelated stories to the successful first "Monsieur Motte." She dedicated that book to "Mr. Charles Dudley Warner, whose kindly recognition of the possibilities of southern literature has been an encouragement to southern writers."[4] Now she wanted May to meet these friends. By chance, May and Brevard would be visiting Washington at the same time that the Warners and Clemenses expected to travel there. Grace told May what to expect.

GRACE TO MAY

New Orleans, March 12, 1888

[. . .] You can imagine how excited I am over the prospect of you all meeting. Mark and Mr Warner go for an author's reading in the interest of the

3. Three novels by Charles Dickens, the first and third in his short-lived (1840–41) weekly serial *Master Humphrey's Clock.* The full title of the third is *The Old Curiosity Shop.*

4. Grace to Susan Warner, March 2, 1888.

Copyright, the reading is on the 17th.[5] If you are there at that date be sure and go. I will telegraph you, if I hear where they will be all staying so that you can call on them immediately. Mrs. Clemens is so simple and shy you will be very cordial and pleasant to her, I know. She will be delighted to meet you, as for Mrs Warner she will take the initiative with you. [. . .]

May wrote later, "I do not wonder that you were carried away by these people, their society is intoxicating to me, I hope I showed them how I appreciated the privilege of knowing them." Mrs Clemens was not staying with the friends, but May sent a message to her by way of the Warners.[6] In fact, Olivia Clemens began to miss other events due to bouts of illnesses, some quite serious.

ANNIE PRICE TO GRACE

Hartford, April ?, 1888

My dear Grace,

I have just been over to see our dear friend Mrs Clemens, and I know you will be glad to hear the very latest news of her.

She saw the children last evening for the first time, and I was permitted ten minutes audience this morning—

Mr Clemens seemed to think as I finally carried no dynamite with me I was a safe visitor.

She is slowly recovering and of course has had every thing that love and her wealth could give her—

The children have taken their dancing lessons and practice here for the last two weeks.

Yesterday their two or three weeks vacation commenced, tennis is the order of the day, doing their driving about is the only real sign of the coming of summer that we have—The ther[mometer] has not soared much from 48° for several days and the trees are as bare as in mid winter. [. . .]

Mrs Clemens is going to leave for Koto did not come off during her

5. As writers, Clemens and Warner would have been concerned that cheap books were flooding the American market in the 1880s due to the absence of an international copyright law, which finally was passed in 1891. Periodic revisions were also fought for later.

6. May to Grace, March 22, 1888.

vacation every chance of that kind is good for her. The invitations were out and had to be recalled on account of Mrs C.'s illness. Many were thoroughly disappointed about it. [. . .]

With sincere love
Annie R. Price

CLARA CLEMENS TO GRACE

Hartford, April 29, 1888[7]

Dear Miss King,
I don't want to burden you with letters but I have got to write & thank you for the most delightful letter I have ever received.

I did enjoy it so & do now when I read it over, but it makes me have such a longing to see you I hardly no anything. How I wish I could see your sister that paints so beautifully.

When we receive that picture you spoke of sending us we *will* thank you so.

I think the weather up here must be as warm as it is down in New Orleans, it is simply suffocating. We have found a good many flowers, snakes, & toads & butterflies.

Then I think we are friends Miss King if you are fond of the theatre for there is nothing almost that I enjoy as much.

Koto had a little evening last Friday & we enjoyed it ever so much.

I have been riding a great deal this spring, I *do* enjoy it so. We also have played a good deal of tennis. Perhaps in my last letter Miss King I told you I was going to read Plutarch's Lives, but now I am reading them, & I enjoy quite a good deal. I am not going to write more than a sheet now because I wrote you such a short time ago. If Cousin Charlie is there yet, I wish you would give him my bestest love.

With a *great* deal for you Miss King.

I am always your loving
Clara

7. The letterhead has a childlike drawing of a little girl.

GRACE TO CLARA

New Orleans, [May 31 or June 1, 1888]
23 Rampart Street, South

Dear Clara,
The little Louisiana scene I promised to send you & Susy is not in Mr Warner's trunk. My sister Nina, persisted that not one she had was the thing to send away she wanted to paint one especially for you. As this was so much to your advantage I did not hesitate—so you must wait, and you will get it one day by mail—a little surprise in store for you when perhaps you least expect it.

I heard of your dear Maman's illness. I sympathized with you all very much, it must have been a great grief to have her suffering, how thankful you all must have been when she recovered. I am sure you did not need Mr Twichell to suggest thanksgiving to the proper quarters.

I am so glad to hear that you are reading Plutarch's lives. I enjoyed them so much when I read them. I always liked to commence as far back as possible in my reading, and then read down to the present time. When you once get accustomed to reading history you will find that it satisfies you better than almost any other form of writing. It is so wholesome.

It will be a year, in a day or two, since I entered Hartford for the first time. I can't tell you how much your family contributed to my pleasure when there, you and Susy doing so much in your own unobtrusive way. Give them all my love, from your Papa to Jean. Remember me to Miss Foote.[8] Ask Susy if she does not owe me a letter.

Ever affectionately dear Clara,
Grace King

June 31st [?]
1888[9]

8. Lilly Gillette Foote, the girls' governess.

9. King seems to indicate a wrong date. She meant either May 31 or June 1, since June has only thirty days, and she arrived in Hartford in early June 1887 (MS, CU-MARK, UCLC 44078, University of California, Mark Twain Papers, The Bancroft Library, Berkeley).

Warner must have kept Grace abreast of Olivia Clemens's health. On May 30, 1888, he wrote that Livy was recovered but still delicate and that she had "good satisfaction in your friendship," and an appreciation of Grace's character. Finally, Livy's own voice emerged. Her illness had interrupted the letter she had begun some time earlier. It reveals a kinship already established over several months of the previous year. Obviously, the two had shared intimacies and engaged in literary conversations. Now, Livy issued an exciting new opportunity for Grace.

OLIVIA CLEMENS TO GRACE

Hartford, June 17, 1888 [and August 7, 1888]
FARMINGTON AVENUE,
HARTFORD, CONN.

Dear Miss King,
Mr Clemens and I are sitting on the Ombra this hot Sunday afternoon, as we used to do last Spring when you were here, and how we do wish that you would stop in now and have a little visit with us. There are so many things that I should like to talk with you about. I never read a book that I don't feel that I should like to know your opinion regarding it.

I have just finished Monsieur Motte (I think I don't care about your opinion of this book. I am afraid it would not be a just one) a copy of which Mr Warner gave me. It is simply charming—every line—the book delighted me. I had never before read the last two sketches in the book. Of course now I read it right through together. I don't believe you can know how fine it all is.

Quarry Farm Elmira
August 7th 1888

Shall I go on and finish this letter to you, dear Miss King or shall I begin a new one? I will send this one simply to show you that although I have been so remiss I have not been without thoughts of you.

I read an evening or two ago a notice of "Monsieur Motte" in the N.Y. Evening Post, which I want to send you thinking it possible that you may not see it altho' I suppose Mr Warner sees to it that you receive all the pleasant notices.

I feel as if something personally pleasant had been said to me when I read a pleasant thing said of you or your work. You have a very tender spot in the hearts of this Clemens household. How I wish we could find you in Hartford when we return there!

I am just now reading the new Life of Emerson by Cabot.[10] Have you read it? I enjoy it exceedingly, but, I don't think I like Emerson as well as I did before reading it. He seems so very cold, so removed from the passions and struggles of other men.

Yet the things that he says have a power over me. It seems to me that what Harriet Martineau said of him, which is quoted in this book, is eminently true—"that without convincing any body's reason of any one thing, (he) esalts [assaults] their reason and makes their minds of more worth than they ever were before." I don't think that Cabot has given a picture of Emerson on the whole that would increase your love for the man.

The children are all well, they ride horse back a great deal and are out of doors most of the day. I hope all this is giving them good preparation for next Winter's work.

Mr Clemens is now very busy, doing rather fragmentary work just at present.

What are you doing? Writing I hope. We have had a taste in "Monsieur Motte" and we are greedy for more.

Mr Warner told me when he last spoke of you to me that you were not very well. I do hope you are better. If you are not, don't you think it would be well for you to come north and spend the month of October with us? We should be perfectly delighted to have you do so. We go home the very last of Sept: if you could come to us on the 10th of Oct: and spend a month you would give us great pleasure.

With kind greeting to your mother and sisters believe me

lovingly yours
Olivia L. Clemens

10. James Elliot Cabot (1821–1903), later Emerson's literary executor.

☙ CLARA TO GRACE

Quarry Farm, Elmira, New York, July 29, 1888

Dear Miss King,

I don't think I have *yet* answered your last letter in which you spoke of your sister's painting a picture for us.

You can be sure without my telling you, that we should of course be delighted, & value it very much. Seeing you seemed interested in the books I am reading I will tell you how I have read since I have been here.

Mrs. Custer's two books, (which are perfectly *delightful* I think) "Monsieur Motte" (I won't give my opinion on that) "Old Curiosity Shop," & have again, about finished "Tale of Two Cities" & it *is* beautiful isn't it? We bought another pony in the Spring, so now we have each a saddle-pony. But I have left the book-subject. I read "She" and one or two others but there is so much riding to do so that reading hasn't much of a place in our daily occupations. Next I think I shall finish "Great Expectations," & then perhaps read a life of H. Clay.[11] But Miss King what books would you advise me to read?

Our largest pony we also drive in a buggy now so we have chances often to take our meals in the woods, in that way.

We have been going to a *great* many ball-games, but they have subsided for a week or two. I think they are perfectly fascinating. Cousin Susie, & Charlie, have been in Virginia this Spring, as I suppose you know. I wonder if she saw Amélie Rives. I hope so.

We are having a most delightful, & cool Summer, & I suppose you are also.

Now my dear Miss King with a *great* deal of love

I am yours lovingly
Clara L. Clemens

Elmira N.Y.
July 29th '88

11. Elizabeth Bacon Custer (1842–1933), perhaps *Boots and Saddles* (1885) and *Tenting on the Plains* (1887); the next three are Dickens novels; the last, possibly Carol Schurz, *Life of Henry Clay* (1844).

Grace had indeed made friends in the Clemens household. She received the thrilling invitation from Olivia Clemens just when New Orleans was at its steamiest. At the time, she was worn down with "house cleaning and servant-driving" in preparation for the wedding of her eldest brother, Fred, by then an established attorney. Grace had internalized the *morés* of family, culture, and class but was determined to put family burdens behind her and make her own way to financial independence and social acceptance. Travel was important in order to establish self. Although the Kings had little money, each member had a turn to travel, for they also considered a change of climate necessary to improved health and spirits. In the summer of 1888, Nina was in Farmington, Connecticut, visiting Maria C. Gay and her daughter, whom Grace had met the year before. Nina's visit was a return favor for the Kings having housed Florence Gay in New Orleans for a few weeks earlier that year.

GRACE TO NINA

New Orleans, Saturday [August 11, 1888]

[. . .] I got yesterday such a sweet, hearty invitation from Mrs Clemens to spend a month with them from Oct. 10th. It was a complete surprise to me, it made me feel happier all during the drudgery of yesterday—and shown like a star, above all the discomfiture of last night. I wish I was certain what I am going to do. If Branch carries out his plans, I cannot leave during his absence, and it may be too late when he returns. I was too anxious for Branch to have the trip, to feel any disappointment of pleasure, if I do not get away—but I am shaken when I think of the profit. I feel that I may be put in the way of doing some well paid work, by frequenting these masters of literature. However, I am not going to hurry to a decision either way. I shall quietly make my preparations, and will be able to start on a day or two's notice. Branch will know by Sept 1st what he intends to do, two weeks after you are with Florence. Of course, privately I am dying to go—but this need not be published. Perhaps Mr Warner and you together may concoct some scheme, by which the complications may be straightened out. A good deal depends upon the humor Nan is in when she gets well—

After the lights of your travels what do you think I had better do with my white silk dress? If I stay at the Clemens I will need fine clothes. I shall get the blue Japanese silk at Lyons[?][12] and have my long black made over.—Do not let the Warners suppose that I do not want to come to them first. They are so sensitive about their friends staying at the Clemens, and I know Mrs C, invited me because she supposed I would not like to make another long stay this year at the Warners. I should like to stay at the Warners about two weeks—then go to the Clemens; for you to stay a little at the Warners and then go to New York to Miss Meta—all coming home the first weeks of November—As soon as the wedding is over, I hope we will settle down and I shall get to writing again. I am full of things that I have not time to put on paper. [. . .] I have not answered Mrs Clemens letter yet. I shall be forced to accept conditionally and after consultation with Mr Warner.

Wednesday.

[. . .] I am crazy to hear how you like Farmington. Isn't it lovely—and Mrs Gay—I know you take to her—Sis.

GRACE TO MAY

New Orleans, Sunday Morning [August 12, 1888]

[. . .] I was surprised the other day by a cordial letter from Mrs Clemens asking me to spend the month of October with them in Hartford. She gave me a general invitation last year, but this is a very unexpected compliment. I do not see much prospect of my getting away. The probability is that Branch may get a trip in September; in which case I would stay with Mimi and Nan. It would be heartless for me to go and leave Nan, and in case of any excitement about Will. Mimi is very hysterical and unmanageable. Whenever I try to infuse some of my courage into Mimi, she protests that she is an old woman and cannot be expected to control herself. You know when women begin to talk that way, what a burden it is on the children. Life is very simple to me when one has an object to work and suffer for, but it is very complex when the daily suffering is made the object. I wish every woman who is not married was as lucky as I. I can see when I do not work, what a wretched desultory affair existence is. I am not going to martyrise myself for Fred and Will, that is sure, and I am go-

12. Unidentified store in New Orleans.

ing to resist vigorously any attempts to connect me with any martyrdom proposed. [. . .] We have Maud Howe's story[13]—it is pretty poor, I think, but the papers think it rather good for her. Well—this is about all, I believe.

Always your loving
Sis

GRACE TO OLIVIA CLEMENS

New Orleans, August 15, 1888[14]

My dear Friend.

What pleasure your letter gave me! I was in the parlors putting flowers in vases and plants in windows, trying to enliven the place for a festivity in the evening—a kind of reception to my brother's fellow Judges—and his fiancée—to whom he had made up his mind to get married all of a sudden. Maman was up stairs, grieving over the prospect of losing her eldest son (overlooking the conventional gain of another daughter, which she protests she does'nt care about), Nan, my sister crawling through a slow convalescence after a fever. Your letter came—the only one by the mail—and it invigorated me immediately—I carried it around in my heart all day, the feeling that you would care to have me spend some time with you—in your family—under your house roof—to talk about books—life—and a little of our experiences—I felt it more, the letter coming as it did, when life had given me a new and not altogether joyful experience—

Whether I can get away or not in the Autumn—is a doubt, which I confess afflicts me sorely. I need the change a thousand times, and I want it, a million—that is just the proportion—the pleasure I would derive from it, swells and burdens when I think of it—until I think it is all a pleasure, and I am selfish and pleasure seeking alone in contemplating it.—Mr Warner (and Susy too) have written, urging me to come—I did not care to monopolise their room as I did last year so it was decided for

13. Perhaps *Atalanta of the South* (1886), a novella that Maud Howe (1854–1948) wrote after her stay in New Orleans at the Cotton Centennial Exposition in 1884–85.

14. This letter appears in full in *GK of NO,* 380–82.

me to pass a short while with them—and then go to the Inn, where I would be in hailing distance if they wanted me. To substitute your house for the Inn would be a delightful prospect. But to avoid any complications caused by my uncertainty, you must not hold your room for me. I know the exigencies of your hospitable heart—until the 1st of September, I cannot say whether I can go or not. Then I shall, D V[15]—make some plans.

I have not read Cabot's Emerson—only read about it. I admire Emerson, but to tell you the truth he is too excellent for me. Besides he makes goodness and success—almost indistinguishable to me. He converts my brain, but he does not touch my heart. He makes it so *sensible* to be good. It is a kind of a profitable investment—It is more profitable to be high principled I feel that—but I like to lose sight of it—I want it to be disinterested—from the heart. I read Emerson's axioms and really think at times I live in an Emerson attitude—but the least grievance—drops me right down—philosophy does'nt seem to prop me up at all. Browning can. Mr Clemens converted me to Browning and this Summer, he has helped me amazingly—bless his fat, fleshy, pudgy face!

"To see a good in evil and a hope in ill success"[16]—is what I for one must strenuously strive for, I who live amid so much evil, and am confronted by so much ill-success.—I have been writing very assiduously—you know what that means; happiness as long as the work lasts, misery the moment it is out of one's hands. I would pray for self-confidence if I did not think that resignation were a better state for the writing mind to be in. It is an immense relief to be patted on the head by the "Post" when one expects a fool's-cap.[17] I wish I did not so much feel that I had simply escaped punishment.—

My brother was married yesterday—today it is raining in torrents. Last night there was not much sleeping done by any of us; I am groping sleepily after my ideas. I write such beautiful letters in my mind! I wish you could have received not one, but the dozen I wrote to you since last

15. Deo volente (God willing).

16. From Browning's "Paracelsus Attains" (1835).

17. A positive review in the *New York Post* was welcome. Either King read it in New Orleans, or Olivia Clemens included it in her letter of August 7, 1888.

Friday. I am sure you would have enjoyed them—I quite enjoyed them myself—My heart expresses itself exquisitely to me, it is such an appreciative little heart, so full of gratitude for kindness, so afraid that its love will not hold out, to the end of a life where there are so many good people.

I owe Clara a letter—a nice letter to repay her's—and I owe Susy for the intentions to write. Give my love to them both—Jean will soon be large enough to remember transient faces too—when she must have her message—Remember me to Mr Clemens—the dutiful salute of a subaltern to a brigadier general—I am sorry that I did not have the pleasure of meeting your mother, but I venture to send her, as we say here—"Mes amitiés"[18]—Believe me dear Mrs Clemens, Sincerely and Cordially your friend

Grace King.

23 Rampart St, South
New Orleans,
Aug: 15th 1888[19]

Grace knew well the shaping powers of family and place, as did Livy. She applied those and her gift of language, emotion, and wit to her letters and stories to build her measure of success. May wrote: "I am so glad to hear that your Lippincott story is off your hands & mind so satisfactorily, & I know it must feel nice to have five hundred dollars in your hand all at once, & just at this depressing season of the year. I trust you will be able to take your northern trip." The story was Grace's novella *Earthlings,* which would appear in *Lippincott's Magazine* in November 1888. May rightly called the amount "a great deal of money."[20] Grace had alerted Nina that she hoped to go to New York to see Lippincott, then to the Clemenses, and to "the Warners if at all, last of all. If we have got to spend money on boarding it is better to do it in New York

18. "My good wishes."

19. MS, CU-MARK, UCLC 44127, University of California, Mark Twain Papers, The Bancroft Library, Berkeley.

20. May to Grace, September 3, 1888; May to Grace, September 29, 1888.

than Farmington. Don't you think so?" She expected the Warners' house to be "full all October; and in September he is going to Canada."[21] Grace might not have expected a complication in the arrangements, but she was wrong; she would later realize that Susan Warner was miffed about being second place in the competition for Grace's attention. But for now, there was rejoicing in the Clemens household about her upcoming visit.

OLIVIA TO GRACE

Elmira, New York, n.d. [late August, 1888]

Dear Miss King

Your letter filled this entire family with rejoiceing, to feel that there was a prospect that you might spend some time with us in the Autumn.

I simply write you a note now to say that we shall keep a room for you, and we all hope that you will occupy it.

If you find that the time that I have set does not entirely suit you and you would prefer to spend November with us rather than October, that will be just as well for us.

Anytime after the 10th of October we shall be more than happy to have you come to us.

Mr Clemens intends to do some writing at home this Fall, so he does not want for six weeks or two months any company that will be a tax to him. That is gentlemen visitors that he has to give up his days to. Mr Clemens says "Tell Miss King that I give her the handsomest salute that ever general officer gave to subaltern and that she will not receive any where a heartier welcome than I shall give her back to Hartford" he says further "she will not be a mar to my work but an inspiration."

The children are not here so I cannot give you their words as I have Mr Clemens.' I can only say they are in a state of jubilation at the prospect of seeing you again, and already worry for fear Mr Warner & Susy will take too much of your time.

My address until the middle of Sept: is here, Elmira, New York; after that Hartford.

21. Grace to Nina, August 23, 1888.

I wish in my most brilliant moment I could write such a letter as you do in your sleepy ones I should be content. With many thanks for your most delightful one. Greeting to your mother & sisters

Affectionately your friend
Olivia L. Clemens

CLARA CLEMENS TO GRACE

Elmira, New York, n.d. [August 1888]

Dear Miss King,
You *can't* realize how *delighted* I am that you are coming to visit us.

It will be simply *scrumpious* to see you again, it does seem such *ages* since we have. You *must* come, you *do* intend to don't you? It will seem like old times to have you back in Hartford again.

I am reading "Martin Chuzzlewit,"[22] & it begins very delightfully. I think we do a great deal of riding here, some reading & a good deal of base-ball-going. I think base-ball-games are fascinating don't you?

Now Miss King dear I will stop for I intended simply to write you how happy I was that you were coming.

With a great deal of love
I remain yours faithfully
Clara Clemens

SUSY CLEMENS TO GRACE

Elmira, New York, August, 1888

Dear Miss King,
We are all rejoicing in the hope of having you with us this Fall. Mamma read us your letter when it came, as a special treat, which we had the promise of as we were starting off to enjoy another treat (a long horseback

22. *The Life and Adventures of Martin Chuzzlewit* (1844), picaresque novel by Charles Dickens.

ride in the moonlight) and which was made more delightful, with a pleasant thing to anticipate.

After she finished reading it to us, we began to make plans and we are still making plans for cosey times reading and dancing with you.

We still play the waltz you gave Clara, and dance the dance you taught us, one of the last evenings you were in Hartford.

Dear Miss King you do not owe me for intentions to write, but for letters written & then not sent. For I have written you three at least, which I did not send you because I lost them and when I found them, the news was then ancient.

I shall write you a long letter next Sunday, and I shall *try* to send it.

This must go now with Mamma's. So good-bye till then,

With love from
Your friend
Susy Clemens

On Monday, August 27, 1888, Grace wrote Nina: "I got letters this morning from Mrs Clemens, Susy and Clara, with a message from Mr Clemens—they seem so cordial and genuine in their wish to have me. I will enclose Mrs Clemens' to you just to show." She also noted: "I see you don't take to Mrs. Warner. She is rather trying as I found, but Northern people are so queer. Isa Cabell is Mr Warner's Laura West, only she has been clever enough to conquer Mrs Warner too." In King family gossip, Laura West was their Uncle Tom's paramour. "One reason that I want to go to the Clemens instead of the Warners is to avoid her. I have taken a strong prejudice to her and no mistake." The Warners, however, had been hospitable to Nina, squiring her around Hartford and hosting her overnight. The sisters owed them courtesies.

GRACE TO OLIVIA

New Orleans, September 5, 1888

My dear Mrs Clemens,

This little note will explain itself. Will you kindly play postman between

Mr Clemens and myself and forgive me for countenancing even in this small way a habit, which I am pledged against by Sex.

I have never in my life received so much heartiness at one time as came in your envelope of letters last week. I can only say as our negro beggars do down here; a touching way of thanking for a gratuity: "God is good!"

I can see no reason now, why I may not be with you on Oct 10th—unless some of those surprising events happen, which large families hold in reserve to frustrate plans; you can count upon me, for that date.—If I cannot have this pleasure, you shall know of my disappointment promptly.—

Like Susy and Clara, I am already planning what we shall do together. It is going to be my vacation, no work at all; myself and time at the disposition of you all. We can play, read, talk or fancy-work, just as the opportunity offers.

I hear from Mr Warner that Nook Farm, has pretty much filled up its room for October—so you must not imagine that your guest is going to be in serious demand over there.

The prospect seems at times too pleasant to be realised, but I cannot help dwelling on it—

What a good Summer Susy and Clara are having—so much out door exercise and reading. They will never enjoy novels or history again as much as they do now. Experience, I think, is the sharpest critic of fiction we have; out of our own lives we are constantly challenging the author—I am so glad you are letting your daughters nourish their imagination; a woman's mind is pretty arid without imagination—yet modern education makes so little provision for it.—With sincere love for you all, believe me, dear Mrs Clemens

Your friend
Grace King

Sept: 5th 1888[23]

23. MS, CU-MARK, UCLC 43563, University of California, Mark Twain Papers, The Bancroft Library, Berkeley.

GRACE TO S L CLEMENS

New Orleans, September 5, 1888[24]

My dear Mr Clemens,

If your Express Co: is animated by the same spirit as ours, you will in the course of a week receive a package which starts the same day as this note. The package contains a "carrot" of tobacco.

Now for the history of the tobacco.

It is not supposed to be the common ordinary weed that grows from the vile populace (whatever you may discover it to be.) It is tobacco of pedigree, strictly private and exclusive grown by an amateur on Cane River in Nachitoches Parish.[25]

The Amateur, sends it to my brother Branch as a high favor and distinguished compliment. My brother, who smokes only cigarettes and mild cigars, looking around for some one to pass favor and compliment on to, remembered my describing you smoking a pipe. He asks me therefore to send it to you from him, the gentleman; in fact a general send from the country to "Mark Twain"—

I have told you the best I know of the Tobacco; but I know also that whiskey and tobacco are made (by the devil I candidly believe) specially to order for each constitution—and this may not be your brand.

One merit, you see it has, it can easily be given away. You know you must cut it with a sharp knife and rub it fine, thumb on palm, but you have'nt got the kind of thumb or palm.—I have seen them, they grow down here on the darkies—

Sincerely Your's
Grace King

Sept: 5th, 1888[26]

24. King's letter to Twain was included with her letter to Olivia Clemens, in a separate envelope.

25. In Louisiana, counties are called parishes. Natchitoches Parish, established 1805, is in the center of the state.

26. MS, CU-MARK, UCLC 44149, University of California, Mark Twain Papers, The Bancroft Library, Berkeley.

Grace also wrote to Susy Warner, gingerly tucking in the news of the invitation from the Clemenses. The rest is chatty and deflective, almost as if she anticipated that her former hostess would find fault with her plans, especially since the Warners had invited her earlier.

GRACE TO SUSAN WARNER

New Orleans, September 6, 1888

I had my paper all ready to write this letter; but I waited for the Postman.

Surely I thought that lazy little Nina "will have provided a letter for to day—and give me some news to start on"—and a letter did come—a volume, we have just read it, and such exclamations and ejaculations and comments on your's and Mr Warner's kindness! If I were to fill these four pages with nothing but "How good you are!" I would only be following the reiterations of my heart. I cannot say or think anything else, when you and Mr Warner come to me, in the little odd moments between work or pleasure, when the mind has time to "take stock" of its pleasant memories. Nina goes into ecstasies about the house, and—Christina's cooking!—I can picture to myself the delight the dear little body takes in it all. She has known very little of pleasure in life, and has had few opportunities of knowing such an example of harmonious existence, as is contained in your house. She will bring home seed, to plant for her own future out of this Summer's experience.

How distressing the death of Mrs Gillett[27] must be to you all! It must have been hard for her to die—and it will be pretty hard I imagine for her husband to live without her. I was very much pleased with the glimpse I had of her; a sweet, tender face.

This has been a long hot Summer—and we have been going through a little disciplining—I don't like being disciplined at all—and, the resignation that sweetens this bitter cup, was left out of my composition. I manage to take things very hardly, and to see all the blackness possible, in the silver lined cloud.

Did Mr Warner tell you of Mrs Clemens sweet invitation to me? I

27. Helen Nichols Gillette (1860–1888), wife of actor/playwright William Gillette. She was just twenty-eight at her death.

wrote yesterday, accepting for Oct 10th. Instead of being at the Inn, I can pass my month there—and be where I can see you and Mr Warner every day. I am afraid my position will be rather trying I shall always be wanting to go over to you all—but with you and Annie to help me out I hope to manage creditably, not to myself but to you all, for I feel, that it is the wish principally, to be kind to *your* friend that has prompted Mrs Clemens' good heart.

I am going to try and be in New York, Oct 1st, and spend ten days there seeing Mr Alden, Mr Armstrong—etc—before going to Hartford. I am dreadfully afraid I shall run out of work. For the first time since I began writing I have no engagement ahead. Yesterday I sent a little paper to "America" the Chicago weekly, Mr Warner gave my name to. I have done lots of reading; not so much as last Summer, with your opulent choice of books—but I have done Wordsworth and Browning very thoroughly—and some American history I stood in need of; with one volume of Heine's Prosaische Werke[28]—and a good many volumes of French.

Is'nt Robert Elsmere a fine book?[29] Mr Warner wrote me that you liked it. I really believe that it warded off a fit of illness from me. I commenced it feeling wretched—but forgot myself entirely—and came out of the book cured. I got immediately one of George Eliot's for companion—Robert Elsmere—comes nearer to my heart, but I could feel that Mrs Ward's head was not so heavy with wisdom and science as ~~Mrs~~ Geoge Eliot.

It is so delightful to think that I am going to be in Hartford again, see you all and hear some of your music! I hope that a disappointment will not be considered necessary for my usual discipline.

I suppose Mr Warner is not there to receive a message from me—What a cheerful happy Wandering Jew he would have made! I declare I think the Harpers should pay you a handsome indemnity.

If this sounds very hot, stupid and tired to you accept it as an indubitable proof of its genuineness, as a complete and perfect picture of myself.

28. Heinrich Heine, German writer of the *Prosaic Works.*

29. *Robert Elsmere,* a novel by Mrs. Humphry Ward (1888) that was an immediate success, selling more than a million copies.

Remember me kindly to Mr Foote—and Mrs Geoge Warner. I sympathise with her and hers sincerely. Believe me always.

Your grateful and loving—Grace.

September 6th 1888

Letters from Sam Clemens to Grace were rare but fun when they came, as is this one about the tobacco she sent him from Louisiana. He anthropomorphizes the carrot of perique in keeping with its mummy-like shape.

S L CLEMENS TO GRACE

Elmira, New York, September 12 and 13, 1888[30]

Dear Miss King:
The handless fore-arm of the mummy has arrived; & if the whole mummy was as good as this fragment, he must have been the very most principal Pharaoh of the very most principal dynasty, & worth the ransacking the Great Pyramid, to get at the rest of him. I thank you; & also your brother; & also his friend, & do hold myself under great & special obligations to all of you.

There is power in that tobacco; it makes the article which I usually smoke seem mighty characterless. I am a robust smoker, & equal to a hundred pipefuls of the ordinary thing in a hundred consecutive quarter-hours; but a single pipefull of this masculine persuader makes me want to go & curl up & take a rest—& I do it. Of course I could modify its enthusiasm by mixing it with the baser sort, but that would be to modify champagne with beer, & no truly righteous person would do that.

[*Sept. 13*]

All of us are glad you are coming with the other splendors of October—& together you'll make a team, now I tell you! You'll be welcome—give yourself no concern about that.

30. King included this complete letter in *Memories,* 203.

Sincerely Yours,

S L Clemens

And then, at last, Grace could put home matters aside and turn her face northward for business and pleasure.

Grace King and two younger sisters, Nina Ansley (*center*) and Annie Ragan (Nan) (*right*) with the family dog, 1880s. Grace would have been in her thirties and not yet embarked on her literary career, Nina was nine years younger than Grace, and Nan, four years younger. *State Library of Louisiana.*

Sarah Ann Miller King, Grace King's mother—"Mimi" to her seven children and a force in the family. She wears mourning garb, perhaps with a photo of the loved one on the table. Photo dates from either 1888, when her brother died, or 1901, when her youngest son, "Will," did. *William W. King and Family Papers, Mss. #1282, Louisiana and Lower Mississippi Valley Collections, LSU Libraries, Baton Rouge.*

Charles Dudley Warner, Grace King's most important mentor, ca. 1890. A longtime editor of the *Hartford Courant* and essayist for *Harper's* and other magazines, coauthor of *The Gilded Age* with his Nook Farm neighbor Mark Twain. *William W. King and Family Papers, Mss. #1282, Louisiana and Lower Mississippi Valley Collections, LSU Libraries, Baton Rouge.*

Susan Lee Warner, earliest hostess to Grace King in Hartford and an accomplished amateur pianist. *The Mark Twain House & Museum, Hartford, Connecticut.*

The Warner House, situated in the Gilded Age Nook Farm neighborhood in Hartford. Next-door neighbors were Harriet Beecher Stowe and Mark Twain. Demolished late 1950s or early 1960s. *The Mark Twain House & Museum, Hartford, Connecticut.*

The library of the home of the Charles Dudley Warners, to which Grace King had access, especially when she was alone in the house. *The Mark Twain House & Museum, Hartford, Connecticut.*

The Clemens family on their Ombra, ca. 1885. *From left:* Clara, Samuel/Mark Twain, Jean, Olivia/Livy, Susy. The scene shows Sam Clemens the way Grace King knew him: as a loving husband and father. She was also a friend to each of the girls and a confidante for Livy. The adults spent many hours on this Ombra talking of life and literature. *Mark Twain Project, The Bancroft Library, University of California, Berkeley.*

The Mark Twain House in Hartford, Connecticut, as Grace King probably first saw it. The twenty-five-room structure was designed by architect Edward Tuckerman Potter with interiors by four designers of the Tiffany Company. The Clemenses moved there in 1874, and King was privileged to be a frequent visitor and house guest in 1887 and 1888. *Library of Congress, Prints & Photographs Division.*

The dining room of the Mark Twain House, showing, on the right, the spinet-cum-glass-front cabinet that Grace King described in a letter. She also regularly detailed the settings, food, guests, and table talk. *Library of Congress, Prints & Photographs Division.*

The library of the Mark Twain House, showing the fireplace before which Samuel Clemens liked to lie while talking. Family and friends spent many hours here telling stories, reading Browning, playing games, and taking pleasure in stimulating conversation. *Library of Congress, Prints & Photographs Division.*

The Elm Tree Inn in Farmington, Connecticut, ten miles from Hartford. Here, for the first time in Grace King's life, she was an independent boarder, enjoying the freedom to dress and act as she pleased and to spend long stretches alone writing in a room of her own. The building still exists just down the street from Miss Porter's School. *Postcard in author's collection.*

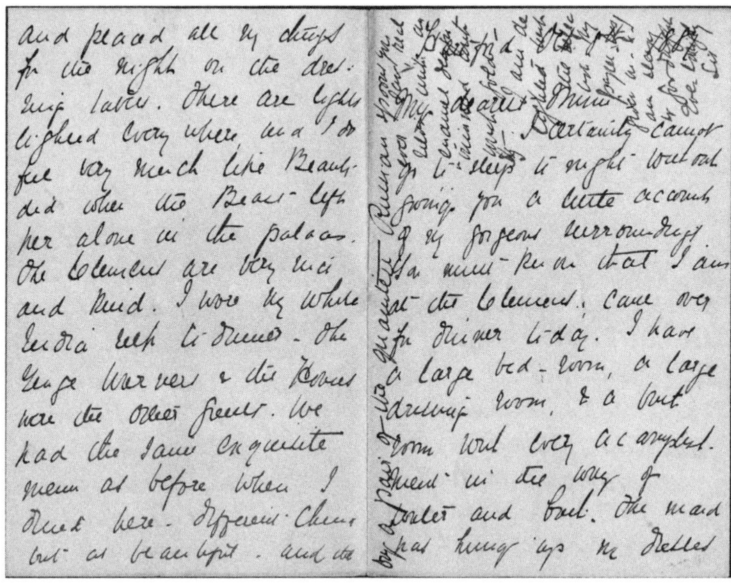

and placed all my things for the night on the dressing table. There are lights lighted every where, and I do feel very much like Beauty did when the Beast left her alone in the palace. The Clemens are very nice and kind. I wore my white India silk to dinner. The George Warners & the [illegible] were the other guests. We had the same exquisite menu as before when I dined here. different china but as beautiful. and the

My dearest Mimi, I certainly cannot go to sleep to night without giving you a little account of my gorgeous surroundings. You must know that I am at the Clemens. Came over for dinner to-day. I have a large bed-room, a large dressing room, & a bath room with every accomplishment in the way of toilet and bath. The maid has hung up my dresses

A typical letter from Grace King, this one to her mother, Mimi, telling of her first stay in the Clemenses' house. She was impressed by the suite of guest rooms she occupied, feeling "like Beauty did when the Beast left her alone in the palace," a line still quoted during tours of the Mark Twain House. Note the cross-writing here; in other letters, it was more pronounced. King also wrote with her left hand on occasion to save her right for copying manuscripts, which made her handwriting rather inscrutable. *Grace King Papers, Mss. #1282, Louisiana and Lower Mississippi Valley Collections, LSU Libraries, Baton Rouge.*

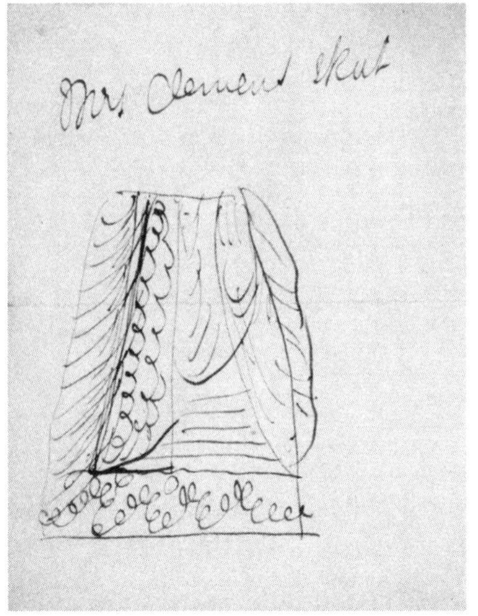

One of Grace King's drawings, this one of "Mrs Clemens skirt." King was dazzled by styles, fabrics, and prices when she accompanied Livy Clemens to a fancy New York dressmaker. Letters are filled with detailed descriptions of what people wore. The King sisters strove to be as fashionable as their diminished finances would allow, often remaking older garments. *Grace King Papers, Mss. #1282, Louisiana and Lower Mississippi Valley Collections, LSU Libraries, Baton Rouge.*

The front of the cottage where Grace King stayed as guest of Elizabeth Burnap at Watch Hill, Rhode Island, in 1887 and 1891. She approached the back of the house from steep stairs that led up from the ocean. With Burnap and her unmarried friends, King found the "jollification of single women" an important lesson for an independent single woman. *Photo by author.*

The Lakelands mansion of Schuyler and Elizabeth Steers, with whom Grace King stayed in Cooperstown, New York, in 1887. The Steerses also owned a residence in New Orleans and were hospitable, but King kept her trunk packed for a fast exit. *Photo by author.*

Otsego Lake in Cooperstown, New York, known as Lake Glimmerglass in the novels of James Fenimore Cooper. This would have been Grace King's view from Lakelands, the Gilded Age cottage of Schuyler Steers. *Photo by author.*

Olana, the elaborate Moorish castle of Frederic E. Church, a leading artist of the Hudson River school of painted landscapes. Grace King accompanied the Charles Dudley Warners and the Clemenses there in 1887 and stayed again on her own in 1891. The grounds are still vast, the house laden with treasures from around the world. *Photo by Richie Lasansky.*

The Ombra room at Olana. A note near the door states, "It is currently set to portray its appearance during the 1887 visit by writer Grace King, who stayed in the room." The shelves in the library of the house also hold her *New Orleans: The Place and the People* and a set of *Parkman's History* that King sent Frederic Church in gratitude for hospitality. *Photo by Richie Lasansky.*

Clara, Olivia, and Samuel Clemens in London, 1900, with Livy already in a weakened condition and seeking health cures overseas, as she often did. *The Mark Twain House & Museum, Hartford, Connecticut.*

The King sisters in mourning, ca. 1903, possibly upon the death of their mother, Mimi. *From left:* Annie Ragan (Nan), Nina Ansley, and Grace Elizabeth. *Grace King Papers, Mss. #1282, Louisiana and Lower Mississippi Valley Collections, LSU Libraries, Baton Rouge.*

The house at 1749 Coliseum Place, New Orleans, photographed in 1930. Grace King's brother Branch bought it in his sisters' names after their mother's death in 1903. It was the first house the family had owned since antebellum days. The four unmarried siblings lived there until each died—Branch only a few months after moving in, Grace in 1932. *State Library of Louisiana.*

CHAPTER 6

DEEPENED FRIENDSHIP

Isn't this a splendid opportunity!
—GRACE TO MAY, NOVEMBER 14, 1888

In September 1888, Grace and her brother Branch headed to New York. They stopped at the Willard Hotel in Washington so Grace could have a broken front tooth replaced before going on to the New York Hotel, as she wrote May, "paying $3.50 for board when I can only eat pap!" She was to meet Nina and their aunt Sally Miller in New York. Despite dental hindrances, her imagination forged ahead. "I am quite wild just at this moment over a scheme which has come to me like an inspiration to dramatise Monsieur Motte—[. . .] I am going to consult Nina about consulting Will Gillette. Perhaps there will be millions in it!" she wrote, repeating the shibboleth from Twain and Warner's *The Gilded Age.*[1] That letter almost made May "weep with disappointment" for Grace's physical pain, but she granted she was "almost as much excited over your plan for M. Motte as you are."[2]

Grace's route to the Clemenses had been circuitous, but Mimi was relieved when she was finally "safe after all your wandering."[3] Upon arrival, Grace recorded a second impression of Mark Twain in her journal, calling his fun "personal" and "autobiographical," his frankness "startling." He felt no obligation to "apologize or explain" his actions, and if anyone else did "anything absurd, or philistinish—or mean and stingy—he will notice it—and no doubt tell it on you some day when your character is being discussed. But he does not pick at your words, or test your sincerity."[4]

1. Grace to May, September 26, 1888.
2. May to Grace, September 29, 1888.
3. Mimi to Grace, October 15, 1888.
4. For the complete impression, see *To Find My Own Peace,* 35–36.

Once more among northeastern literati, Grace would deepen the social and professional bonds. She wrote Nan a long, revealing letter.

GRACE TO NAN

Hartford, n.d. [October 15?, 1888]
Monday Morning

Dearest Nan,

Before I commence work, I shall start this letter to you, and then may-be it will sprout into something more worth two cents postage than the things I have been wasting my money on.

Mr Clemens is very funny—he does tell the most remarkable stories and picks out the staidest and most respectable people here to foster them on. They are a pretty close set, and have got ahead of Mark in several transactions. After the next election he is going to cease his citizenship of Hartford, and become a citizen of Elmira, because they removed the electric lamp from in front of his house, to put it before the Chamberlain's[5] who had influence in the council.

He said he would do it before the election day, but he wants to have the pleasure of voting for Cleveland. They are all in a tight place here as to politics, they are afraid to vote the republican ticket and confess themselves, as Mr Clemens says—scoundrels—and ashamed to vote the Democratic ticket. The Courant is floundering dreadfully, but manages to get caught in some pretty shady electioneering lies. Goodrich the editor,[6] is a sleek pious, slow speaking Yankee. Mr Clemens says that at Mrs Hawley's funeral, when they were all standing around the open grave convulsed with grief—that Goodrich took his handkerchief off one eye and peeped around to see who was near. Mark Twain was next to him—he sidled up to him—and between his sobs and sniffles said—"Land—(sniffle, sniffle) is raised mightily around here!" burying his face in his handkerchief—After a while, peeping out again. "I own some! (sniffle, sniffle) paid twenty five dollars for a lot." Buried his face in his handkerchief—The minister

5. Franklin Chamberlin (1821–?) attorney, head of firm Chamberlin, White & Mills, representative in general assembly. His wife was the former Mary W. Porter.

6. Arthur L. Goodrich, treasurer of the Hartford Courant Co.

commenced the prayer. "Worth two hundred and fifty now! (sniffle.) But I've got a son in it."—Charlie Clark (Mr Clemens rode in the carriage with him & told him of it) said that Goodrich was not up to his usual enterprise or he would have offered to sell lot, son, and all.

Howells, stayed here with his son once, when the boy was very young. Johnnie got up early in the morning and reconnoitered all around examining every thing, until George came in to the dining room to set the table. He ran to his father who was in bed and said, "Get up Papa! Get up—time to get up! the *slave* is setting the table"—

Eziro, Mr House's Japanese valet was very much puzzled over the milk of this country, it tasted & looked so different from the condensed that he had been accustomed to—He ran in to Mr House radiant one morning from the dairy—he had found out all about it. "this milk was from the *living* cow."

Tuesday.

I managed to do a nice little piece of my work yesterday: the dramatization. I told Mrs Clemens about it—she is delighted with the plan and full of enthusiastic encouragement; she insists that I shall come immediately to my room after breakfast. It is a very good plan; she teaches Jean at this hour, Susy studies and Clara goes to school. She cuts Mr Clemens short in all his speeches—for like all men he is fond of haranguing—and dismisses every one to work. She is a wonderfully clear-headed managing little woman; the most conscientious creature I ever saw, and the least self-assertive. I am very much taken with her.

After lunch yesterday, I took a little walk. It was the first day that the sun shone, since I came. The trees are changing color, the thermometer about 35—and I really felt every draught of air invigorate me. I paid a little visit to the Warners. Did I tell you that Isa Cabell is coming to Hartford to live, Mr Warner has given her a position on the Courant. Mrs Warner is going to New York tomorrow to bring her back; she Isa, is to stay some time with the Warners, then she is going to board. My opinion is that it will end by her living with them. The Hawleys are to be there next week too, to stay until after the election. I am crazy to see them.

At half-past-four, the carriage came to take us to Mrs Colt's tea. It was a brilliant affair. The whole establishment is princely, it is so large, and the furnishment so handsome. Mrs Colt was lovely in a steel gray satin, trimmed with cut steel passementerie. She was very nice to me, and all my friends were warm in their greetings. But I get tired so easily! and I must get very pale, for the first thing I knew Mrs Clemens was hustling me back to the carriage, and apologizing for keeping me so long. She is going to give a Whist party to Koto House—next week and a grand tea to me, some time afterwards. A dinner party is on the tapis for next Sunday. Mrs Warner is going to give a tea to Isa Cabell & me, she says. By the way—if Aunt Sally wants to dispose of that exquisite green dinner dress, Annie bought her, I want it, if the price is not too high. There is no one in the family it would suit so well as I, and I should think I might have a better chance than the community at large. As soon as Uncle Tom is well enough to receive a letter I shall write to him, so you can let me know. I see that you must have got my order for a hat in all the excitement. It is such a pity! But I was too dreadfully hard up in New York to buy one, I had to borrow from Nina and so deprive her of the pleasure of her little treats. I am very much afraid that the $50 is lost. I did not leave the N Y Hotel until the 10th, mailed on the 5th—it had ample time to reach me—I should have had you send it to Armstrong's care. Of course a hotel is not responsible for mail—and I should have known it—I know it now, but I wish I had'nt to pay so extravagantly for the information—Did you ever see anything like my ill luck? Every other letter has followed me around through Westchester, back to New York, and here—only this one miscarried! I don't think either of the clerks of the hotel above opening the letter & taking the money, and unless you made it payable to Grace E King—they would find no difficulty in imitating my handwriting. I shall telegraph you tonight if it does not come today. I suppose you had better draw out the rest & send me for I have only 1.15 in my purse. How does the poor house look with all the ornaments gone? I am looking around here for ideas—I shall give you the benefit of them—& my observations on dress making—Good bye, love to them all—Devotedly

Sis

Grace must also have been mollified that Richard Watson Gilder, who had rejected her first story, was now courting her.

❧ RICHARD WATSON GILDER TO GRACE

New York, October 18, 1888
EDITORIAL DEPARTMENT
THE CENTURY MAGAZINE
UNION SQUARE NEW YORK

Dear Miss King,
Mr Armstrong was kind enough to tell me that I might call upon you at the New York Hotel. In the confusion of moving my household gods and goddesses I was unable to call until too late. They told me at the Hotel you had left, and I understand that you are staying with Mr Clemens.

This note is simply to say how disappointed I was at not meeting you, and to add that I hope your engagements will permit you to send something to "The Century."

Sincerely
R W Gilder

Miss Grace King.

No matter how idyllic a stay Grace expected with Sam and Olivia Clemens, home troubles inevitably intruded. Her uncle Thomas Miller died. Numerous letters from Mimi poured out every grieving detail, planned every mourning wardrobe, and speculated endlessly about who might receive what in the will. Mimi's brother was the only family member with noticeable wealth. It was rooted in his cotton and sugar factoring businesses that had brought him plantations and other landholdings. Would Mimi inherit something that would at last revive the Kings' fortunes? Would Branch benefit from his years of service and servility as Uncle Tom's right-hand man? Amounts kept changing, but it appeared that Mimi and Branch would each receive about ten thousand dollars[7] and that Branch would be executor of the estate, according to a telegram from him on October 20, 1888. They foolishly thought there would be no squabbles with Miller's family over money and possessions. They were wrong. May went to New Orleans for the funeral; Nan's telegram advised Grace to stay

7. Ten thousand dollars would be $265,269.47 in today's dollars.

in Hartford,[8] but her spirits weakened and her nerves were on edge from the stress. Livy Clemens was sympathetic and provided essential remedies.

GRACE TO MAY

Hartford, Saturday Morning [October 20, 1888]

Dear May,

Your letter came this morning with one from Mimi. I am so glad you have gone home. Nothing I can think of could do them so much good—and now that you are there I feel assured that Nan, Nina and Mimi will be made to take care of themselves. That was my great anxiety—I have just got Branch's telegram—The will is about what I supposed it would be. I infer, that Uncle Henry gets the same as Mimi, and the rest is divided between Annie and Aunt Sally.[9] I could not help writing to Branch, the other day—to look after his interests, as regards the business, and in the settlement. Had Uncle Tom lived I am sure B—would have been the principal heir—and I think every year added a little to his interest in us. It is a great relief to think that Mimi is still to have her $50 a month—Branch promises particulars by mail—I shall wait in patience until all the letters come in.

It is just a month yesterday since I left home—it seems six. I wish that I felt free to return immediately—but I really cannot, I see that. I must make arrangements for next year, and one month more is absolutely necessary.

I have canceled all engagements for outside gayeties—but I insist upon coming to Mrs Clemens dinner party this evening, given to some friends from New York. I have had to assume enjoyment so often before, that I have got kind of used to it—only, when I get to my room, I am utterly exhausted—barely can undress and get to bed. Mrs C, has put a decanter of Scotch Whiskey—and some sugar in my room and she insists upon my taking toddies—she says I really need them—and I believe I do. I am so tired and heavy headed, and heavy hearted all the time. For-

8. October 17, 1888.

9. Sarah Whiting Gordon "Sally" Miller (1824–1924), wife of Uncle Thomas Miller; Annie was their niece, daughter of Henry Carlton Miller (1828–1899).

tunately I look it—which makes them all attentive and kind. These are really lovely people. I am glad that I am here & not at the Warners, it is so much more restful, and in a way I can be so much more retired. Before I forget it—Will you send some of my music to me, for the girls here—I can take it back with me. I want the Faust ballet,—the Waltz from "Nanou" the Spanish Mazurkas—Roses & Thorns & Maria—Bells of St Peterburg Waltz.[10]—I believe that will be enough. They will come cheaper separately by mail. I had a letter from Miss Burnap this morning, begging me to stop over and see her in Baltimore—I won't think of it, unless you and I could be jogging home from New York together—and so make the visit.[11]

We have had the most doleful rainy weather imaginable—sun only two days since I came—if I could only get out and have a rousing walk I might feel more like Grace King and not so much like a woman in a novel.

It will gratify Nina to know that my silk shirts are the most delightful garments in the world—and that every body pronounced the brown hat she gave me as decidedly the most becoming one I wear. The Récamier Cream, too.[12] Mrs Clemens uses it—so I do not have to conceal my obligations to it. It is curious how my pleasure is crossed all through life—I could have such a nice time here if I had a free heart.I cannot think of anything more to add—I had better lie down a while, too—shall write again to morrow—Ever devotedly

Sis

In the middle of Grace's visit, the Clemenses made a trip to New York, leaving her in the house.

10. The Faust ballet is by Charles Gounod; "Waltz of Anomalies" by Nanou; "Spanish Mazurkas" by Frédéric Chopin; "Roses & Thorns & Maria," perhaps the German carol; "Bells of Petersburg Waltz" by Carl Czerny.

11. King had met Elizabeth Burnap at Watch Hill in 1887.

12. Récamier cream, sold as an emollient, was used at night and washed off in the morning, to remove sunburn, pimples, blackheads, red blotches, and other imperfections of the skin (*Lippincott's Monthly Magazine* 45 [April 1890]: 633).

☙ S L CLEMENS TO GRACE

New York, [October 24, 1888]
Murray Hill Hotel, Wednesday, P.M.

Dear Miss King,
This is to require you to understand that you can't count in the time we are absent as a part of your visit. No, we allow nothing for intervals of this sort—they have to be made up. The visit has to be extended to cover them & make full count. It would be unreasonable & inadequate for you to regard the matter in any other way.

Mr & Mrs Crane arrived at 9.20 p.m. in pretty fair condition, somewhat tired, but not overmuch.

Please hide Jean's candy till we come—it will save her from sin.

Sincerely Yours
S L Clemens

Mrs Clemens would have a message, but she is visiting her sister.

The Clemenses returned to Hartford just in time for the presidential election on November 6, 1888, between Democrat Grover Cleveland and Republican Benjamin Harrison. Grace regaled her family with an amusing account of Mark Twain's adventure to vote Democratic. To family, she could freely express her hatred of Republicans and could vent about politics, which was every King's passion. None of the women in her family, however, demanded a vote of her own. In 1888, they were all supporting gubernatorial candidate and former Confederate general Francis T. Nicholls, the avowed anti-Lottery candidate. The Louisiana Lottery was the country's oldest and most corrupt such vice, and its twenty-five-year contract with the state was coming up for renewal in 1892. "Lotteryites" were busy lining the pockets of legislators and the current governor, Samuel McEnery, to grease the way for a new contract. An anti-Lottery movement was agitating in 1888, however, and the Kings were in that number.

☙ GRACE TO MIMI

Hartford, November 6, 1888[13]

13. A portion of this letter was included in "GK and MT," 41.

Dear Mimi,
I told Mr Clemens last night that I thought I would have to borrow his secretary to write my letters home for me—When you don't get letters you may be sure I am working—if I don't write them in my working time I cannot write them at all. After that it is generally a long drive until dinner—then a talk then a game of Hearts—about which Mr Clemens has gone crazy. He insists upon playing it every night; and almost all night.—

Here it is half past seven—nothing but talk done! Annie Price, Mr Warner, and long talks with Mrs Clemens between times. Mr Clemens went off with Mr Warner to vote—He takes the most exquisite delight in voting for Cleveland—Mr Warner, of course votes the Straight Rep:—

Mr Clemens has just come in—he said that at almost every step he was met by some one offering him a Rep. ticket—and he told him that was not the kind of ticket he wanted—if they had any for Cleveland, he would be much obliged.—When he got almost up to the polls, a man stepped up and said "Mr Clemens, you had better let me look at your ticket—there are so many split tickets—and the regular one is the thing for you." Mr Clemens, gave his ticket—The man looked at it and exclaimed: "Why this is the Democratic!" "Yes" said Mr Clemens drawling more than usual—"that's what I thought it was!"

The Warners are very indignant over Mr Clemens conversion—that is the women part of the family—Mr W does not say anything—in his secret heart he wants to do the same; but he has been whipped into line by his wife and Gen: Hawley. There was a grand Republican procession yesterday morning—and a torch light Democratic procession last night—But we are out of all excitement living in this rural Forest St. In driving through the Town I have noticed most of the handsome private residences on particular streets, with a big U S flag floating in the breeze with H & M's[14] names in great letters—It looked so peculiar to me, and the little boys and girls waving little Yankee flags—some of them dressed in red & white striped clothes, with brass buttons and blue caps.—

I think I have equanimity enough to stand the result; which ever it is—I have thought it judicious however not to read any newspapers, for

14. Benjamin Harrison and Levi P. Morton. Grover Cleveland won the popular vote, but Harrison won the Electoral College.

they are so exciting, that I have no confidence in my ability to keep my mouth shut after they get their work done.

I am so glad you like the obituary—It seemed to me that I never could write anything appropriate—and respect for Uncle Tom prevented my indulging in the usual eulogisms—If it is printed do send me a paper. Mrs Clemens likes to read every thing about him. She appears to be interested in every item concerning the family. Isn't it curious her grandmother was named Eunice King?—a Massachusetts King—

I got a nice nice letter from Nina this morning—I was dying of curiosity to know what was in the little box the Gay's forwarded to her—has she any idea who sent the garters? Tell her not to worry about the dresses in New York—I am going to send for them myself—I have plenty of money for that and more; the *more* being particularly—vestibule curtains. If I were only in New York I would buy them immediately—I have not looked here for any thing. I insist if you need money for anything that you shall take mine—Branch will give you $50 as well as not. Nina must ask him for it any how to pay for my dress-making—My idea would be to give Mrs Harris[15] a regular percentage on any thing that we procure through her—She would get interested in it, and perhaps help us still more. You should insist upon it. Tell Nina that I am going to buy in New York some little sweet bread dishes like Mrs Clemens—(they are quite reasonable) I think of getting an extra dozen for Nina to give Lilly, or Adele just as she likes—She must write me and tell me if she approves—May—I know would like some—As soon as I finish my drama—Mr Clemens is going to send it to Abbey[16] for me—He you know is *the* man—Gillette is off playing an engagement in New York, so I am not going to refer to him unless Abbey rejects.

I am getting along very well only I find myself excessively nervous; so easily excited. Mrs Clemens is the best of all companions for me, she is so soothing—such a perfectly wholesome character—They are all exceedingly complimentary about "Earthlings"—Mr Warner told me frankly that I had astonished him—he did not think all those conversations were in me. They seem to like it as well as Monsieur Motte—which is saying a great deal for them.

15. Perhaps a dressmaker.

16. Henry Eugene Abbey (1846–1896), American theater manager and producer.

—Well, as I was saying—Nan seems to be having a good time at the plantation—I wish she *would* stay there a month. "She surely could do it, if she put her mind to it"—She must need it—and it will do Nina just as much good to stay at home and manage. She needs employment for her activities—

How I wish you and Nina could look out of this window and see this lovely view—The weather is as warm as Summer—it is slightly cloudy—and there is a haze over every thing—hardly a leaf is left on the trees—and there is a perfect interlacing across my window of satiny grey boughs and twigs—as for the distant hills they are too ethereal for anything—Here is a dish for you—Irish potatoes sliced fine as if for "Saratoga"—laid in a deep dish, with seasoning,—and the top covered with slices of bacon—and all baked—. the top should be crisp & brown like baked beans—underneath very delicate and pleasant. A splendid lunch dish is hard boiled eggs—taken out of their shells and rolled heavily in bread crumbs (& something to make 'em stick) then browned. The crust around should be as thick as the crust over veal cutlets.

There now—this is the very last. Love to all
Sis

In a week, Grace moved to the Republican household of the Warners, but her heart seems to have stayed behind with the Clemenses.

GRACE TO MAY

Hartford, November 14, 1888
"At the Warners"

My dearie—It seems an age since I wrote to you. I know it is'nt an age—only since before election—and that hateful 6th—is just a week gone to day!—How I loathe, despise and hate the Republicans!—

It was most imprudent for me to write this and leave it, for Isa Cabell is in the house and I am sure she belongs to the species that listen at doors, read peoples letters—and rummage in trunks and drawers—Mrs Warner called me up stairs to look at a dress she is having made, one of the wildest things you ever saw, in white and yellow. I am getting more and more rigid every day about gowns—I begin to believe there is no salvation, in a toilette way, out of the regulation dress-making shop. These original devices, are so trying to the nerves of the beholder.

I moved over here Monday—I hated to leave the Clemens—I was so perfectly at home there and I liked the children—& Mr Clemens was fun itself all the time. It is sweet and lovely here and natural—but with my bête noir, Mrs Cabell—it is trying—you know, she is Mr Warner's Mrs West—and her overtures to me are simply oppressive—and the more she overtures—the less I respond—Well, I hope Mr Warner will not be so foolish as Uncle Tom, that is all.—

Sunday, I finished my dramatization—went down stairs to talk it over with the Clemens, who were spending church time lounging in the library. Mr C, is a great friend of Augustin Daly's.[17] He had offered to send my MS, to him—now, he proposes that he, Mrs Clemens and I go to New York next week—that he fetch Daly around to see me, that I talk him into the whole thing—Isn't this a splendid opportunity! Mrs Clemens sister,[18] is at the "Murray Hill"—we would stay there a day and a night—for so short a time, the expense would'nt be appalling—we will go to the theatre in the evening—If Daly sees possibilities in my arrangement of Monsieur Motte,—it will necessitate perhaps a longer stay on my part North—but I have made up my mind if that is the case to go to you in Charlotte—From there I can return to New York in twenty four hours—the travelling expenses would not be more than board in New York—If there is no outcome from my project—then I can go quietly home. I hardly think I shall return to Hartford, next week from New York—I don't dare mention it—but it seems unbusiness like for me to spend the money, in making short excursions—and then I am anxious to see some of my own family—I must talk over all the changes at home. And I do want to get some where, where I can speak my mind about the Republicans—Here they are all so happy and triumphant. I am so glad that I am not going out in society here. I would'nt go to Church last Sunday—I knew the minister was going to pray out his thanks for a Republican victory—and a literary

17. John Augustin Daly (1838–1899), premier American stage director, critic, manager, and playwright.

18. Susan L. Crane (1836–1924), activist, humanist, reformer, businesswoman.

society met at the house of one of the editors of the Courant—I excused myself on account of mourning—They were going to discuss the future of the French Republic—instead of contemplating the present of this Blaine ridden government—

Mrs Warner is practicing Chopin—she is a wonderful musician—To night, she has a musicale as usual—It is a regular concert given by her and Mr Meyer, her professor and very enjoyable—only we dare not speak even in a whisper—and Mr Warner is continually getting into trouble because he will try and get up a conversation with some one.

Mrs Warner told me to give you her warm love—she takes a great interest in you—and she insists that I shall insist upon Kreuznach—

I am going to the Chrysanthemum show to day—Mrs Clemens hot-house was a perfectly beautiful sight with them—she had a hundred pots all in full bloom at once—all the new varieties—her gardener has sent twenty specimens to the show. I wonder how Mrs McDowell's turned out this year—The Chrysanthemum I most admired was the "Timbale d'Argent"[19]—but the gardener told us it was not new—the "Lord Byron" is a beauty—dark red—

It was very nice of your Charlotte newspaper man to notice me—but I prize Brevard's judgment more—I know he does not say what he does not mean—and wouldnt praise anything out of mere politeness. The Xmas story is what I most count on, however—This seems a poor kind of a letter—but it will show at least that I thought of you this morning—

Ever lovingly,
Sis.

Samuel Clemens generously applauded Grace King's new novella, *Earthlings,* and exhibited the goodwill he heaped on friends, writers, and artists. More than most of these recipients, Grace gained a distinctive place in his family. She posed no competition or threat, and Twain was apparently comfortable in the company of women. The two writers might easily have shared travel experiences on their beloved Mississippi, and in addition to Grace's genuine talent, she brought conviviality from a South that Twain knew well. In fact, some

19. A snowy-white bloom.

lines in *Earthlings* could describe how Sam, Livy, and Grace spent their time: on "questions of the day, society topics, books, opinions expressed, explained, combated" in "rapid conversation" that "produced a genial warmth."[20] The story struck Twain just right.

S L CLEMENS TO GRACE

Hartford, November 16, 1888[21]

Dear Miss King,

I do suppose you struck twelve on Earthlings. It does not seem possible that you or any one else can overmatch that masterpiece. I cannot find a flaw in the art of it—I mean the art which the intellect put there—nor in the nobler & richer art which the heart put in it. I *felt* the story, just as if I ~~had lived it~~ were living it; whereas with me a story is usually a procession & I am an outsider watching it go by—& always with a dubious, & generally with a perishing interest. If I could have stories like this one to read, my prejudice against stories would die a swift death & I should be grateful.

Sincerely Your friend,
S L C

Then her friend went beyond praise of *Earthlings* and gave her perhaps the most terror-filled and exciting days of her trip. He pushed her out into the theatrical world of New York.

GRACE TO MAY

Hartford, November 22, 1888[22]

Dear May,

This is not your letter, but Nina's—I only let you read it first because I got such a nice letter from you, on my return yesterday from New York—and

20. *Earthlings, Lippincott's Monthly Magazine* 42 (November 1888): 609.
21. This letter is published complete in "GK and MT," 41, and in *GK: A Southern Destiny,* 100.
22. A sizable portion of this letter was published in "GK and MT," 42–44.

I had already made up my mind to write to Nina because, I thought of her every minute of the time I spent there. What a good time we had together!—I smiled when I tried to get the Broadway car—and got in a 6th Avenue, by mistake. Nina would very soon have put me straight.

We made an early start Tuesday morning; took breakfast at 7.30. I got up four times after daylight to see if I couldn't begin to get ready. I never knew a morning so slow in getting to 7 OC—Mr & Mrs Clemens, Clara, Jean and the German maid were besides myself the party. We got a chaise car—and New York is just far enough off from Hartford to have a good long confidential talk; and take a little nap—Mrs C is an easy "napper," and availed herself of the opportunity but I was too excited. The Cranes, Mrs Clemens sister and brother in law, were expecting us at the "Murray Hill."[23] They are thoroughly nice, congenial people, our "taking to each other" was instantaneous and complete. The hotel rather overpowered me with the magnificence of its interior, but I soon recovered my equanimity after seeing the bed rooms and eating lunch. In no one respect, for comfort, could I see that it was better than the shabby old New York.[24] The cooking is wretched, the bath-rooms vile smelling and ill lighted. The Clemens like it because it is so near the 42d st station—but for the price I am sure one could be better accommodated elsewhere. It is 7.50 a day for a single person—but $10—for two rooming together. Fortunately I roomed with Clara. As soon as we had eaten lunch, Mrs Clemens ordered a carriage & we drove to her dressmakers—a Madame Fogarty—38, East 22d—She is what Annie[25] would call a "swell" dressmaker—Mrs Clemens asked to see her pretty things—and you never in your life beheld a more superb collection of gowns and cloaks—The cheapest dress was about $250!—I got lots of ideas—and enjoyed the show hugely. Then we drove to Mrs Clemens tailor—De Luray, on 6th Avenue. It amused me very much, this performance, seeing a fat, pudgy man, pinch up her jacket at the waist, and chalk up the arm holes—which he called "Harm oles"—We went to "Charles Jones"—on Broadway, where I wanted to get some pretty china "ramekin" saucers and pudding dish, like Mrs Clemens—but

23. A popular hotel built in 1884 on Park and Fortieth across from Grand Central Station; it was demolished in 1948.

24. The New York Hotel, where Grace and Branch had stayed.

25. Annie Miller, King's cousin.

the wretched creature had sold them all out the day before—and I was disappointed—the only thing that consoled me was that you (May) could get them for us later in the season and have them sent by express. If I had only had time and money, I could have filled a trunk from this place. It is filled with all the domestic and kitchen utensils we have been hankering for for years.

We landed at the hotel at 3 OC—went to our rooms; Mr Clemens was just putting on his coat—to receive Augustin Daly—whose card had just been sent up. The Cranes had offered their rooms for the interview—as they are quite handsomely installed there. I seized my MS—and we all went in a body to the Cranes—I as you may imagine in a tremor.

I was never more surprised in my life—than when a slouchily dressed, thin, most *un*theatrical looking personage was introduced as "Mr Daly." He has a literary look—and a very artistic face. While we were all talking, Will Gillette—who boards at the Murray Hill—passed by and seeing us all through the open door, came in—Then I felt very dramatic indeed. Soon every body went away and left me with Mr Daly—and Mr Clemens who was chaperon. I had no difficulty in talking, and managed to remember what I had composed to say—Daly said that he was looking all the time for some one to write for his theatre; that he was tired of it himself—that a dramatic success, paid better than any other literary venture—that he hoped I had made one in this—but if I had not, not to be discouraged; he himself had had five plays refused right straight along, when he first commenced. He would see if "Monsieur Motte" were actable—then if it were adapted to his theatre he would take it; if he could not use it he would advise me about what to do with it. If it did not do at all, I must not be discouraged but take my time and try my hand again. When I went to get a string and paper to do the MS—up in—I made Mrs Clemens come back with me—and we had a general good time all together. He invited us to the theatre that night, and said he would wait for us at the door.

As soon as he was gone, we started off in a carriage to call on the Howells. Mrs Clemens insisted that I must know them. They live on Stuyvesant Square, in the third story of a flat. The Janitor took our cards up—and reported that they were in—but after we had climbed up to the place we found that the Janitor had made a mistake. A very lackadaisical young girl of about sixteen clad in faded greens received us, and said that she was sorry—but no body was in but herself—Mamma was ill in bed—Papa was out shopping for something—Winnie was over in Philadelphia "under the charge of Dr Weir Mitchell"—Mrs Clemens, who never goes up stairs if she can avoid it, sank in an arm chair perfectly disgusted. Mr Clemens walked around the room and looked at the pictures—I gazed about me in silence while Miss Mildred Howells went on in her languid voice giving her family news. She is a very pretty girl; talks just like Cora Urquhart[26] used to. The room we were in seemed to be parlor, dining and sitting room—furnished with the inevitable Turkish rugs on the floor, and striped portieres dangling from the door ways—with some bric-a-brac and otherwise artistic attempts scattered around on tables, and pinned to the walls.

We took a good glass of wine when we got in the hotel again, and laid down until dinner time. Over the dinner, we naturally fell to discussing the episode, and criticizing the selfishness of the girl for not running down stairs and explaining herself that no one was in—Mr Clemens saying how distressed and mortified Howells would be when he heard of it. I raised my eyes and was just going to say "Why there he is now"—when Mrs Clemens saw him. I recognized him of course from his pictures. He sat with us during dinner—I found that he was every thing the Warners & Clemens had described. Unaffected, modest, but perfectly charming in conversation and manners. He and Mr Clemens laugh and talk together like two school-boys. He was exceedingly pleasant and cordial to me. We went into our rooms after dinner—sent for the children, and until theatre time, were just as sociable and family-like as possible. How the man can write his stories, is a puzzle to me—there is nothing cold and critical about him—but he has a sad face—and a hopeless look about the eyes, which shows that he is a pessimist, at heart. His language in talking is as exquisite as his writing—his division of sentences, exactly the same as in his books.—

The performance at Daly's was "the lottery of Love"[27]—A regular side splitting comedy. We had Daly's own stage box—and Daly's company,

26. New Orleans acquaintance.

27. Either a French play by Pierre de Marivaux, dating from 1720s or, as in "GK and MT," 44, *The Lottery of Life: A Story of New York* by John Brougham, French, 1867.

most of the time. Mr Clemens of course attracted great attention from the audience, and stage too—we could catch the actors and actresses casting side glances constantly in our direction. Oh it was all great fun! I wondered at my temerity in offering Daly any thing—and when I saw what a good thing his dramatization was—and what a capital witty epilogue he had written—I made up my mind that Monsieur Motte would not suit him or his'n—I told him that I wished he would send me my MS straight back—that I was convinced—but he laughed, & declared he would read. He has a mouth like Cartwright Eustis's & laughs just like him[28]—

Nearly all of yesterday morning I went looking at the Vereshchagin collection of pictures.[29] As Howells says—"they are Tolstoi in paint"—"perfectly dreadful, but as real as the tooth-ache"—I bought all the books and catalogues, so I can "exhibit" a little, when I can get back, and give you all an idea of them. The man's power is simply immense—colossal—I am not an art critic—so I cannot classify Vereshchagin's place in Art—but he must have tremendous influence in the outside world—I was carried away by the whole thing.

Last night Mrs Warner's Wednesday musical was in full blast on my return. Mr Warner was sitting in the dining-room smoking with a modest quiet, Haynes-ish looking individual. He turns out to be the future Earl Grey—Mrs Warner is a good-deal impressed by the fact, I think. To me—he is rather unimportant. He is to be here until Wednesday—

To morrow I go over to Northampton to visit Smith College on Mary Barton's invitation. Monday, I spend the day with the Gays—Wednesday morning D V—I pack my trunk, and start for Baltimore. A good deal depends however, upon what I hear from Daly. If he should care to talk the thing over with me—I will stay a day or two in New York—I am prepared though for disappointment—this letter, send this home—I will not be able to write again until day after tomorrow—

Ever devotedly
Sis

28. Eustis was a prominent New Orleans citizen (1842–1900) who had a pouty mouth.
29. Vasily Vereshchagin (1842–1904), Russian artist, particularly of war scenes.

☙ GRACE TO NAN

Hartford, n.d. [November 24?, 1888]

Dearest Nan,

Every thing is frozen, hard and fast; boys are skating on the little pond and the little river looks like a winding strip of isinglass. They say it is going to snow to morrow; woe is me! I wish I were at home; I wouldn't live in this climate for all the riches in Connecticut.

All day yesterday I was over in Northampton, visiting Smith College. We left at 9 OC, in the morning. Patrick the coachman, enveloped in furs, looking like one of Tolstoi's Russians—with his tog cap and shaggy tippet.[30] Mrs Clemens was all seal-skin except the tip end of a very red nose. I thought I would freeze in my seat as the open carriage dashed at full trot through the icy streets.

You ought to be very thankful my dear, that you were born on the other side of Mason & Dixon line—and so escaped a college education!—Of all doleful, depressing places, of all ugly uninteresting girls! Four hundred of them—being trained into science and homeliness—They may know lots—but oh the beauty of our ignorance in comparison! the charm, the grace—Well—there ought to be some punishment for being Yankees and I think the females who are in the colleges here—are going to get it—

One poor little creature jumped in a river and committed suicide a week ago—one of the students—and I am not surprised—only I would have loved to drown some of the others too, if I had been she.

I send you a sample of smocking—it is on every thing—I got Annie Price's sempstress to show me how to do it—I never should have hit it in a life time I am sure. It must all be done by measurement. Tell Nina to take her soft black silk sash and tie it around in front in a full bow—they are all the rage—tied just as she would tie it behind, only the bow does not come on *top* of the stomach—but slightly *under* it—There is no other way of expressing the position.

Isn't this a nice letter from Lounsbury—I begged it as a souvenir—I adore Mugwumps, and am still hating the Republicans & raging against them.

30. A shawl-like strip of cloth worn over the shoulders.

I send Will's last to Mimi with the note from Miss Barton to him.[31] We have drifted into quite a correspondence. I enclosed $5 to him, as it appeared very fortunately. I offered to take him home with me—I knew I would feel easier if I made the offer, being pretty sure that he will not stay North all winter. If Daly's answer is favorable—I shall send Will enough to buy flannels with. The Xmas story is just out here,[32] and every body is complimenting me about it—Now I must go to work & write some more—but I am going to take a walk to the P O now—

I wish I could get presented to the Clevelands—but the trouble is I can't stay in Washington—I could go over any day from Baltimore—if I had some one to meet me, and take me to the white house. Who is Gen Hooker?[33]

How I wish Judge Rogers would be there about that time. Give him my love when you see him.

Ever devotedly
Sis.

By late November, Grace had heard from Daly, and the news was discouraging. It would be decades before she tried again to write for the stage.

AUGUSTIN DALY TO GRACE

New York, November 24, 1888[34]
Daly's Theatre.
under the management of Augustin Daly

31. Clara Barton (1821–1912), founder of the American Red Cross. King's brother Will was then working with the organization in Washington City; he wrote that Barton promised to help place him in a better position.

32. "The Christmas Story of a Little Church," *Harper's New Monthly Magazine* 78 (December 1888): 463.

33. Joseph Hooker (1814–1879) was a Union army general whose last name is attached to the term "hooker," as in prostitute. Although the word preceded him, he seems to have earned the reputation by having an abundance of camp followers at his encampments.

34. The spacing of lines in this letter is unusual, gradually descending from the left side on an angle all the way down to the signature.

My dear Miss King,

I regret that I do not find a play in your book. I find some very good acting scenes where Marcelite is engaged, and quite touching bits where Marie is concerned; but it does not begin to be an actable one until your fifth or sixth scene—the previous half being simply dialogue without movement, or at least without movement of interest to a spectator.

I think your instinct is dramatic—and you could write very effective "speaking" dialogue—as dialogue for the stage as we distinguish it from dialogue for the reader, most of the latter being absolutely "unspeakable"—or if spoken would be laughed at by a mixed audience of strangers.

In constructing a work for the stage you should avoid so many changes of scene—Your piece as it stands would require about a dozen sets.

If I do not make myself understood, & you happen in town any morning & will call at the theatre I may be able to give a suggestion or two in plainer terms—

Sincerely
Augustin Daly

Any further need for Grace to stay in New York now settled, she made a short trip in December to revisit the jolly spinsters with whom she had frolicked the previous year at Watch Hill, Rhode Island.[35] Then she left Hartford and the cold North to spend some weeks in North Carolina with May before returning to New Orleans. She wrote Susy Warner from Charlotte, apparently hurt and confused by a confrontation as she had boarded the train. Something had gone wrong with that friendship over her closeness to the Clemenses and the gossip about Isa Cabell that Grace had repeated. The letter alternately fawns, justifies, and confronts.

GRACE TO SUSAN WARNER

Charlotte, December 1, 1888

35. Heloise Cenas, Elizabeth W. Burnap, and artist Lizzie Adams, sister of writer Annie Adams Fields, who was the wife of publisher James T. Fields and *intimate* of Sarah Orne Jewett.

My dear.—I hope never as long as I live, to merit such a good-bye as that of last Wednesday morning. I say merit, because you evidently thought I merited it, and Mr Warner sustained you in his disposition towards me all the way in the carriage to the station—and at the station, wanted to know "if I had anything to say for myself"—expecting I supposed an apology—or excuse, or whatever—I could say, that he might be warranted in giving me a pleasant word to carry away, with me on my journey. I was too startled, too demoralized to say anything—consequently I had nothing to carry away with me except the sense, made certainty, that last morning by you both—that I had done something to offend, to estrange you.

I had intended, when I kissed you good-bye—to say something to you—what I have forgotten now—but the way in which you said for the crowd to hear that "you wanted to see whether I would not forget to tell you good-bye"—made me feel, that I wanted nothing but to hurry away—and hide my mortification. I blessed Mrs George Warner for the kind expression in her eyes, and I was glad to kiss Daisy—I am not cold, unfeeling, nor ungrateful—I never for one moment forgot when I was with you what I owed you and Mr Warner—I never can forget it as long as I remember anything. It never occurred to me to suppose that you and Mr Warner could seriously disapprove or snub me. I knew that education, blood, sectional differences, even opinions about religion, separated us—but I thought that we all could meet in our natural characters and enjoy even the expression of such differences. For Mr Warner in his kindness had come to me, and laid me under those obligations which only a great heart can impose—and which I thought, only a great heart could accept. —Perhaps, it was in the assurance that I could not be misunderstood that I allowed myself liberties which a more discreet person would have avoided. It is a pitiable excuse to profess—but the very wretchedness I felt, both of health and spirits, made me careless of trying to please.

I saw that you were a little surprised at the great intimacy I fell into with Mrs Clemens but you were not more surprised than I, myself. I went to the Clemens in great uncertainty, and only after consultation with Mr Warner. I never expected them to like me; more than the ordinary liking between a pleasant hostess, and a most ordinary kind of a guest. I love them now, all of them—and I do most sincerely hope that the friendship will endure—a little while at least. The kinder they were to me, & the more I loved them—the more grateful I felt to you and Mr Warner for bringing us together, I did not mean to make myself absurd by any undue impressions of sentiment about them—but I candidly thought that as you loved Mrs Clemens too, that you would be gratified at my pleasing them—and that such a common friend would strengthen our own friendship. To think that I had gone over to them as you expressed it last Monday—was an insult which you did not mean—I do not "go over," either from my country, my religion, or my friends. I cannot feint love—that is all—and I have not a discriminating brain when my heart is touched. I should be inexpressibly wretched now, if I did not have the hope that you will come to New Orleans next Winter. I want you to see my own home, my own people—to let them love you, not more than I do—but as much—and I want you to love them a great deal more than you have ever been able to love me. I don't dare say you have done me injustice. Heaven knows you may be doing me justice—but the position of ingrate is one of such abhorrence in my mind that you must grant me an opportunity to plead for myself again; not with word but with deed.

I am sure you will do this; that you will do it not entirely for yourself—but for Mr Warner.

Do you really think that my friendship for him must be discouraged? It was a friendship I was so proud of—I hoped it would give him pleasure, some day. However it rests entirely in your hands. I think he is prepared to follow your lead in the matter—I must of course submit to your decision. I intend to do it—although with me it will mean almost despair. I have not much confidence in myself. You can very easily convince me that I was simply found "not worthy."

But if love, and friendship mean any thing in this world—I am not to be separated from either of you. My own heart tells me to have faith—to trust if not in you two—in God. A gravity of this kind can not be eradicated from my heart—is it to be uprooted from yours? then let me try over again—some day—I will furnish the seed, the cuttings—may be you will give me a little corner of your hearts to plant them in—

Grace.

Then, perhaps, Grace got closer to the source of the problem between the three.

GRACE TO SUSAN WARNER
Charlotte, n.d. [December 1888]

My dear Friend,
I see that I wrote too impulsively to you; I saw that after I received your first letter. But my heart and mind were so troubled that I had not judgment to wait for the calm that time brings. I rushed at once to you to seek relief from the thoughts that had overcrowded me in the train all the way to Charlotte.

Mr Warner was so strange to me in the carriage the morning I left; his goodbye was almost unfriendly. I did jump from conclusion to conclusion; my premises as you say were wrong, but they were a little less painful than to suppose he was acting entirely from his own views in regard to me.

I felt acutely what a miserable failure my whole Northern trip had been—I had been disappointed in almost every hope, and in every business calculation with which I had set out. I was not prepared to accept the gain of the Clemens friendship as an equivalent for the loss of your's and Mr Warner's. The remembrance of his kindness to me and the innumerable little gifts which represented your good-will to us, at home convicted me easily of ingratitude. I was entirely too miserable for the occasion and acted as I usually do with little worldly wisdom.

No, you did not accuse me of going over to the Clemens that morning in the dining room. It was the evening Mr Gillette returned to me the Daly letter.

The morning in the dining room—you are right the moment was badly chosen for a confidential talk. I was so preoccupied and distressed about a family matter that at the time the rearrangement of a friendship was almost a mockery. All the friends in the world were nothing to me that morning. I was in doubt and really in great trouble. I felt your kindness but it hurt me to think that you thought I could deliberately accuse you or complain of you. If I ever felt a momentary smart over anything you said or did I settled it in my mind by thinking I had deserved it. I am not egotistical enough to think I was right and you were wrong—I saw how others could please you—and how quickly you understood and responded to others—both you and Mr Warner. I felt no change in my feelings to you. I was unconscious of any difference; but I did not dispute your impression that I had changed. I felt too unequal to it. I had a hopeless certainty that I was fitted by nature and education to occupy but a very small place in your lives—and it did hurt me very much to think when I was in such distress of mind, that loss of appetite and even moroseness would be attributed to a childish pouting—

Any little explanation I tried to have with Mr Warner was unsatisfactory after his anger with me, about what I said about Isa Cabell. After that impression upon him—I offered, even tried to release him from the invitation to stay with you—I wanted to go straight home. I did not wish to give you any more worry about so unsatisfactory a protegeé—I envied you the tears in your eyes that morning. I have had to suppress my tears so much during life that I have almost lost the ability to shed them; except at night when I am entirely alone.

Well, your letters have reassured me, and I do not intend ever to allude to this again—I am in hopes even that it will be a good lesson for me the rest of my life.

But it is hard, that contact with people—the inevitable comparisons, between self and others, should work so much to my discouragement.

May sends you her love and always her thanks for the kind interest you take in her. She is carrying on her life very bravely here, is full of energy and work for other people; but I wish that her eyes looked better. If Christmas were not in the way I would stay a long long time with her. [. . .]

Give my love to Annie, and remember me to Ellen and Christine, and believe me, I beg, always your loyal Grace

Whatever had occurred, a stray note from Livy is suggestive:

Dear Grace,
I am a little scared after your talk this morning but I love you and I wanted so much to do it so you wont mind will you?

With much love your
Livy L. C.

Letters from Sam and Livy and Susy and Clara Clemens tell how close they had all become and must surely have assuaged Grace's dismay over the chill from the Warners. By now, the Clemens girls had a private and playful name for Grace.[36] As well-raised daughters, the two older girls wrote notes of thanks. Clara replicated Livy's practice of expounding on books she had read and theater she had attended. Livy, confident in her friendship with Grace, was generous about the Warners' need for her attentiveness.

OLIVIA CLEMENS AND S L CLEMENS TO GRACE

Hartford, December 4, 1888

FARMINGTON AVENUE

HARTFORD, CONN.

Grace dear,

I cannot tell you how I have delighted in your two letters.[37] It is not as good as having you here still it is very good.

I have lost my stylographic and so feel quite put about this morning.[38]

My sister and my brother-in-law arrived on Wednesday as they expected. Mr Crane seemed better for two or three days, Thursday night he greatly enjoyed our frolic and we hoped great things from the change, but now for two or three or four days he has been perfectly wretched. He has had no appetite and has been in the deepest darkness as to his spirits.

We did have a good and jolly time Thanksgiving evening and I wished for you all the time, and all the time too I was thinking in my heart I am richer than I was last Thanksgiving I have found a friend. Grace you may be very sure that I love you and trust you and you may write just as many letters to the Warners as you desire, I feel that you are my friend and that is enough.

36. In *Memories,* King recalls the nickname as Tweety (83). The girls write it as Teety or Tety but might have pronounced it as King suggests. Perhaps it originated with little Jean's inability to pronounce "sweetie."

37. The letters are missing.

38. Engraving stylus. Twain liked this new pen and wrote Twichell that it could be "a genuine God's blessing" once "the dullest ass" spent "a royal amount of cussing to make the thing go" (*MT and Twichell,* 98).

Don't ever feel taxed to write but when you do write you may be sure that your letter will have a most hearty welcome at this end. There is no hand writing that I more rejoice to see than yours.

Mrs Charles Webster, Mr Clemen's niece is now with us and is to be for a few days. There is the "bridal chamber" left[39] and I wish you were in it, we miss you greatly. My sister has been taught "hearts" so we still play. Last night the German class met and Mr Clemens did not retire to the billiard room. I think that speaks well for Miss Corey.[40]

I am glad you are going to stay for a time with your sister. I hope you will leave there in better health and spirits than (woe is me) you left here in.

With kind regards to your sister I am
Your loving friend
Olivia L. C.

Dec. 4th 1888

Me, too. S L C

[Livy left me to address the envelop, & suspects no overstepping of my privilege.]

SUSY CLEMENS TO GRACE

Hartford, December 6?, 1888
FARMINGTON AVENUE,
HARTFORD, CONN.

Dear Tety,
How I miss you! I knew that I should, of course, but I did not know how much, how very much.

39. The suite of rooms in which King stayed is now the recently renovated Mahogany Suite at the Mark Twain House.

40. Susan (Susy) Corey (b. 1865?) taught music to Susy and Clara and also taught German to the two girls and to Livy.

Still perhaps the missing you will help me to be good for whenever I think of you I add at least one kick to the height of my "ideal." It has been pouring every day since you left. I wish I could say that I have been keeping fare. But I have not lived up to it one day, no, hardly one minute yet. The first time that I really do, I will write you.

You sent us such beautiful messages in your letter to Mamma only they made her cry. It was a blessed thing! that *box* of candy, I am sure it brought us much more pleasure than boxes of candy generally bring.

Constantly we run across little things and sayings that remind us of you, you will never cease to seem very simply near I am sure even if we should never come together again.

As long as you stand before me as clearly even so effectively with your "how Susy!" how can it be otherwise?

You are telling me through my ideal that I musn't write another minute. I will be obedient. I love you. I wish you were here, and we could take a walk together.

You *must* come back next Fall.

And now good bye
Your ever devoted
Susy Clemens.

SUSY CLEMENS TO GRACE

Hartford, n.d. [late December 1888]

Dear Tety,
What *made* you write me such a beautiful letter? I suppose because you felt it, but I was surprised, I couldn't believe that you did at first.[41]

I have never had such a letter before, I am sure that is true. The first paragraph especially was so wise.

Mr. Meyer is down stairs and Clara is playing him her last new piece, it is a beauty but what it is, I have not even asked.

We have had a very beautiful peaceful, Xmas, I think. I wish you could have been here.

41. The letter is missing.

Yes I shouldn't wonder at all if the German Rounds would be played tonight, it is such a pity that you will not be able to enjoy your favorites.

In my next letter I will write you in more detail about the Greek, but now I have stopped it for these two weeks, you know. I like it more & more, tho,' and Mr Chapin too, I think Miss Jan[?] Fleck is wonderful in her algebra teaching, ~~I think~~ I know.

Poor Miss Lima! has just buried a sister. I dread taking my next singing lesson of her, I am so sorry for her.

We all go to New York next Monday. We shall see the wonderful child Elsie in "Little Lord Fauntleroy," I think.

It is raining a slow, drizzling, summer, rain. Cousin Charlie is satisfied "this is the only decent Xmas we have ever had here.["] The poor, funny deluded man! it has been lovely weather, but our snow, and sleighing Christmases are the ones richest in sentiment, and other ways too.

Dear Tety, I must say good bye now, with no end of love, and hopes that I may soon have another letter from you. Every one sends love and a Merry Christmas, and happy New Year, and everything imaginable in such messages.

With love
Your own
Susy Clemens.

CLARA CLEMENS TO GRACE

Hartford, [December 19? 1888]

Dear precious Teety,

Perhaps you have thought I have neglected you, maybe I have in pen & ink but not a second in my thoughts, for all the time have *longed* to have you back again.

How short your visit seemed here, but we did get quite a good deal accomplished in that time. Tety it is very too bad you were not here last Wednesday, they played *most* delightfully, & Rubinstein & Liszt.

They did *not* play the "German Rounds," nor the "Ballet," Max Smith was there, and he played us a piece afterwards, & didn't seem at *all* scared.

But Thank Heavens! *we* did not have to play. The examinations begin next Wednesday, I dread them very much indeed, I hope they wo'nt be very difficult. I anticipate the Xmas vacation immensely, which begins next Friday & lasts until a week from the following Wednesday.

I hope to get a lot of time for reading then. I am now reading "John Brent" & enjoy it so very much. Do'n't you think his description of the black horse in the first part of the book is very striking, & it is quite exciting I think where Armstrong, Wade & John Brent, pursue the murderers & Ellen.[42]

After I have finished this & read "Cesil Dreams" j'ai l'intention, to read Hypatia,[43] which is very interesting is it not?

Mary Foote is coming to spend Xmas, & most of the vacation with us. I think we shall have great fun, we did last year when she staid with us. I only hope there will be sleighing, it looks today as if it were going to snow.

I do *wish* it would snow the Monday before Xmas, & Christmas also. We are going to New York for the last three days of the vacation, to see my beloved Ada Rehan, & dear little Elsie Leslie.[44] The whole family is going & we anticipate it muchly. I suppose you are glad you wont have to hear my jabbering after we come home from the theatre, but Susy will have to bear it, that is if I can get in a word now & then.

Dear Mr. Gilette is over at Mrs. Warner's & he was coming to see me today, but he does not seem to be coming very fast.

Both my thumbs are now maimed so that I don't know *when* I can practice, it is *very* annoying I think. Teety Sweetie, I seem to have no more to day, so I shall end this epistle with no end of love & kisses,

from your loving & affectionately fond
Clara.

P.S. was that end too-too?

42. Characters in *John Brent* by Theodore Winthrop (1864).

43. *Cecil Dreeme* by Theodore Winthrop (1861); *Hypatia, or New Foes with an Old Face* (1853) by Charles Kingsley.

44. Rehan (1857–1916) was a Daly theater star known for "personality" acting; Leslie (1881–1966) was the theater's first child star.

The year 1888 ended with a sort of reconciliation with Susan Warner, who sent "all the good wishes in my heart for you" and assured Grace that the two were "in the same dear old place with each other, are we not?—& we will never refer to it again—no never." Then she gave news of friends and acquaintances in Hartford, including that the Clemenses were going to New York, leaving the Cranes behind. "Poor Mr Crane is very wretched most of the time" and was using "Clara for his mouth and Jean for his eyes—& the others for fun I suppose."[45] Grace and Susy Warner seemed to be back on track, but they would never share the easy comity that Grace and Livy enjoyed. Peace-making Livy would not perturb her exacting neighbor, but she was inadvertently drawn into the storm, apparently by whatever Grace spoke in her library.

45. Susan Warner to Grace, December 30, 1888.

CHAPTER 7

BUSY TIMES AND TIME APART 1889–1890

Whether you are on the Matterhorn or in the valley
I am always your deeply loving friend.
—OLIVIA CLEMENS TO GRACE, MARCH 24, 1889

Declarations of reconciliation aside, Grace's friendship with the Warners cooled somewhat, especially when Isa Cabell was staying or traveling with them. When Grace wrote Susy Warner, she couched justification of her "judging and condemning" of Isa's motives in a declaration that she was the one who risked loss of their good opinion.[1] To Warner, she wrote mainly literary talk with some condemnation of his political choices. She congratulated him on essays and admitted that she "only wrote scraps here and there, nothing to count unless the relief to the imagination be of value."[2] He skipped his usual trip to New Orleans in 1889 but did meet with Grace in August in North Carolina, and he bucked up her confidence and goaded her to write more continuously. Although she still relied on him to recommend her, she was assuming her own agency with publishers and editors. As was her style, business often included a personal component.

Over the next few years, Grace kept in touch with the Clemenses, a friendship of equals, absent of recriminations. Although Grace showed little interest

1. Grace to Susan Warner, February 15, 1889.

2. Grace to Warner, February 1, 1889. King fervently stood for white men handling racial issues in the South and feared another Republican reconciliation (Grace to Warner, May 28, 1889). One piece she did write at this period was a four-thousand-word story for Decoration Day ("A Silenced Battery") for *Harper's Bazar;* she made fifty dollars (Margaret E. Sangster to Grace, May 10, 1889). Sangster cut King's story down to three thousand words and had to "do the best I could" when she discovered a page missing from the manuscript.

in children at home, her pen pal relationship with the Clemens girls extended to nine-year-old Jean, now old enough to write. Fifteen-year-old Clara's letters showed an increasing discernment about the arts. They also suggest the lessons Grace tried to teach and the passions Livy sought to curb.

CLARA CLEMENS TO GRACE

Hartford, February 3, 1889

Dear Tety,

I was so delighted to receive your sweet interesting, letter, & hope to hear from you pretty soon, for it seems like months since I have.

Rosenthal[3] gave a recital last Wednesday; & oh! such *playing* such playing, I never heard. I do'nt think Aus der Ohe compared with him in any way, certainly not in technique, but her music never stirred me, as his did.

Stirred, I could have laughed & cried at once. It was supernatural, superb, marvelous, I would have given anything if I could have sat next you, for I know that you would have appreciated it in the same way.

He played among the other things the 1st (I think) Rhapsodie Hongreuse,[4] oh! it did not seem as if the man could be mortal; if I had been a man, I should have risen & *shouted shrieked* Rosenthal! oh! Rosenthal! would have done anything.

There the audience sat, hardly clapped, & never thought of even calling him back on to stage; & to realize, there was Mr. Meyer, Mr. Cooly, Mr. Welch,[5] any of those men, who had it in their power, to make the whole house resound with applause, & *none* of them did it, I suppose because they were self-*conscious,* or feared they might lose their reputation; oh! what fiends! they were. There sat Rosenthal, that genius, that wonder! & they hardly condescended to clap, thourough selfishness.

It was well mamma was there for if she had not been, no one knows what I might not have done.

He was so attractive personally & *most* distinguished-looking. Tomor-

3. Moriz Rosenthal (1862–1946), "the Napoleon of the Pianoforte."

4. "Rhapsodie Hongroise" by Franz Liszt (1811–1886).

5. Meyer was Susan Warner's teacher; Francis R. Cooley and Archibald A. Welch were members of the supporting organization for the Hartford Philharmonic Orchestra.

row night Aus der Ohe, Emma Guch[6] & a number of others give a concert at the Armory; to which mamma is going to let us go.

They are going to give the last scene of Faust, but it can't *approach* the Rosenthal concert, in any respect, Mr. Stanchfield[7] has been here, & was as lovely as ever.

We took a number of rides together. But Tety your talk that evening did me so much good, that I did not mourn for more than a week after he went, & if your talk had not continually presented itself, I should have made myself miserable for a long time.

As for your saying I must have been studying french very hard, I fear I must say that then I had studied comparatively none. But since Xmas I have studied very hard on all my things, & when I have had any spare time have either practised, or read in Shakespeare's plays; have not brooded on John Barry Stanchfield

Do'nt you think Tety, dear I have grown better, since you left, its only when I go to bed that I take any time for Ada Rehan & the other, & then usually, I do'nt think long; & I certainly don't gush to any-one I keep all my feelings to myself.

I suppose you heard all about Mr[s]. Cabell's serious illnesses. Mamma stayed with her a good part of last night; & is over there now.

About a week ago she raved fearfully & "writhed & went on," no "he was writhing & going on," I believe. I don't feel someway that she will live, I do'nt know how it is with the rest.

I think I have told you all the news, & told you a few of my sentiments, so Prescia, I will close this boonlet, with love no *end* of it!!

Your loving
Clara.

P.S. I have learned any-way nine, irregular french verbs. I thout it would please you to know.
Sunday Feb 3rd 1889

P.S. We went with Mamma last night to hear Bill Nye, & Reiley[8] read, & I

6. Unidentified musician.

7. Stanchfield (1855–1921), American lawyer and politician from Elmira, New York.

8. Nye and James Whitcomb Riley, known for wit and humor.

never laughed so hard in all my days, if Mamma had not been there, I am sure I should have grown too silly. But do'nt you think they are amusing.

I laughed harder at Nye than at Ryley. They came out to the carriage afterwards, & were just as nice as could be.

Clara.—

JEAN CLEMENS TO GRACE

Hartford, February 10, 1889[9]

Dear Miss King,
I thank you *very very* much for the two valentines. they were so pretty. I am so sorry that I did not write you sooner than is, I never remeber to write notes that I ought to write, Mamma allways has to remind me of them and then I write to all that I have to. and this is one of then that I am writing now.

Good bye
Jean

CLARA CLEMENS TO GRACE

Hartford, March 7 and 8, 1889

Dear Tety,
I have not written you since I was laid up with a sour (or is it sore) back.

There has much happened though since.

Mr. Welch is as nice as ever & I am just as fond of him. I danced with him a week or two ago here, one whole evening. He dances sublimely & we went perfectly together.

We have gone to the music regularly & they have ceased playing "new music," but they play Siegfried, Tannhaüser, Meistersinger, the most wonderfull of all Preludes (Liszt) etc. etc.

We have had spring from the time you left us, & now we are to have 3 more months of it. I love it, I can not say that I am fond of winter with all its cold gray disagreeable days. I adore the sun, & the days that are so

9. On children's stationery, in a childlike handwriting.

clean & fresh. I always feel radiantly happy, when these first real warmish summer windy enspriting days arrive.

I have been out all the afternoon, first driving then *riding* (oh! *such* a ride) & then lastly walking. It is Thursday & we do not have school again 'till Tuesday.—

Miss Howe[10] said I had been getting on very well of late, both in the reading & in the grammar (French).

It is an other beautiful morning so I am going to ride before breakfast. I began this letter last evening & stopped at the top of this page.

I have been reading short lives of Wagner Liszt & Beethoven. The one of Liszt is the most fascinating of all I think, oh! how I *wish* I could have seen him & heard him. I suppose Tety sweet that you have read "Guenn" by Miss Howard. It is a beautiful story I think & Guenn Rodellec is my ideal of a young girl.[11]

The end was horrible but of course there would have been no strength in nor object to the story, if it had been otherwise.

I am reading now the Life of Bayard Taylor by his second wife.[12] It is very fascinating I think, though I have allways hated scenery descriptions I revell in his, you can truthfully see the sunsets & woods before you.

Proff. Johnston sent me "Two Gray Tourists" (by himself) with a word in it from him.[13] Next week I think I am going to see beloved Ada Rehan in "Taming of the Shrew" which of course delights my heart, for I should prefer to see her in that than anything else. I have 42 photos of actresses now, & the wall is all filled so that I shall have to buy an album.

Booth & Barret[14] are coming to town next Thursday, & I am going to try to get papa to invite them here to dinner. Mary Anderson[15] comes down in Winter's Tale, & Aunt Clara (she always hated her fearfully) says she was beautifull in that & was so enthusiastic that mamma may let us go possibly. I have been practising a little more of late & so Mr. Meyer has been complimenting me on my playing, a thing he never does.

10. Apparently, Clara's teacher at school.

11. *Guenn: A Wave on the Breton Coast* (1884) by Blanche Willis Howard (1847–1898).

12. Taylor (1825–1878), poet, author, critic, diplomat. His wife was Marie Hansen.

13. Richard Malcom Johnston (1822–1898), "Two Gray Tourists" (1885).

14. Edwin Booth and Lawrence Barrett, famous Shakespearean actors.

15. Anderson (1859–1940), "Queen of the Drama!"

Tety love, the horses are waiting so I must close this epistle & soon write another.

With oh, so much much love & many kisses & hugs
Your loving
Clara—

March 7th or 8th '89

Warner also sent news of the friends in 1889. In March, he wrote that he was to join "Sue" and the Clemenses in New York to go to the home of Dora Wheeler together.[16] Lilly Warner wrote that "Livy and I are always talking of you and ending up with a hearty declaration of affection for you." Lilly added that she had misjudged Isa Cabell, and she seemed to be trying to persuade King that Isa was more a "daughter" to Warner than a paramour.[17] However, even Mark Twain and minister Joe Twichell would later exchange gossipy innuendoes about Isa's presence, disruptions, and bizarre actions.[18]

Then Livy's own letter to Grace suggests the kind of intellectual and professional talks they must have relished when together and the uncommon directness that existed between the two women. Livy, the peacemaker, also counseled Grace to be more forbearing with her friends. The dustup over Isa seems to have exposed Grace's principled but sometimes ill-conceived frankness and, perhaps, a bit of jealousy.

OLIVIA CLEMENS TO GRACE

Hartford, March 24, 1889
FARMINGTON AVENUE,
HARTFORD, CONN.

Grace dear,
I desperately want a visit with you, and although it is nearly bed time I am at least determined to begin my visit.

16. Warner to Grace, March 14, 1889. Wheeler was an artist and daughter of Candace Wheeler, decorator and friend of the Clemenses. Her home was at 124 Twenty-Seventh St., New York City.

17. Lilly Warner to Grace, March 27, 1889.

18. See *MT and Twichell,* 208, 210, 226.

Mrs Church is coming to us for a visit on April 1st How we wish you were coming too, she has a great desire to know you better. She says when you were here in the Fall she wanted to ask you to come to them, but they were both so miserable that she had to give it up, now she hopes next time that you come north that she will be able to have a visit with you. And you know it is not to be so very long before you come again. If you wont come any other way I shall be compelled to get sick and need you and then you will have to come you know, because I have not forgotten that lovely promise that you made me.

In your letter before the last one you wonder what I thought about when I sat beside Mrs Cabells sick bed and whether I remembered your bad temper &c &c.[19] I don't think I thought about any thing except a desire to relieve her, but what ever I thought, I thought nothing of you that you would not have entirely enjoyed knowing. I never do think anything of you except thoughts that are pleasant and loving, and admiring. I have chosen you for my friend and I am mighty proud when you write affectionately to me. Gracie dear I am pleased beyond measure for if I was to confess the truth I should have to write that it surprises me very much that you care much for me, because I am so deadly common place, and you know yourself that you are not, even your worst enemy could not accuse you of that crime. I don't find common place people interesting even if I am one myself and so as I said before I am very proud and thankful for your friendship. There is no letter that comes in our mail that is more eagerly looked for and devoured than yours; and while I do not want you to be for one moment taxed to write me, do send me a letter as often as it is not a tax.

Now good night it is rather late bed time, I will write you more tomorrow. I wish you were going up stairs with me I would just step into your room for a five minutes chat.

March 25th

Here it is, evening again Mr Clemens has gone to the billiard room for an hours work and so I will have some more visit with you.

You ask if Mr Warner shows any sign of repentance.

19. The letter is missing.

I think he is about as disgusted a man over the appointments as a man can well be. I don't suppose he would really say that he is sorry he voted for Harrison, because he thinks he did his duty, but he is evidently very far from satisfied with things as they are going.

It seems to me people never had so good an opportunity to say I told you so as the people who voted for Cleveland.[20]

Get up on your Matterhorn again, and write Mrs Cabell, it will please Mr Warner and what's the use in holding on to things any way. I really do think it was rather natural for her to tell the Warners about the talk in our library, when they found her crying and *would* know the reason why. I think I could have gotten some of it out of you Grace dear in the same case. I think so often of what you said that you found after all that the house was pleasanter with her in it than out of it. I find that true too. Much more amiability when she is there than when she is not.

An other friend of the Warners who was to visit them wrote to a mutual friend that if Mrs Cabell was there she could not visit them she was not in the mood to be in the house with her. It begins to seem very funny to me and makes me want to laugh, it begins to look as if the Warners were not quite independent in their house or at least, if they keep Mrs Cabell they must let some of the older friends go.

Mr Warner is a good friend of yours and it would be such a pity for you to forfeit your pleasant relations with them. Give it up (that is the fighting). You wont be deceiving any body you have been honest about your opinion and they know just how you feel. So it is only an act of graciousness on your part.

I have had "pink eye" a most unromantic name and disease both, the only reason that I remember the matter now, as it is nearly a month ago that I had it, is that it has left my eyes so that I am unable to use them for reading, that is a terrible trial. So do tell me just what you are reading so I may make the more plans of what I will read when I can use my eyes.

Did you read Mr Warners "Simplicity"?[21] I think it is beautiful, don't you? It seems to me the best thing he has done lately.

20. Bypassing traditional patronage, Harrison named lawyers and businessmen to his cabinet instead of active workers in his campaign, and he swept out nonclassified civil servants.

21. Published in *Atlantic Monthly* 63 (March 1889): 309–13.

Please give my loving greeting to your mother and sisters and kind regards to your brothers, and know Grace that whether you are on the Matterhorn or in the valley I am always your deeply loving friend

Olivia L. Clemens

News from the Clemenses began to further tell the toll that illnesses were taking in 1889, and the girls' letters were important links to family concerns.

☙ SUSY CLEMENS TO GRACE

Hartford, n.d. [March 25–31?, 1889]

Dear Teety,
Mamma's eyes are still useless after her pink eyes, and so she wants me to thank you from her for the orange flower candy, and to say that it was lovely in you to send it, and that she was very proud to show it to her friends saying from whom she had received it; we have all enjoyed it, it is so pretty and so fragrant.

Soon I shall write you a long letter in answer to your last beauty to me, but not today.[22]

You are not the one to write when I am cross and willful and rather void of resolutions.

No, I must wait till I am my better self, and willing to say "Life is *not* a strife, *or* a battle, *or* a dread, man is *not* a little boat afloating down the stream," for now I rather think life *is* a strife etc etc.

I hope Mamma will have the use of her eyes soon it is very hard for her to be deprived of them, she always uses them so constantly.
With much love dear Teety from her and from me,

Your affectionate
Susy Clemens.

☙ SUSY CLEMENS TO GRACE

Hartford, April 1889

22. The letter is missing.

Dear Teety,
It is lovely here now so green and springy and warm. Clara and Daisy are having their vacation.

Some of the rides I have had, have been perfect dreams of bliss. The sky so blue! and the air so balmy!

Day after tomorrow Cousin Susy has one of her musicals, we are to play. I am going to play an Impromptu of Schubert.

I believe I wrote you that I have dropped my Greek for the present and am preparing in German instead, the preparation for the classical course is too hard to accomplish in one year more. I hope to take Greek as an Elective in College.

I want to read "The Witness of The Sun" so much, but the story is forbiden fruit to me.[23]

Grandma comes Thursday of this week, and Saturday a Miss Lizzie Slee[?] from Elmira, for whom Mamma is going to give a large tea on Monday. Clara [is] exited at the prospect. I admire Clara for this I wish I might be exited by such prospects, my exitements are far more exiting than teas.

I have read Miss Trumbull's story "An Hour's Promise,"[24] I believe Mamma is going to send it to you. Their are two pretty pictures in it of a village station, and a girl on horseback there waiting for the mail.

I wish I could see you this minute, and that I could see you for a long visit and that you could go to the Farm with us.

Jean has just been in with lips drawn down, and brows contracted in distress about some much desired strawberries which seem to be, judging from what mama says, *her* forbiden fruit for today.

The wind is blowing the clouds away. I must go out for a few seconds for the sky will be a glory when the sun setts (our T!)

Your letter to me was beautiful and long. Perhaps my next to you will be longer, perhaps not.

Very, very lovingly,
Susy Clemens.

23. By Amélie Rives, whose novels were called "wild literary oats" by the *Saturday Review of Politics, Literature, Science and Art* 67 (June 22, 1889): 765.

24. Annie Eliot Trumbull (1857–1949), story published 1889.

Mamma has received and enjoyed your last letter, but does not know when she will be able to answer it because of her eyes. She sends her love.

☙ CLARA CLEMENS TO GRACE

Hartford, n.d. [April 5–12?, 1889]

Dear Tety,

It seems as if it were years since I have heard from you but of course you are too busy to write.

I am having quite a vacation now, so that I am reading a good deal, riding & practising. I have just read The Heir of Redcliffe.[25] I think it is the most or *one* of the most delightful books I have ever read.

But I could not be resigned to Guy's death I thought that was dreadful. How I did l*ove* that character.

Have you read Mrs. Burnett's new story ["]The Pretty Sister of José"?[26] It is quite nice.—Tety what *do* you think?

I did not tell you did I that *blessed* Ada Rehan sent me *three* photographs of herself with "Never to man Shall Katharine give her hand,"[27] written on one, From Katharine on an other and Yours Truly A. R. on the 3rd you can imagine I was overcome. You know I saw her as the Shrew this winter so my wish was granted. This was the way it happened. Papa went to a Daly dinner & I gave him two very good photos. One of A. R. & an other of John Drew for them to write on so Drew wrote on his & papa brought it back & then he took hers to her & she wrote on that & sent t[w]o extra ones wasn't that *grand*!!!

I am now reading "A Noble Life," & then I think I shall "pitch in" to Scott for a while.[28]

Soon now my career will be over in the H. S. oh! how happy I shall

25. *The Heir of Redclyffe* was a popular romantic novel (1853) with a religious tone, by Charlotte M. Younge (1823–1901).

26. Published in 1889, by Frances Hodgson Burnett (1849–1924), British novelist and playwright.

27. A line from *Shakespeare's Comedy of Katharine and Petruchio*.

28. A sentimental Victorian novel (1866) by Dinah Mulock Craik (1826–1887); Clara next plans to read Sir Walter Scott.

be! The fascinating Henschels[29] have just been here & they gave the *most* charming concert that ever was given here.

We met them afterwards, & they were both extremely attractive & refined, & she was quite a beauty.

I have 53 photos now, but I dread tremendously taking them all down for the summer but I have to because they get all milldewed.

I am going to begin the violin again I don't know just when, I should like to, right away.—I have worked quite hard Tety since Xmas, & now am sorry I did not before. Mr Meyer has been saying some grand things about my music so that I am encouraged more about practising.

Supper is ready & I am not, so that I must say "adieu kind friend adieu," with a *great great* deal of love & a *heavnyish* hug

Your loving
Clara.

Contacts with the Clemenses and Warners continued sporadically. In June, May wrote that Grace needed a trip: "I can tell it by your hand writing it looks nervous and I am quite sure you are tired out" with work and the irresponsibility of brother Will. In August, Susan Warner wrote she had found a place for Grace to board in Farmington, but Grace made no plans to go north that year. And her publisher Armstrong had written that her book *Monsieur Motte* had not been profitable. By August 1889, she was in Blowing Rock, North Carolina, boarding with the educator Emily Prudden.[30]

She saw Warner at Grandfather Mountain near there, where he fired her with "energy and determination," as she wrote May. He also annoyed her with news of the sickly Isa, who so easily manipulated the Warners: "He cannot

29. Sir Isidor George Henschel (1850–1934), German-born British baritone, pianist, conductor, and composer and his wife, Lilian June Bailey Henschel (1860–1901), an American soprano.

30. May to Grace, June 10, 1889, about needing a trip. Susan Warner to Grace, August 12, 1889, about boarding in Farmington. Armstrong to Grace, July 5, 1889, about *Monsieur Motte,* which had made only $113.37 for Grace to that date. Emily C. Prudden (1832–1917) worked closely with the American Missionary Association to found schools in Blowing Rock (Skyland Institute, 1887 to 1912) and elsewhere. King helped fill the library (later named the Grace King Library) with books from her publishers. (William S. Powell, *Dictionary of North Carolina Biography,* vol. 5 [November 9, 2000], 152).

understand, why I do not work all the time—and seems to think the excuses I made too trivial to talk about even. He rather provoked me with his confidence, serenity and great share of happiness and contentment. He suffers from nothing but Isa Cabell's troubles—told me at length all about them—and her great intellectual ability, powers of work etc—until I got rather bored."[31] On the other hand, Livy Clemens's letters were a balm when she wrote Grace and Nina "begging us to pay them a visit during the Fall, she is surely a good friend,"[32] as Grace wrote Mimi. Two months later, however, she queried Warner: "Is anything the matter at the Clemens? I have not heard from them for so long."[33]

Grace had returned home from North Carolina and focused on work. Relieved that Alden rejected one story as it was, she began another about the celebration of All Saints Day, "the *fête par excellence* of the city" that eventually became "Madriléne; Or, the Festival of the Dead."[34] Finally, on New Year's Day, 1890, she wrote Warner that the Clemenses "relieved my anxiety by sending me" Twain's *A Connecticut Yankee in King Arthur's Court*—which the family read aloud—and Annie Trumbull Slosson's *Fishin' Jimmy,* both published in 1889: "In every letter I wrote you I asked you if there was anything the matter that they didn't write me—and, do you know—you never answered me—so I concluded woefully that they were ceasing to care for me." It seemed a repeated concern for which Grace needed reassurance. Then she received news from a source in the family and, finally, from Livy's own pen.

❧ SUSY CLEMENS TO GRACE

Hartford, n.d. [January 1890]

Dear Tety,

I thought it was your turn to write me, but perhaps it is not, at any rate, I must be with you some way now, if not by hearing from you, why then, by writing to you.

31. Grace to May, August 19?, 1889.

32. Grace to Mimi, September 17, 1889. Olivia's letters are missing.

33. Grace to Warner, November 21, 1889.

34. *Harper's New Monthly Magazine* 81, no. 486 (November 1890): 869–86. In the same issue was "Princeton University" by Sloane and "Our Italy" by Warner. King earned two hundred dollars for the story (Alden to Grace, February 12, 1890).

If your Southern winters have more blue sky and sunshine than we have had this season, I am sure I should like to live South for many reasons. Today it is raining & yesterday it was dark, but it is long since we have had two successive dark days.

A short time ago Mamma & Papa went to Albany to visit, and Miss Price and I met them in New York on Saturday, and went to Daly's and the opera. We had [a] beautiful little trip. Miss Price asked me to call her Aunt Annie, and we had some extremely gossipy, confidential, talks.

I am so devoted an admirer of the doctor that cuts and burns me that he could decapitate me and I should still anticipate going to his office. Why, you were here when he visited us, Dr. Rice, you know.[35] I have his photograph, but every one ridicules it, and criticises his features. No one in this neighborhood tho,' has half as fine eyes, I will contend.

Since we came home Mamma and I have both had the pink eye, and have been unable to read or write. It was so ridiculous, such an unromantic kind of a disease.

I am reading Xenophon now perhaps I wrote you. I like it very much indeed. The narration is flowing, and pleasant, far above Caesar. Cicero I like too more and more, and my algebra and algebra teacher both extremely well. I don't know when I shall take singing again. Miss Lima is coming no more this year, I doubt if she ever comes again

Jean is taking violin lessons, with true mathematical zeal, which perhaps will surpass musical in its results, still I doubt it. She practices constantly, and tunes her instrument between times.

I have just finished Miss Howard's story "Gueen," and was carried away with it; it is so nice and romantic, and touching, and thrilling.

Clara plays your beloved "Danse Macabre" now, and we have also your ballet music in duet, don't you wish you were here to hear us play it? Perhaps I have lived up to my ideal one day, since you left. I think I have been creeping nearer it, a little in my studying. I really like to study very much. I think I would make a student if I had strength of character enough to force my love of study to hold the reins of my love for drumming on the piano, and "writhin' & goin' on." For this week I find I have missed studying very much and all my ambitions are to be a slug, and learn things; and

35. Dr. Clarence C. Rice (1853–1935), family physician of the Clemenses.

all my most natural instinct to do nothing except dance & sing and be a lazy good for nothing.

Our word *agony* comes from the Greek ἀγῶνα, which meant, games. I think that's good. I suppose their games were often pretty brutal were they not? If they were our English derivation is unsparingly severe, in its statement of the truth.

Cousin Susy is down stairs I have not been able to see [her] since the pink eye, for fear of giving it to her.

Now, I know I am perfectly well, and still have to keep my distance It is very tantalizing.

How I wish you were here! Well, I am sure you must be again—before long, it couldn't be any other way. Write me please, as soon as you can I love you.

Good-by &, with much, much love

Your Susy.

LIVY TO GRACE

Hartford, February 25, [1890]

Grace dear,

How I wish you were here with me this evening! There is a German class down stairs but as I am just getting well from an attack of Quinzy[36] I am staying up here in my room.

We talk of and wish for you often and there is nothing that delights this household more than a letter from your beloved self.

I have had no eyes and even if I had eyes I am absolutely lacking in letter-writing gift. Therefore as you have such a rare gift in that way, do send me a letter with out waiting to have me send you one of my poor ones.

I went to New York two weeks ago to consult an occulist. I went to him once, was then taken with Quinzy, staid in my bed for nearly a week in New York with Mr Clemens as nurse and then returned home.

We hope now that we may go to Europe this coming June for the

36. Quinsy is an abscess or inflammation of the throat near the tonsils.

Summer months. We are not yet entirely decided where we shall go but if we can find some pleasant place on the Northern Coast of France that is where we want to go.

There the children can get French and we can have the sea and if possible the country and some very retired spot.

If we cannot accomplish what we desire in this way perhaps we shall establish ourselves on Lake Geneva, there I think we can get good French and beautiful rides and drives beside the rowing. We are afraid however that it will be a good deal more populous than we desire.

What are you reading now-a-days write and tell me all about it. I am reading just now, rather late in the day, Ibsen's "Ein Puppenheim" how clever it is and how discriminating of character. Have you read his "Ghosts"? I intend reading that next.[37]

Have you read Mr Howells "Study" in the last Harpers? It seems as if Ex-Minister Phelps could have very little to say in return.[38]

I have not seen Mr Phelps article, but as Mr Howells quotes from it, it would seem that he had allowed himself to say some very weak and unprovable things. I am *very* sorry that Mr Howells should have made so much however of the slips in grammar. If I had been asked to edit the Study I should have taken some of those remarks out.[39] It seems as if some of Mr Phelps errors must simply have been careless proof reading. Nevertheless I think Mr Howells article fascinating. Do you enjoy his Study very much? I do almost always—I don't know but I may say always. I turn to that first when the Harper comes.

We have had a real disappointment in the fact that the Prince & Pauper is not better put upon the stage. In the main it is poor and does not in the least do the book, we think, justice. Such inferior English is put into the mouths of the actors in many places.

Perhaps you better not quote this from me because I don't know that Mr Clemens would like me to say it. Then Mr House's attitude toward Mr Clemens has not added to our happiness this winter. It has not worried

37. Both plays are by Norwegian playwright Henrik Ibsen (1828–1906), the "father of realism." They are considered commentaries on nineteenth-century morality.

38. "Editor's Study" was William Dean Howells's regular column of criticism. Edward J. Phelps (1822–1900), envoy to Court of St. James's in Britain from 1885 to 1889.

39. Olivia Clemens edited Twain's works.

Mr Clemens as much as I was afraid it would. I think it has not greatly fretted him because he felt so free of guilt in the matter. Then he is not sorry, as Mr House has taken the initiative, to cut away from that tiresome friendship or semblance of friendship.[40]

Since writing the above there has been a little interval during which I have finished "Ein Puppenheim." I never discovered the sort of man Helmer was until he said "Ich bin gerettet."[41] There must be loads of just such people in the world. Was it natural for her to think that he would take the sin upon him? I suppose her life had led her to feel that every thing would be carried for her. The ending is strong and yet would any mother leave her three children in that way? and that sort of woman? Her soul was suddenly born. Good bye I love you and want to hear from you as often as you can write.

Always lovingly

Livy L. Clemens.

Grace's return letter is her most definitive observation of the position of women in the late nineteenth century; another age might label her response feminist. It is also the deepest expression of her search for religious faith, previously having been more indifferent than earnest.

GRACE TO OLIVIA

New Orleans, March 3, 1890[42]

I thought *my* eyes had a disease my dear, when an envelope came with your handwriting on it this morning. How good it was of you to give your evening to me!—and as usual, since getting your letter, I cannot fasten my

40. Twain and Edward H. House were estranged over a suit concerning the play. House claimed Twain had given him the rights to adapt the book, thus cutting Twain out of royalties (*MT and Twichell,* 154).

41. "I am saved."

42. Although King dated this letter as May 3, internals suggest that it is from March and thus coincides with its accompanying envelope. She was accustomed to writing to her sister May, so the month was probably a momentary slip of a distracted mind.

hand to anything—it will run on so; about what I want to say to you—"right off"—As you see I am humoring myself.

Yes—I have read "A Doll house"; and it produced the most vivid impression on me. We have discussed it in the house—and outside considerably, and it seems to me, people reveal their characters a good deal, in the judgments they pass upon Nora and Helmer. I have always thought, that New Orleans, with its European ancestry—its past wealth and present poverty—its war times—and its peace struggles—its politics—and its pleasures,—offered the only American counterpart to the life depicted by European novelists.

As I found a great deal of Tolstoi, right down here—so, I imagine, I find a great deal of Ibsen.

I hope it won't shock you, when I say that I have seen a great deal of untruthfulness in the women down here—and it must not set you against us—I have known some Nora's—who were engaged in a constant deathly struggle—standing in front of husband and children—battling with desperate energy—against, bills, dues—liabilities of all kinds—sacrificing a great deal of truth, dignity—and conscience—all for love—They would have gladly sacrificed their limbs—instead of truth—mutilating themselves physically—instead of morally—but that would not have served the purpose—these women represent the highest type of unselfish devotion to me—I cannot admire them, but I do love and pity them.

And I have always remarked here, that such women were married, invariably to Helmers; the refined, selfish, high-minded—moralistic husbands—Helmer could have confessed crimes to Nora—and she would have forgiven him—and loved and pitied him the more for his weakness—I think Nora was wrong in hoping that Helmer would take upon himself such a lie as owning the forgery; It seems to me that she could only hope—for his standing by her, exonerating her—loving her motive although condemning the means she made use of to realize her object. When a woman's object is the life of her husband—what man can spurn her—for any thing, but personal dishonor!—She left her children, because in her self-abasement, she did not dare rear them. After her husband's words, how could she remain as their mother?—I understand that feeling so well—I could have done it myself—I could never have lived with a man after those words—I could never have raised his children—

but instead of going away for self improvement, I should have gone to the nearest pond.—When a woman's motives are misunderstood—her affections—despised—her very parents—condemned—by her husband—the father of her children—I do not see anything but death left for her—Helmer's after words of contrition, were calculation—the first outburst, was the spontaneous language of his heart. I do not like "ghosts" at all. It is powerful enough—but if heredity—be only for the transmission of *bad* qualities—then were we all long ago—totally unfit to live! there is also the heredity of the good—and so bane and antidote—flow into us—a livin[g] stream—there would be no hope for us otherwise—I suppose it is well, that such a book as "Ghosts" should be written—in a day particularly—when such a Prince of Wales—is heir to the throne of England—But—out of the very royal families of Europe—come our best arguments—against the hopeless view of life contained in Ghosts—Good is stronger than bad—and—thank God! If men are bad—they are still not bad enough to seek *bad* women for wives—to mother their children—And so, the struggle goes on through eternity and the Prince of Wales, who had a good woman for mother and a good woman for wife—has transmitted to his descendants—the antidote—of his own vices.

I approve so little of Rosmerholm—that I conclude that I do not understand it—the Pillars of Society—is full of moral, applicable to America.[43]

Besides Ibsen—I have read Marie Bashkirtseff[44]—If you had been that poor child's mother—how different the journal would have been!—I could not help thinking this all the time I was reading it.

I liked Howells "Hazard—etc"[45] very much. It seemed so much stronger—and "human—naturish["] than his later—previous works. But—oh, those petty squabbles with his wife!—and I do so loathe, those "funnies" and trivialities, with which he meets her silly carpings.—Why cannot Mr Howells (and Mr Warner) treat wives, in print with serious earnest-

43. *Rosmersholm* (1886); *Pillars of Society* (1877), both by Ibsen.

44. Marie Bashkirtseff (1858–1884), Russian diarist, author, painter, sculptor; perhaps best known for her confessional *Journal de Marie Bashkirtseff* in two volumes (1887).

45. *A Hazard of New Fortunes* (1890), a novel of social injustice.

ness?—The husbands are henpecked—and chicken-pecked—And the wives are made fun of—by the husbands—

I have been enjoying the new Spanish School of novels very much—But what I am most interested in, has been the methodical, careful reading of the Bible—according to the Episcopalian table of lessons—With it—I have been reading Liddon's University Sermons—and his: "Some elements of Religion"—a fine, noble work.[46] You remember, when I was at the North—I was dissatisfied with my attitude towards religion—I found that I must get nearer—or go away entirely from it. I could not go away—for life was too serious with me—too full of sorrows and responsibilities—I could understand life, as a part of religion—I could not understand or be resigned to it as mere existence—And I found, on examination, that I admired people who believed, more than unbelievers.—From these fragmentary premises—I started out—and am so relieved to find—that I am not separated—in belief—from what I admire—that life and religion (to me) are one—and that I can—be resigned—to what I am to suffer.—You see—I had travelled pretty far in life—with only the religious provision provided in the Catechism and Sunday School—I imagined—that that provision was all—but I find—that there has been nutrition provided for my hunger all along—but I did not know where to find it.

The Church's passed through here last Friday. Mrs Church was very, very ill, in Mexico—had Pneumonia—They are gone now to Thomasville, Ga: to remain, I do not know, how long. I saw Downie but for a moment. She was pale and harassed, in deep distress about her mother—There are, I hear grave doubts whether she will ever recover.[47]

I knew you would be worried about Mr House's conduct. I saw a brief account of it, in the Critic; our papers not taking any notice of the difference. I am not at all surprised at Mr Church [House].[48] You remember

46. Henry Parry Liddon (1829–1890), *Sermons Preached before the University of Oxford* (1869); *Some Elements of Religion* (1870) were Lenten lectures.

47. Frederic Church (1826–1900) and Isabel Mortimer Carnes Church (1829–1899), whom King visited at "Olana" near Hudson, New York, with the Warners and Clemenses in 1887. "Downie" was Isabel Charlotte Church (1871–1935).

48. King mistakenly writes Church; obviously she meant House.

from the first, I did not like him. He had not a good countenance—I really believe it impossible for a man with his expression, about the mouth, to be frank, generous, and grateful. I was almost sure that Mr Clemens would not worry—when a man's conscience clears him, he does not worry; but the most unselfish women will brood over an accusation of meanness; women will doubt their own uprightness.—

I have not seen the last Harper yet—We have neglected to renew our subscription, and are constantly forgetting to get the Magazine when we are near the shops.—We live pretty far away from shops now.[49]

I dearly love Howell's literary essays—for they are really not criticisms. What a good one that was on the "Yankee etc"[50] I was so afraid that some scruple would prevent his noticing it. It seems to me that Howells has solidified his reputation by his editorial work in Harper's. His novels were rather—(on account of his theories) a meagre exposition of the real knowledge of the author.—What a beautiful Summer you have planned! I am so glad you are going to Europe. It will do the dear girls good.

I love to write to you, as you see—but I get timid about it when I don't hear from you all. It seems conceited to imagine that with your surroundings, you can care to hear from me—

I find I must add this page—to tell Mr Clemens that ever since Autumn I have had a "carrot" of Perique tobacco—given me to send to him—I have always forgotten in my letters to ask him if he wanted it—If he cares for it—I shall express it to him if not—I can suppress it as well—and more economically at this end, than at the other. It is supposed to be very fine—but he must *temper* it, with a milder quality—He may be able to temper a thing mildly—I never could.

With dear love to all,
Ever devotedly Your's
Grace

49. When the Kings lived at 23 South Rampart Street, they were in the first block off of Canal Street. At the time of this letter, they lived at 530 Baronne (old numbering), which later would be in the 2100 block, twenty-one blocks from shops on Canal Street and probably not near shops on Magazine Street.

50. Twain's *A Connecticut Yankee in King Arthur's Court.*

530 Baronne St.
New Orleans[51]

☙ S L CLEMENS TO GRACE

Hartford, May 8, 1890[52]
To Grace E. King

Dear Miss Grace,
What a noble hunk of tobacco it is! I would God you were here with me to help smoke it; then would we have a serene & improving time, & unspeakable enjoyment. As it is, I will smoke it solitary, & think gratefully of you all the time.

Some time ago I was in my office in New York & said I wanted my new book sent to the "Grace King Library" in North Carolina, but my partner was in England, then, & the boys were uncertain about the address, as I have given books to other libraries in the South. Now perhaps I can save time & a letter by enclosing an order to you—hey? Do me the kindness, please, to mail it.

We keep up a great affection for you in this fambly, & we all want to see you.

Sincerely Yours
S L Clemens

Nina confirmed his charity when she wrote Grace that an acquaintance had discovered in a library a *Book of Sermons* that S. L. Clemens had gifted. It included a poem by Richard Burton and sermons by Timothy Dwight and Joseph Twichell.[53] His friendships and generosities were widespread. It is likely that Grace did not expect to receive more than occasional mail from Clemens himself. He was friendly and entertaining with her, but he wrote only short notes

51. MS, CU-MARK, UCLC 44990, University of California, Mark Twain Papers, The Bancroft Library, Berkeley.

52. MS facsimile New Orleans Auction Galleries catalogue, sale of June 29, 1996, lot 191, UCCL 11906, University of California, Mark Twain Papers, The Bancroft Library, Berkeley).

53. Nina to Grace, July 6, 1890.

and those infrequently, perhaps out of propriety. He seems to have appreciated her as a writer and southern friend but valued even more the intimacy she shared with his precious Livy.

LIVY CLEMENS TO GRACE

Tannersville, New York, September 10, 1890
Onteora + Club
Catskill Mountains

Grace dear,
You will see by the heading of this page that we are not in Europe, nor have we been there this Summer.[54]

Mr Clemens found that on account of business connected with the machine he should be compelled to take us to Europe and leave us there. That I did not like. I did not at all fancy the idea of putting the ocean between us. So we decided to give up our trip for this Summer. Our main object in planning to go was on account of Susy's French. When we decided that it was not best to take the trip we secured the French teacher at Smith to come here and give Susy lessons. She has gotten on extreemly well so that Mlle Duval (her teacher) thinks there is little doubt of her passing her examination and says she knows more French after this short time (she began the 21st of July) than many girls know in more than a year's study.

I feel hopeful and yet there are so many chances that she may have something given her that will happen to be too difficult.

Oh Grace do come and have a talk with me! I would give a great deal for a two or three hours visit with you. I *love* your letters and hate mine, so I desire to write you in order to receive one of your beloved letters, but I hate to write because mine seem such poor compensation in return for yours.

There is a real down pour of rain today and it is such a good time to sit by the fire and talk with a friend—such a friend as Grace King.

This is a pleasant spot and we have enjoyed our Summer here very

54. The letterhead has a graphic of animal figures before a mountain and information about the Onteora Club in the Catskill Mountains post office in Tannersville, New York.

much, when we decided not to go to Europe, I did not quite want to go to the Farm at Elmira because, as my brother and his family were in Europe my sister would have to remain with my mother and that would make it necessary for me to do the house keeping, that I did not care to do as nine months of the year is quite enough of that for me.

In one or two ways our coming here has been most fortunate! We found a Miss Pinney here, a very fine pianist, pupil of Liszts, she had been a fellow pupil with Aus der Ohe in the conservatory &c &c. Well! she interested the children, of course, very much and apparently became interested in them in return. The result of it all is that we have given up Mr Meyer (which I have long desired to do) and the thought of College for Clara and have put her under Miss Pinney's piano instruction. She is to try Clara and if she works well she will keep her as a pupil, because she thinks she has musical talent, if she does not work well she will not keep her, because she can only take a few scholars and she only desires those who are willing to work hard. Clara is to go down to her twice a month in New York.

We have had an other pleasant little exc[i]tement in the fact that Miss Pinney was married here last week, to a Mr Baldwin. Hence the reduction of pupils.

I tell you all these particulars feeling sure of your interest in what concerns us.

We look forward with a good deal of dread to the prospect of having Susy away from us next Winter. There is still a possibility that she will not leave us until February.

I am entirely delighted to hear of the great success that Mrs Hinks has made in London. I am delighted that her persevering effort should be rewarded, and also I am afraid a little malicious delight swells the accounts, that some people who sneered should find themselves in the minority.

Grace come to us next November and bring one of your sisters with you. Will you?

I have still very little use of my eyes and you can be of great service to me by coming and reading with and talking to me. I long for a sight of you. It will then be two years since you were with us, can't you manage to prevent the time from extending itself more than that two years?

I have just had my mother's pride piqued, what vain creatures we mothers be, by a lady saying to me in a rather blunt way "I am glad Susy is going away to school it is what your girls need they have not touched enough against people. they show that, in the way in which they estimate people." I assented even adding that I thought it was still more necessary in teaching them how to estimate themselves. That there were faults in any mode of teaching and so on. It is probably true that they do need it, but I hated to have an *acquaintance* venture to tell me so.

How delightful it must be to be as full of reading as you have been this last Summer, and always are for that matter. I have done almost none, having had so little use of my eyes.

I brought some of Parkman's Histories[55] to read but have not been able to even finish one.

Will you come to us in November?

If the family knew I was writing they would all send love so I will send it for them. For myself I am now as ever your most loving

Livy L. C.

Sept. 10th, 1890.

For the remainder of 1890, there was a lapse in correspondence. The Warners and Isa Cabell sailed for Europe and the Near East. Grace worked on two historical biographies, her problematic Bienville and one on LaSalle. New Orleans suffered a yellow fever epidemic almost as devastating as the one in 1872, she reported to May.[56] In the north, Livy's mother died of more natural causes, but she wrote only after the depth of her loss had passed.

LIVY CLEMENS TO GRACE

Hartford, January 14, 1891

FARMINGTON AVENUE,

HARTFORD, CONN.

55. Francis Parkman Jr. (1823–1893), American historian, especially of western trails and in seven volumes about France and England in North America.

56. Grace to May, January 1, 1891.

Grace dear, dear,
How I wish you were here so that we might sit down by the fire and talk, talk together. These have been such hard days, and I carry about such a heart-broken feeling. I should so like a long quiet time with you.

So very often lately I have wished so deeply that you had known my mother and that she had know[n] you. She heard me talk so much of you and she would thoroughly have enjoyed you. I feel so much older since mother was taken away. When you are no ones child When no one will pet you as your mother had always done, When you are the oldest generation of your family, then you begin to feel that you are growing old. My mother was eighty and I try to realize that I had a long lovely life with her—yet I am very lonely for her.[57]

I am truly sorry that your work has not gone to suit you. What is the trouble? I can not but feel that whatever you want to do, you can do, and I feel that you deserve and merrit all success.

My sister and Susy were with me for a little more than two weeks. Now they are gone and Mr Clemens is off in Washington so Clara, Jean and I constitute the family.

Clara is very busy with her music she practises from four to five hours a day, three on the piano and one on the violin. She likes her new piano teacher in New York and I think she is doing extreemly well under her teaching. She certainly ought for she is very faithful and industrious.

Jean takes the usual little girl studies. She has begun latin this Winter and enjoys that. She was very ill while I was in Elmira with mother, so that I felt that I must be in two places at once but she is very well again now.

Susy is quite settled in her work at Bryn Mawr. She enjoys the work there extreemly, but she is home-sick, the life outside the work does not please her very well. If she remains well I shall keep her there this year, but if she is not more contented I shall not send her back next year.

We all so often talk of you and wish for you. Our plans for next Spring and Summer are entirely unmade, but if we should be at home could not you come up to us for a month? You cannot imagine what a quiet

57. Olivia Lewis Langdon died on November 28, 1890, the day after her daughter Olivia's forty-fifth birthday.

neighborhood we have. I think it is just as you would enjoy it here now. Probably you know of the Warners movements as well or better than I do, at any rate Annie has gone to her brother in the South and "Isa," the worshiped one, has gone with the Warners to Europe. The last news from them they were going into Egypt and up the Nile for seven weeks.

Tell me, Grace dear, every thing that you are doing particularly of the books that you are reading. Have you read "The Light that Fades"?[58]

Do you know that I love you and that loving you I long for you?

Please give my cordial greeting to your mother and to your brothers and sisters and know that I am your deeply loving friend

Olivia L. Clemens

The two women were fortunate in their friendship.

58. Probably *The Light That Failed* (1890), by Rudyard Kipling (1865–1936).

CHAPTER 8

EUROPEAN PLANS, 1891

I really am going to Europe to work—not working to go to Europe.
—GRACE TO MAY, OCTOBER 24, 1891

By 1891, the Clemenses and Grace King were independently contemplating European travel. The Warners were already there, so changes were unavoidably afoot. Grace's own plans depended on her completing enough work to be able to afford the trip. Perhaps she wanted to escape the heated battle over the corrupt Louisiana Lottery into which her family was plunged. Perhaps she was weary of the roller coaster of emotions inside the house. Will's short-term sobriety and employment, followed by alcoholic stunts, caused even the mild-mannered May to call them outrageous enough "to embitter the existence of the rest of the family."[1] Perhaps the sojourns of Grace's friends whetted her appetite to further widen her world.

In the meantime, she had apparently made overtures to Twain asking if his Webster and Company would publish the autobiography of her old friend and mentor Judge Charles Gayarré. He declined.

TWAIN TO GRACE

Hartford, February 17, 1891[2]

Dear Miss Grace,

You see my partner[3] says the straightforward thing in the business-like way. That is, let Mr. Gayarré's friends gather the stipulated subscribers &

1. May to Grace, March 9, 1891.

2. Complete letter is included in "GK and MT," 45.

3. Frederick J. Hall (1860–1926) replaced Charles L. Webster in 1888 and managed Webster and Company until 1894.

the money, without commission, & we will undertake to manufacture and deliver—dividing the *profit,* over & above all legitimate costs (cost of *any* kind which would not have been entailed upon us but for the book) between the widow & our firm in the proportion of ½ to each.[4]

As I am going to send this through Mr. Hall for his approval or emendation, I shall withhold those eruptions of affection always sure to happen in a letter to you from Mrs. Clemens or me. She has been ill but is better.

Sincerely yours
S. L. Clemens

The friends were trying to coordinate their schedules, but Grace's attention was necessarily on business. It would be a strain for her to afford the trip under any condition.

LIVY CLEMENS TO GRACE

Hartford, May 28, 1891

Grace dear,

What a shame that you are not to sail on the 6th of June for that is the very date on which we sail.

We go directly from here to Havre on the Gascoigne. We stay a day or two in Paris, then a day or more in Geneva and then Mr Clemens my sister Sue, Jean and I go to some German baths. Mr Clemens is greatly troubled with rheumatism. The girls we shall leave in a French family in Geneva—

We intend to be for ten days at the Bayreuth festival[5] then perhaps in a French town for six weeks. We shall settle in Berlin for the Winter where the children will go on with their work, particularly music. Clara has made great progress with her piano this Winter and we hope Susy can cultivate her voice.[6] (Grace dear do excuse these blots. I do not know where they came from.)

4. Gayarré had not yet died; Twain misunderstood.

5. The annual music festival, held in Bayreuth, Germany, still features performances of operas by Richard Wagner in a specially designed theater, the Bayreuth Festspielhaus.

6. Although Susy Clemens studied voice and piano and received encouragement, she did not develop a profession as did Clara as a contralto singer.

If you go to Paris next Winter you must come to Berlin to visit us.

I write in the greatest possible haste, because it seems as if every thing must be done and *at once.*

I am truly thankful that your brother Will is doing so successfully and that you like your new sister.[7]

Be sure and tell me when you write what the matter is with your right hand.[8] You write marvelously with your left.

How delightful it will be to visit on the other side.

I suppose the Warners will return in the Autumn or early Winter.

I must send you this scrawl this time. The girls will write you before we go.

With deepest love
Livy L. C.

Write me soon our address is Brown Shipley & Co
Founders Court E. C.
London.

O. L. C.

Grace missed seeing the Clemenses off, but by July 1891, she began a northern trip that would eventually lead to Europe and a reunion with them. She and her bachelor brother, Branch, set out together, spent a few days in New York, and then parted on separate journeys. Her route was meandering, taking her again to the Hudson River mansion of the Frederic Churches for a month, to Farmington for a week, and to the cottage of the jolly single women at Watch Hill for another month. One of the women, Elizabeth Adams, began a portrait of Grace while she was there: "I suppose to day we shall decide upon the dress—The sittings will be a novelty—my 'experience' as the Clemens girls said the death of the coachman's child would have been—if it hadn't recovered."[9]

7. William King married Jennie Conner (1864–1916) in 1891.

8. Grace had started writing with her left hand to rest her stiff right one after copying her stories up to six times. She would do so intermittently for several years. Louisa May Alcott also resorted to the same practice.

9. Grace to Mimi, August 24, 1891. Grace sent the portrait as a gift to her mother when it was completed.

Grace's novella *The Chevalier Alain de Triton* appeared in the *Chautauquan* that month[10] and was praised by family and friends. She expected to meet with her publishers in New York; Europe was as yet uncertain. She would have to sell four interconnected short stories—her "Balcony Stories"—to Richard Watson Gilder of *Century Magazine* and her biography of Bienville to Henry Mills Alden at *Harper's* in order to have enough money for the trip.[11] She wrote May from the Churches' mansion, "Olana."

GRACE TO MAY

Hudson, New York, July 17, 1891

My dearest Partner,

[. . .] You tell me not to bother about writing, it would bother me also to keep from it. Every thing I see everything I do or hear, I want immediately to write all about it to my own people—and I don't believe I could stay away unless I did write.—What a curiously different world all this is from our world!—I don't get discouraged over it as I used to do at the Warners. I take it all in, and reflect upon it afterwards—but the day cannot contain reflections and observations too—There is always something left over to start the next morning—and all the time, I am down stairs I am playing two roles, that of observer—& commentator—People's interests up here are so small, their sympathies so narrow—I am always brimming over about the lottery, or my family, or interests at home—they don't here seem to brew ever about anything but looks, early vegetables, and the wild flowers—and how curious they are about the wild flowers—Not a daisy is allowed to be pulled, or a cat's tail—and as for golden-rod!—The other day we drove miles to get some yellow daisies, & sweet fern, when there were prairies of it all round about here—but that would have dispoiled the place—taken a little from its beauty—what self control of the people—to deprive themselves when there is abundance all round about.

10. *Chautauquan* 13, no 4 (July 1891): 409–64. A short sketch by Annie R. King (Nan), "The Spanish Creole," was included in the same issue as part of the "Woman's Council Table" section, 502–3.

11. Jean-Baptiste Le Moyne de Bienville (1680–1767) founded the city of New Orleans in the crescent of the Mississippi River.

There is a most beautiful bath-room here—and although the hot water does not flow freely in it, I delighted for the mornings in icy cold baths—then Mrs C with great delicacy & ample apologies informed me, that the scarcity of water did not permit the enjoyment of the bath, here—she said, that often when Englishmen came to visit them, they left in a day or two most unexpectedly—she was convinced, because they could not bathe—I should think so—Any thing more discouraging than dabbling yourself all in a basin, I cannot imagine—and at night, it has to be done by the feeble light of one candle. Mr C. is very strict with the boys, Mrs C, very lenient—so there is a little friction constantly between the worthy pair—that breaks out in peevishness in her.[12] I think if the whole family had some hard work to do in the world, they would all improve. The boys try to interest themselves in the horses & dogs—& in natural history; Mr C won't let them give an order, or touch any thing on the place. I doubt if either of the boys could make their living if forced to do it. About every two weeks Mrs C gets a letter from Downie, a little four-paged note paper affair,—filled with her great pleasure & happiness in her new home & surroundings—not a word of regret for the people or home here—or the wish of an only daughter, to be with her invalid mother—All this, as you may imagine, is most strange to me. [. . .]

We have been driving all the morning from 10 until 1. The day is perfect. Yesterday was hot, with a cold unfeeling wind rushing in the house at every door and window; a wind that went to the bones while the skin burned with the heat. It made me feel pretty wretched; but to day, thanks to a flannel petticoat & an undersacque, I am all right again—I would not live in this climate if the whole thing were given me—as it is, I do not know but that a course of "Dr Luminous"[13] would be as agreeable. I am in hopes Branch will come back from his next expedition about the time my visit is ending here; so I can have another little fling in N Y; with him. If he does not I shall go straight to Farmington and spend a week with Mrs Gay—& then—instead of going straight to Watch Hill—I believe

12. The "boys" were Frederick Joseph Church (1866–1914) and Theodore Winthrop Church (1869–1914).

13. This reference might be to the Luminous Brotherhood, a male Afro-Creole spiritual circle in New Orleans from 1858 to 1877.

it would be better for me to board for a week or two in or about Farmington—to work off if possible my Bienville. I shall go wild, dabbing at it, as I am forced to do, on visits—between meals & driving—and then I'll have the field clear for the Balcony Stories—about which Gilder is so optimistic. If he pays as he talks—I would not be surprised if I really did cross over to Europe—I shall talk it over with Branch if I see him. We could go together to Low's Exchange & make all arrangements.

I really don't feel like going anywhere or seeing any thing else but—I am lacking a "regulator"—and I suppose Europe is necessary—all places are the same to me when I am away from home.—

I wonder if you & Brevard are started on your trip yet?—I wish it was up this way and through the White Mountains—then I'd go with you. I suppose Mimi will send you Branch's enthusiastic letter on the subject.—I haven't heard from home in a day or two—I do hope they are getting along well there—Of course they will never let me know if they are not. Why can't I make thousands instead of hundreds!—Oh My!—If my family were only rich enough all to travel together, what a time we would have! [. . .]

With a heart-full of love and devotion.
Sis

Grace and Branch met up on the train and "talked straight along all the way to N Y," spent a short time at their favorite New York Hotel, and pondered the possibility of a European trip. Then Branch set out on a steamer for home.[14]

Grace first considered going to Paris alone, to "stay there very quietly & economically" until a sister could join her in the spring for a grand "European jaunt." She figured that a year's travel for two would cost about $1,500: "You see I can stay alone by myself, but I can't travel alone—& we could just buy Cook's tickets if necessary & 'go it.'"[15] By mid-August, Branch offered to help sponsor Nan to accompany Grace to Europe: "You two being away would somewhat reduce expenses at home, and my business outlook is rather encouraging so is

14. Grace to Mimi, Farmington, August 3, 1891.

15. Grace to Nan, Watch Hill, August 16, 1891, written with her left hand. In today's dollars, $1,500 would be $39,790.26.

yours, and maybe we can manage to give you both a year in Paris—I will do my share." Mimi also promised help, as the trip would advantage Grace professionally and personally. It was left to Grace to decide.[16]

LIVY TO GRACE

Marienbad, Bohemia, August 23, 1891

Grace dear,

I want so much to hear from you. I hate this getting news through news papers. I wanted so to see you last Spring that I might tell you fully all our plans, more fully than I could write them. Did you receive my letter telling you of what we expected to do next Winter? I wrote you as soon as I found you could not come to Hartford before we left. I do not know whether you received it.[17]

The papers tell me that you expect to come to Europe this Fall. Is this true? If so you must come to us for a while in Berlin. I wish on most accounts that we were to be settled on French soil. However Clara's music demands the German country. Susy says that she shall take no more piano lessons perhaps it is well, yet it makes me feel unhappy and especially as I feel that this result has been brought about by Mr Meyer's bad teaching. It is too bad, too bad, yet I was too ignorant to prevent it.

The Hartford paper states that you were at Mr and Mrs Hooker's golden wedding.[18] To think that you should be in Hartford and I not there to receive you! It gives me a pang.

We are having a very pleasant stay here. Mr Clemens has been taking the baths and doing some work. Mr Warner is here and there are a number of very pleasant people.

16. Branch to Grace, August 19, 1891; Mimi to Grace, Sewanee, September 8, 1891. Branch sent two checks totaling $100 to King's New York exchange, "1 of $75 & 1 of $25 00 as you requested" (September 10, 1891). King claims in her memoir that Branch and Mimi initiated the trip to keep her out of "a disagreeable participation" in the Lottery fight (*Memories*, 103). Letters suggest that the choice was hers.

17. Grace had received it.

18. John Hooker and Isabelle Beecher Hooker celebrated their fiftieth anniversary on August 5, 1891. The *Hartford Courant* listed Grace King as an attendee (John Hooker, *Some Reminiscences of a Long Life* [Hartford: Belknap & Warfield, 1899], 179).

Mrs Warner and Mrs Cabell are at Franzembad. Now in about a week they finish their various cures and come together again, I believe. They stay a month or six weeks in Vienna and sail for home the last of Nov.

Are you really coming to Europe? and when are you coming? What a pleasure it will be to see you again. These lands over here are desperately interesting and charming, yet I must confess to waves of homesickness, where I should like to see my friends and sit down in our library beside an open wood fire, instead of a stove, for a visit with them. Come! and we will have a visit beside the stove as we cannot do better.

We are all well except for Mr Clemens' rheumatic shoulder which is very troublesome and unfortunately is the right shoulder. With kind regards to your family and the same deep love for yourself

your affectionate friend
Olivia L. Clemens

Grace worried about making too many plans for Europe. She was becoming superstitious that her travel might trigger disaster at home. She wrote May from Watch Hill about news from their eldest brother, "very much shocked at Fred's telegram announcing the death of his baby. The last time, I was North you remember Uncle Tom died—it makes me feel as if my trips boded ill to the family."[19] Nevertheless, she would go abroad if May would help with the family in New Orleans and if Gilder would pay well for her stories. May wanted Grace to "not only endure but profit by the separation" from anything that would otherwise hold her back.[20] Grace agreed.

☙ GRACE TO MAY

Watch Hill, Rhode Island, Sunday, August 30, 1891

[. . .] I don't want to be in N O—next Winter—I would spend my whole time watching politics & nothing else—besides, I need the "ideas" I get away from home. It would cost about as much to live North a Winter as

19. Grace to May, Watch Hill, September 23, 1891.
20. May to Grace, August 21, 1891.

to travel all over Europe. I am perfectly disgusted with the expenses of living here—Well, thank goodness, I have still six weeks before me!

GRACE TO MAY

Watch Hill, September 23, 1891

[. . .] As you may imagine I am getting wildly anxious for Gilder's check for my stories—The moment I hear, I shall write to Mimi about Nan's trip—& they expect to head up by the 15th—so I must hear by the 11th. My idea is to start immediately whether the Bienville is finished or not. It costs more to live in the North than in Europe I am sure—Here, people are fleeced—you have no idea how much I am forced to spend by & for others—While I am screwing myself down to the last point of economy.

RICHARD WATSON GILDER TO GRACE

New York, September 24, 1891[21]

EDITORIAL DEPARTMENT
THE CENTURY MAGAZINE
UNION SQUARE NEW YORK
R. W. GILDER, EDITOR.
R. U. JOHNSON, ASSOCIATE EDITOR.
C. C. DUEL, ASSISTANT EDITOR.

Miss Grace King,
Watch Hill, R.I.

My dear Miss King:—
I believe I like all of these Balcony Stories. The "Little Mammy" is particularly strong, although all are good.

It strikes me, however, that the last words in the story of "Little Mammy" are somewhat flat,—that about drawing morals from it. Could not the ending be a little stronger? I send you a copy of it as it is now.

I was thinking of having a little head-piece to each of these stories. Could you give any hints as to a balcony? Have you any photographs

21. The letter is typed.

convenient? I do not know that it would be feasible as the artist might get them too much away from the actuality.

If I should make a criticism it would be that these stories run too much to painfulness. It would be well, I think, if there were a little more absolute humor or lightness for contrast.

In the story of the deficient pupil (a delightful sketch by the way) I would like to drop the word "red" from "large red nose."[22] Our Catholic friends are rather sensitive, as they have shown, and they might think that this was an attack on the priesthood. I don't suppose you care much about the red in that nose, anyhow. It is more a question of *size.*

Very sincerely yours,
R. W. Gilder

Whatever Grace did with his suggestions, she seems to have approached guidance with a combination of compliance and subversion. She was anxious to please but not to abandon principles.

She wrote more "Balcony Stories" and corrected proofs. She worried and puzzled over the Bienville biography and managed a "big installment" of it while she boarded in Framingham, Massachusetts, where she could please herself alone. Her host there talked and led her "as Mr Warner ever did" but without Warner's "flirting proclivity," she wrote Nan.[23] Tired of waiting for Gilder to commit further than his tacit agreement to publish the "Balcony Stories" with his recommended corrections, she took herself directly to his Century Company. By 1891, Grace had achieved a good measure of the autonomy she earlier craved. Now as an intrepid businesswoman, she used a rival publisher's offer as leverage to get Gilder and his partner, Robert Underwood Johnson, to come to terms. During their meeting, commerce and politics overlapped, as they often did. The personal was almost always the *lagniappe* in her business relationships.[24] That practice also included her extending hospitality to pub-

22. If the reference is to the story "Pupasse" in *Balcony Stories,* King changed the line to "Father Dolomier [. . .] the catechism class said they could dance a waltz on the end of his long nose without his perceiving it."

23. Grace to Nan, October 5, 1891.

24. In New Orleans parlance, *lagniappe* is traditionally something extra given with a purchase, for example, an onion with a pound of red beans.

lishers when they visited New Orleans and accepting reciprocal invitations into their homes when she traveled north.

GRACE TO BRANCH

New York, October 22, 1891
New York Hotel, N Y

Dear Branch,

When I got up this morning—I felt that I had a good long day's work before me—& I planned it out, by thinking what it would be likely you would do in my place—I waited until half past ten—waiting for some one to come from the Century Co—then as it was raining hard I went there myself—Gilder & Johnson (the other editor) were all that was polite—but there was a good deal of preliminary talking before they got to terms—They were so frankly surprised at the prices the Harper's gave me—that they could not conceal it—I was as nice as they were—& finally I saw that printed—my stories were very much shorter than I expected—most of them only 2½ printed pages—and so after I told them—that I got $50 from the Bazar for not so important work & after prolonged consultation they offered $60 apiece for 12—I accepted—I drew from them only $480—for the eight—which I had corrected—this leaves $240 to my account—I then went straight to Low's—deposited the check with him—(getting a receipt)—and engaged passage on the Brittanic—for Wednesday the 28th—

Low is a sensible looking middle-aged man—and he has his business arranged in a marvelously clear way. He is not engaged by any line—and will only recommend ships, which he personally knows to be good—He says, we will be perfectly safe and well cared for on the Brittanic which is one of the best of the White Star line.—He personally will get us off here—We will be met at Liverpool & London—and at his Exchange there as he says, we can even get a laundress if we want one—We deposit our money with him. He gives us a check book—and we can draw checks as we need them—In every city in Europe his checks are negotiable at the banks—He says he has been forced into this—by the thievery on the Continent, that hardly a traveler goes there, but what loses his or her money.—I myself had been a little alarmed at what all the ladies told me—about inside pockets, & sewing their money into their clothing—with Low's check book I shall be perfectly secure—& he says never to draw more than I need at one time—Nan & I both will have a check book, in case of accidents—It seems to me—that arriving in Paris with about $300—with $120. to draw from the Century in November and $120 in December I shall be in no danger of running short of funds, and with the Harper's ready to pay cash for anything that pleases them. I am expecting the $25 Exchange I wrote to you for, and about $10 Nina will have to send me—that will see me & Nan out of New York.—

What made my interview at the Century so long, was the fact that Gilder & Johnston, his partner, wanted to talk Lottery and nothing but Lottery—They are wildly excited about it—and then they told me what they and General Johnson were doing—I tell you, your old adversary has worked hard and well. He has so interested the prominent people in New York that just as soon as the election is over (about the 10th of Nov) I believe, they are going to hold a grand public meeting. [. . .][25]

The Century, are going to send some one to New Orleans—to write up an article on the subject—which is to come out in the Magazine in the critical time (but this is a business secret) and nothing must be spoken about the New York meeting until after the election. The Lotteryites do not suspect it—The Northern meetings are to make public the demoralization caused here by the Lottery, & the amount of money yearly taken up by it—Louisiana is represented as refusing a bribe of thirty one millions—for the sake of honor & morality—If La. is beaten in the contest—every state then will have to fight—single handed against the evil—La. must be helped—and the Lottery given to understand if they do succeed in La—that Congress will crush them—The effect Gilder says will be immense—& I am sure his is right—He sent Johnson to see me at the Hotel. The old fellow was very interesting and impressive [. . .] He says he is being watched by the Lottery but only suspects—are not sure of anything—He talked to me in whispers—sitting on the sofa with me, in

25. In this election, Grover Cleveland defeated incumbent Benjamin Harrison and the Populist Party's James B. Weaver, who was supported by the Grange, the Farmers' Alliances, and the Knights of Labor. These groups would help defeat the Lottery in Louisiana in 1892.

the corner of the room—He said the hotel was full of Lotteryites during the Fall—& they put on great airs of contempt for the hotel—[...]

Lovingly *Grace*

GRACE TO MAY

Metuchen, New Jersey, October 24, 1891

Dearest May—I came over here Thursday evening—as I expected the Aldens wanted me immediately, they telegraphed for me, and I was very glad to obey for I did not at all relish the prospect of a week of $3.50 days at the New York Hotel. As I wrote to Mimi I had a delightful trip to N Y, from Boston—& a good room waiting for me at the Hotel, with Crawford genial & welcoming.[26] The next morning I posted in a coupé to the Gilder office—It was raining cats & dogs—what with their politeness, business & Lottery talk, they kept me there three hours—They give a pretty good price for the Balconies—$60 apiece—I really expected $75—& I think the Harpers would have given that, but when I saw that printed they were only 2½ pages—I had not the face to insist upon more. I am to give 12 in all—and if they are successful—I can easily place 12 more, if not there, in some other Magazine—They are to be illustrated and published in a volume—by the Century Co. I drew $480 from them—& am to draw $120 in Nov & $120 in Dec. I flew over to Low & secured our cabin—He looks old enough to be Clarence's father[27]—pale, wrinkled, careworn—a perfect gentleman—& has evidently perfected his line of business.—I put off all the main arrangements with him, until Nan comes—so that she could have some of the pleasure & excitement of it—my morning's business cost me $5.50 in carriage hire & you can fancy how lugubriously small my little pile seemed in face of such expenditures $9 for one day—However—I determined to be like a business man over it, & not like a penny saving woman—When I got to the hotel Mr Alden's telegram was waiting for me. I packed my hand bag—& until the hour

26. Crawford was the hotel manager, whom King befriended on other trips.

27. The Kings knew Clarence Low in New Orleans; this is possibly his brother.

of departure passed the time talking to Louise Sullivan[28] and one Anti Lottery emissary—old Gen. Johnson there. At 6.50 I drove to the Jersey city—dark & still pouring rain—crossed—got my train, & arrived at Metuchen about 8 OC—Mr Alden was waiting for me, on the platform & his welcome repaid me for all my annoyances, & the welcome of the family—for all the doubts and blues of the day.—

It was such a delight to me—to get into this dear, bohemian, congenial crowd—Supper was prepared for me—beefsteak, & a big cup of coffee, which I did not hesitate to drink, for I knew what was before me—Mr Alden soon got me into his library—& we talked literature, until midnight—He read me the opening chapters of his new work—& seemed to want to discuss the whole subject with me—I enjoyed listening to him—and tried to answer up to his expectations—but oh I got dreadfully tired & sleepy—& was glad enough to get into bed, when midnight came—Yesterday, we had another long talk—about his affairs, and my affairs—& the affairs of the Magazine in general. He has positively engaged from me—an article on Iberville & the Mississippi—(*en passant*—I count upon that money for January)—

He gave me a most flattering note of introduction to the Harper agent Theodore Child—in Paris—asking him to do every thing for me & introduce me to all the celebrities he could, in literary life there—Altogether, I feel very well satisfied—with what I have accomplished, & what I have ahead of me in the way of work—with Nan's assistance, I hope to get through a great deal—& you know that achievement is my greatest pleasure on earth—I really am going to Europe to work—not working to go to Europe—& the little pressure upon me, of having to finish my articles, to get my money—will be just the stimulus—to energise me—I dispel all those doubts & heartaches that dogged & delayed me so much at home—Of course I must be backed by letters of credit from Branch & Mimi—so that I shall never feel the "want" of money—& I suppose Nan will get her usual monthly allowance for dressing.

It has been a close squeeze, getting my stories done—& every thing arranged for this trip—travelling around as I have been forced to do—furbishing up my toilette—making myself agreeable—& thinking out new work—but it agrees with me—I feel better & stronger under it—I try

28. An acquaintance from New Orleans.

to throw off, all worriment about home—I feel I must keep my faculties bright and ready for action and I dare not indulge in sentiment or sadness—Mimi's & Nina's desolation at home—discouraged me awfully—I depended upon their pleasure in the trip—& their hopefulness & cheerfulness for the Winter—to keep me up—I thought, that they would not only say, they were glad that we were going, but be glad and cheery one to another about it—as for Emma & Cécile[29]—I am disgusted with their adding their feelings too, to the situation.—It seemed to me that we were fated, never to do any thing happily or normally—But—it can't be helped I suppose—& I try not to think of it at all. I know what I would do—if I were left at home, & the others went to Europe. [. . .]

I could write lots more—but I had better stop—& do some of my other epistolary duties—Yours & Brevard's ever devoted—

Sis

Finally, the sisters were off on their dazzling journey.

GRACE AND NAN TO BRANCH

[telegram], October 28, 1891
9 Paid 4.30 Pm Oct 28 1891
Dated New York 28.
To Mr. Branch M. King 214 Gravier St
New Orleans

Are sailing all right well and happy beautiful weather.

Grace and Nan.[30]

29. Trusted servants in the King household; King claimed Cécile was a spectacular gourmet cook (*Memories,* 194).

30. Grace and Nan sent the same message to May.

CHAPTER 9

EUROPE AT LAST, 1891–1892

I at last, thank goodness! have found the Paradise of literary women.

—GRACE TO NINA, JANUARY 19, 1892

GRACE TO BRANCH

[cablegram], November 6, 1891

CABLE MESSAGE.

THE WESTERN UNION TELEGRAPH COMPANY

Manchester

Nov 6 1891

Branch King 214 Gravier St

N O

Arrived safe Grace

"It is wonderful that any one can get over sea sickness—& feel as well, as we do—& take interest in life again—I could not have believed it last Saturday," Grace wrote Mimi from the R. M. S. *Brittannic* when land was in sight.[1] She and Nan arrived in Ireland and went on to "London town" by way of Liverpool and Manchester but still with one foot in New Orleans politics, still "fuming & cussing about the Lottery" fight at home.[2] As was customary for genteel travelers, they carried letters of introduction and had contacts waiting to smooth their way. Numerous missives to family detailed the sisters' wide-eyed sightseeing excursions to all the expected sites in London and Cambridge over two weeks, and eventually in Paris, which felt most like home.

1. Grace to Mimi, November 5, 1891.
2. Grace to Nina, November 10, 1891.

☙ GRACE TO MIMI

Cambridge, England, November 13, 1891

Can you imagine us in this beautiful place?—I wish you could—Sometimes I think my being here is a piece of imagination—and I look at Nan to reassure myself. [. . .]

This seems a very commonplace letter to write from Europe—I am always expecting to be inspired to write some of those letters we are always reading in books—the people surely could not have written them without inspiration—for sight seeing is fatiguing & takes a great deal of time—& thoughts increase at such a rate—that to attempt reliving them by letters—is like draining a hogshead through a vial funnel. [. . .]

☙ GRACE TO MIMI

Paris, November 21, 1891

At last we are at the end of our journey—and to our delight we find ourselves in a big fine New Orleans. Our french here seems to pass muster better than our English did in London—We certainly understand the french here, better than the English there.

Madame du Pilouey's [. . .] offered to give us a pretty room lights & board for 150 francs apiece—a little less than $30 a month—It is an "Institut"—where teachers & scholars board—a very excellent idea. [. . .] When we went into the dining room & saw our fellow about 12 boarders, all laughing & talking around a long table, a bottle of wine before each one—not a word of English to be heard, we did begin to feel very much at home. There was a bottle of wine at our place too, and we shall string our visiting card around its neck—just as the others do.—[. . .] There are two English girls, two Russians, three Germans, & the rest all French. Every one seems to speak French fluently and well—Nan & I included. [. . .] I have only room to say—that you must look upon us as perfectly fixed & comfortable—lodged & fed far better, than I was last Summer at the North many a time—enjoying visitors—& I at work for just as soon as I finish this—I get out my Bienville. [. . .]

GRACE TO BRANCH
November 24, 1891.

[. . .] Paris is a great place—but, New Orleans is very much like it—By carrying New Orleans out to its highest possible expression of wealth and beauty, [. . .] you can have an idea of what the Mother of New Orleans is!

Nan and I try to feel strange but we can't—Every thing seems so natural, so what we are accustomed to. [. . .] Paris has not the New York art of making strangers feel uncomfortable—On the contrary to be a stranger here, is to be shown every courtesy and attention. And I cannot imagine where the idea came from that ladies were treated rudely by men on the streets here. Since we arrived Nan and I have passed five or six hours every day on the street and we have yet to see any thing which by the greatest exaggeration could be construed into offensiveness. On the contrary, we never hesitate to go out by ourselves and look for strange places because our questions are so kindly & copiously answered. [. . .] The ladies here all go, two together to theatre and opera—and Nan and I are told that we must not omit to go out at night and take a walk—just to see the brilliancy of the scene.

On her thirty-ninth birthday, November 29, 1891, Grace released her urban wryness on May after describing the majesty of l'église de la Madeleine: "Isn't it curiously typical of the place & people that their most prominent church should be dedicated to Mary Magdalen?" Such incongruity should have been familiar; it was commonplace in New Orleans.[3] She was dazzled by art at the Louvre, by the Luxembourg gardens and Renaissance buildings, but she was surprisingly critical of the excessive number of shops everywhere. She preferred to attend the lectures at the Sorbonne three or four times a week, where Grace heard the French expert Ernest Renan examine the Pentateuch: "the most charming old man in the world—very short & fat—with quite long white hair—raising his eye brows, screwing up his mouth, shrugging his shoulders—

3. Grace to May, November 29, 1891. King's gravestone gives her birth year as 1851, but in a letter to May on November 29, 1885, she calls that "my thirty third birthday," which makes her declaring 1852 as the year she was born.

and talking [. . .] in the most intimate personal tone."[4] In Paris, she discovered that she felt most free, "for I at last, thank goodness! have found the Paradise of literary women, I can dress as I please, & do what I please—and not have to visit—It is rather a negative kind of Paradise in some respects—but the results in comfort and pleasure are very positive."[5]

Despite the pleasures of Paris, Grace had work to do. She had promised Alden her Bienville biography and Gilder more "Balcony Stories." She had tackled "the great pile of proof—which the Harper's sent me for my Xmas week's amusement—and plodded along as pleasantly as I could, considering how I detested my stories—and myself for doing such poor work."[6] Living in cramped quarters with Nan, however, thwarted her ability to write and thereby to earn. At home or while traveling, she was accustomed to a room of her own; having to share a ten-by-twelve-foot one caused tempers to flare.[7] Nan lectured Grace on her "want of self-control," and Grace wrote Mimi: "If you can't tell a person the truth & correct her—the best thing is to soothe & feather—As I was at this moment, the spiritual director of the Clemens girls, Louise Sullivan & the young Russian—I think I shall let my sister alone."[8] Why Grace considered herself a "spiritual director" is unclear, but Livy Clemens later thanked her for "the trouble that you took about our needs in Paris,"[9] perhaps searching out lodgings and lessons for a stay that Livy and the girls aborted.

Soon, the serious lack of funds became an irritant. Branch had promised three hundred dollars for Nan's departure and three hundred dollars more in the spring. By late March 1892, Grace claimed she had only twenty dollars "between me and an emergency. [. . .] I think that the best thing for me to do—is to try & get my money out of Gilder & come home the quickest & cheapest way possible. I never dreamed of being able to keep Nan & myself in Europe

4. Grace to Mimi, December 15, 1891. Joseph Ernest Renan (1823–1892), influential historian, especially on early Christianity, and a political theorist on nationalism and national identity.

5. Grace to Nina, January 19, 1892, written with her left hand.

6. Grace to Folks, Christmas day, 1891. Four older stories would become the book *Tales of a Time and Place* (1892).

7. Grace to May, March 3, 1892.

8. Grace to Mimi, March 12, 1892. The two young women were fellow boarders.

9. Livy to Grace, May 20, 1892. MS, CU-MARK, UCLC 04209, University of California, Mark Twain Papers, The Bancroft Library, Berkeley.

on the work of my pen—but I could do it—if the publishers paid as promptly as they should,"[10] her consistent complaint.

While waiting for payment, the sisters immersed themselves in Paris life. They "cut the American and English quarter entirely" and even attended a French Protestant church, Grace wrote the peripatetic Warner, who was by now back in Hartford. In their *pension,* they enjoyed "all the comforts & familiarities of home life—it is just as if we were boarding in some good old Creole family down town in N O."[11] They entered the intellectual circle of Madame Marie Thérèse Blanc (Th. Bentzon) and Madame Rose Blaze de Bury—a set "most difficult to get in"—whose salons would inspire Grace and whose lives and writings would enthrall her.[12] Madame de Bury considered the sisters "in the 'Movement'" because of their "venality & religion, in politics—in the Lottery fight—The T.D. called us sentimentalists—we are called here idealists or Spiritualists," she wrote Mimi.[13] Of Madame Blanc, she enthused to Warner, "how much I admire—I may say love her! for I have never learned to admire without loving—or vice versa—and through Madame Blanc I am made welcome at Madame de Bury's—and so, on into the very literature of Paris."[14] She began to goad Warner to help the two women to get published in the United States.

Grace's "Paris time" was indeed "tenfold more precious than time anywhere else," but she also began to have the kind of love/hate relationship with Paris that she had with New Orleans. Although she claimed it was "quite wonderful

10. Grace to Mimi, March 27, 1892. One of the stories on which she waited for payment was "On the Plantation," the second story in the "Monsieur Motte" series, published in *Harper's* on January 9, 1892.

11. Grace to Warner, Paris, January 7, 1892.

12. Grace to Mimi, Paris, February 7, 1892. Baroness Marie Pauline Rose Blaze de Bury (nee Stuart, ca. 1813–ca. 1894), author of *Racine, and the French Classical Drama* (1845), *All for Greed* (1868), and other works. Marie Thérèse Blanc (1840–1907) was a prolific French novelist and a literary critic with *Revue des Deux Mondes,* which Grace King and her sister May often read. King became friend and correspondent of both women and tried to get them published in the United States. She patterned her own salon in New Orleans after theirs and cared for Madame Blanc as she was dying. Through them, King became enamored of the teachings of Charles Wagner (1852–1918), a French reformed pastor whose inspirational writings helped form the theology of his time. She also helped to get him published in United States.

13. Grace to Mimi, Paris, February 28, 1892.

14. Grace to Warner, Paris, February 28, 1892.

how strong these European women are—they do not pretend to give up to sickness as we do,"[15] some Parisians and Parisiennes shocked Grace with their disregard for modesty:

> I do not know what Parisian art would do without the naked woman—particularly those who are created with simple provision for the nourishment of infants.[16]

> A nation of men, who so little respect women—as to commit the indecencies in the street they do.[17]

> There may be less drunkenness here, but there is more drinking, than in any place I have been in—and every man of the millions—sipping absinthe—or great glasses filled with black coffee & brandy—I don't wonder they are so worthless.[18]

> [W]herever one could look, there would be a woman stripping up some child, & holding it out at arm's length for it to do what our children do in diapers—& under every tree—boys & girls—up to eight & ten years relieve themselves—without the slightest regard to decency.[19]

> [W]omen, who to within an inch or two of the waist were as naked as they came into the world. We in N O don't know what decollèté means—it simply means naked—I must say that like the men, I could not keep my eyes off the spectacle—It was far more thrilling than anything on the stage.[20]

15. Grace to Nina, Paris, January 19, 1892, written with her left hand.
16. Grace to Mimi, February 7, 1892.
17. Grace to Mimi, January 31, 1892.
18. Grace to May, April 7, 1892.
19. Ibid.
20. Grace to Mimi, Paris, February 7, 1892.

While the travelers absorbed Paris, the fight against the renewal of the Lottery's contract in Louisiana reached a fever pitch. Grace was "sure I would not be able to write a line—if I were at home & in the thick of it."[21] Then finally, "after two years of worry and excitement," it was over. Mimi, the steadfast anti-Lotteryite, announced on April 20, 1892: "The day after the battle! and we have won!"[22] Now they could all breathe easier, as well as those in major cities whose newspapers had attacked the monopoly and its use of federal railroads to transport lottery tickets.

Mimi had kept Grace and Nan *au courant* of every incident along the way. She was the family's news and gossip gatherer as well as its loquacious storyteller. Grace had heard a lifetime of tales on their balcony from the dramatic and effusive Mimi and other women who fed her literary storehouse. She trusted these informants and harvested their reports for the self-proclaimed realism in her stories. That knowledge coupled with deep archival digging informed her historical writing but perhaps also influenced its romantic tone. Mimi and Nan helped with local sources and contacts, but Grace claimed that her own research was her delight and her passion. Paris was a marvelous resource in that way.

In their tiny room, Grace managed two more "Balcony Stories" but ripped up her biography of Bienville and started again: "I am so tired of it—& my left hand pokes along so—& my right hand, is so detestably mean."[23] Stiffness had long since forced her to write to family with her left hand, but that was no deterrent to a mind reeling with ideas: "a thousand projects are careening in my brain—even if they never come out—it is pleasant to have them swarm there," she had written Warner.[24] Armed with the necessary credentials to plumb the stately Bibliothèque nationale de France, Grace then began a "good article" on Pierre Le Moyne d'Iberville and the Mississippi River, and she continued to search for a critical map related to his journey.[25]

On the other hand, her newest version of the cursed biography of Sieur de Bienville, Iberville's older brother, went more slowly, and finances became more dire: "Mr Gilder surely must send the $300, he owes me some—such an

21. Grace to Mimi, April 7, 1892.
22. Mimi to Grace, April 20, 1892.
23. Grace to Mimi, March 12, 1892.
24. Grace to Warner, January 7, 1892.
25. Grace to Mimi, March 18, 1892.

enormity as waiting to pay for stories until after the proof is corrected, I never saw in my 'literary career' before."[26]

GRACE TO MIMI

Paris, March 27, 1892

[. . .] I am driven to my determination, by a calm survey of the situation—& by my little exhaustion, after working as I do, every day—to pass my afternoons worrying—when Gilder means to pay me? How can I get in more work? How detestably mean Branch is?—

I get Bienville off, this week. Instead of 600—it is 1000—pages of MS—but I get no money for it until next year—I shall go right to and at something else, but after the MS is finished—it is a month between sending it off & receiving an answer—I have no doubt, but that simply on my work in hand—I could borrow 3 or $400—from a broker—but I have too much family pride for that.

Grace had written in January to Warner in Hartford that she planned to "pay a little visit to Berlin—principally to see the Clemens."[27] But by late March, the Clemenses had moved on to Florence, and Grace instead began to plan "a short cheap excursion & meet the Clemens in Italy—they are simply inundating us with letters[28]—but I have written to them, not to wait upon seeing me—Of course when I get my money it will be too late—our Spring will have been passed."[29] Branch finally sent 500 francs (approximately $100) and Mimi 1,500 more (approximately $300) while Grace waited for her final $240 from Gilder for the last of the "Balcony Stories." Influential editor and prolific essayist Hamilton Wright Mabie sent her $40 (200 francs) for a short version of her Bienville[30] but had not allowed her to correct her own proofs. "Oh! there

26. Grace to Mimi, Paris, May 8, 1892.

27. Grace to Warner, January 7, 1892.

28. The letters are missing.

29. Grace to Mimi, Paris, March 27, 1892.

30. King recalled in her memoir that her longtime "precious friend" Hamilton Wright Mabie (1846–1916) was the first to recommend her as a biographical writer to Dodd, Mead for their series "Makers of the Nation" (she chose Bienville) and also to Macmillan for their series on American cities (she wrote *New Orleans: The Place and the People*) (*Memories,* 69, 182). Mabie

was so much alteration to put in it!—I am desolated," she wrote May.[31] She had learned to trust only herself since the first proofs of "Monsieur Motte." As a diversion for her upset, she and Nan went off to the Fontainebleau palace and its glorious fields of flowers. But when Grace received a message that the cartographist at the Bibliothèque nationale had something important to show her, they hurried back to their Paris *pension* at 26 rue de Turin.

GRACE TO MIMI

Paris, Saturday, June 4, 1892

[. . .] The old place seemed very homelike and delightful to us—We had to tell all our experiences—just as if we had come home—The first thing the next morning, was the visit to Mr Marcel at the Bibliothéque Nationale—to see what he had according to his message to show me.—And he again, was most cordial—& very excited—He had been rummaging among the maps of the Bib Nat—& had found such a lot of old & precious maps, that he is going to make an exposition of them—& he said he didn't want me to leave Paris without seeing them—So he took me in the next room, where his workmen were at work, getting the exposition ready—& such a good time as we had! Most of it, crawling over the floor on our knees—examining one treasure after another—There are a great many curious maps of La. and one of N O—which we must get copied—[. . .] Nan, who joined me in the Section geographique, could not help laughing, to see me & one of the most eminent cartographists in the world—creeping around the room on our hands & knees. [. . .]

Devotedly
Sis

Gabriel-Alexandre Marcel had uncovered a long-sought map that he believed Iberville had used,[32] and Grace was convinced that no one had seen it for more

---

was an associate editor to Charles Dudley Warner's editorship of the series "Library of the World's Best Literature Ancient and Modern."

31. Grace to May, March 18, 1892.

32. Gabriel-Alexandre Marcel (1843–1909), archivist, cartographist, historian.

than a century, since France and Spain had held so many documents of colonial Louisiana. The map showed how Iberville might have recognized the mouth of the Mississippi River, a difficult stream to detect when approaching from the Gulf of Mexico because of its many fingers of waterways there. This significant find was ample reward for Grace's hours of research and her entreaties of Mr. Marcel. Now she could turn her attention to personal pleasures and a reunion with her dear friends, the Clemenses.

CHAPTER 10

WITH THE CLEMENSES IN ITALY

Only come! We want *you*!

—LIVY CLEMENS TO GRACE, AUGUST 30, 1892

OLIVIA CLEMENS TO GRACE

Venice, May 20, 1892

Grace dear,

Do come and talk to me a little while.

I am only going to send you a scrap of a note today to tell you what our latest plans are. We have given up Paris and have taken a villa in Florence for next Winter.

Mr Clemens had a great dread of Paris and even a suburb did not attract him. We found the singing advantages would probably be good for Susy and so we decided rather suddenly to take a villa a little way out of the town. The distance is perhaps two miles.

I want you and your sister to come and spend the month of Oct. with us. Will you? But you know you must so you may as well say yes at once. I met Miss Mildred Lee[1] last night and she told me that you were planning to go home in the Fall but you wont be able to go until after Oct. You know the steamers sailing from Genoa are now said to be very good.

I am so grateful to you Grace for all the trouble that you took about our needs in Paris, and I am truly sorry that you were given the trouble for naught, but until we got into the enticements of Florence we fully expected to go there.

I soon now go to Nauheim to stay for a few weeks perhaps for two

1. Mildred Childe Lee (1845–1905) was Robert E. Lee's youngest child; she died in New Orleans but was buried in Virginia.

months or more to take the baths there. Our address however is always Drexel Harjes & Co. Paris.[2] When do you go to England and what is your permanent address?

Next Winter I have got to have a good French governess. I have written to Florence to know if that will be an easy thing to find there. I do not fancy that it will be easy to find any where. I want a lady, some one who can go with Susy to teas, go out in the evening with her when I am unable to go and so on. Some one who will always speak French to the girls & teach them. Of course it is quite important that she speak Italian. How I do wish that I could stumble on just the right person, who wanted such a position and did not require extravagantly high wages.

If you should see such a person Grace just tell her to write me. Don't give yourself the least care or thought about it, but you may have seen or may see some one that you would think just fitted for the position.

It is necessary that you see a little bit of Italy before you return to America. The tramway runs near our door, (and we shall probably have a carriage too) so you could so easily go into Florence to study the pictures. As you would be so near Venice it would seem a pity not to see it. In case you think of going there (or rather coming here) I should advise you to do so on your way to Florence as it is said to be lovely here all through Sept. In fact we were here fourteen years ago next Sept. and it was divine. I love Venice. Dont go home without seeing it and then come to us for a month. I want so much to know your sister.

With deepest love
Yours always
Livy L. C.

During this time, Grace also continued contacts with Warner. She thanked him for his good notice of her *Tales of a Time and Place,* a title that suited both her private and public writings. He had called her New Orleans stories "as perfect a representation of creole conditions and social life as Nathaniel Hawthorne ever

2. Bad Nauheim is a resort town southwest of Frankfurt am Main known for its many types of hydrotherapy and salt springs. Drexel Harjes & Co. was a Paris-based investment bank from 1868 to 1895.

made of New England," noting that both authors wrote out of their experience, and neither used "local color" as a varnish. In his "Editor's Study" column in *Harper's,* Warner judged the four old stories as similar to French masters of fiction. The book included "Bayou l'Ombre," "Bonne Maman," "Madrilene; or, the Festival of the Dead," and "The Christmas Story of a Little Church," and Grace dedicated the book to George C. Préot, her "critical friend and friendly critic." She confided to Warner: "Those poor little stories made me terribly sad, going over them in proof—How much older I am now!" She also wrote that she was thinking of writing a novel, "something on the American life here in Paris,"[3] but historical research had greater sway. By then, her biographical essays were establishing Grace King's reputation as a historian and, thereby, as a woman ahead of her time.

GRACE TO WARNER

London, June 19, 1892
24 Goldhurst Terrace E.
S. Hampstead—London

My family think you are the most discerning critic in the world—and I?—I am in that chaotic state of mind and heart, into which any treatment of myself as a personality, plunges me. But, if to touch a writer's aspirations, methods, creed;—(independently of all personal fore knowledge) be a test of literary acumen and a sign of critical ability—I think I can give you an uncontestable certificate. It is not needless perhaps to tell you—that your notice of me has done me an immense amount of good—and that—to be formally introduced, in such a manner, & in such a column, into the literary world, as an accredited writer, will go far to make me one. I can tell you—what I frankly told Mr Alden—that I never read a "study" of Mr Howells[4] without feeling disheartened—and his utter want of sympathy, for the school to which I belong—was aching, I felt

3. Grace to Warner, April 10, 1892.

4. Charles Dudley Warner had, shortly before June 1892, taken over "Editor's Study," a monthly column of criticism in *Harper's* that William Dean Howells had previously written. He recommended the new collection, *Tales of a Time and Place* (*Harper's Monthly Magazine* 85 [June–November 1892]: 155–56).

to the detriment of the literature of the whole country—for he seemed to be trying to confuse literature to life shown, not through many, but one personality—And, if you desire to know when I found a school—& how I define myself—I answer, that in Paris—we all belong to schools—and that name is "realism as we see it!"—which seems to me, to be a very ancient & trustworthy school—and much broader than Howells—which is "realism as Howells sees it["]—

But—I am no longer in France as you see—*only* in London. However, I suppose, London is very nice when one gets used to it. We left Paris for Switzerland and were passing a preliminary fortnight, in Barbizon—in the memory of Millet,[5] & Society of the most eccentric set of artists I am convinced the sun ever shone upon—when a letter from Mrs Clemens—insisting upon our spending a month with them—(October) in Florence; changed all our plans. It was an invitation not to be refused—but it necessitated our seeing England now, and not at the end of our stay in Europe as we had planned;—and our sailing from Genoa instead of Liverpool—And so here we are—quite comfortably situated, boarding with a clergyman's widow—out in the suburbs—and leading the quiet orderly lives that befit boarders of a widow—of the church of England—But the household is not "colourless." [. . .]

Affectionately Yours G. K.

Nan sends love to you. Have you commenced your novel yet?

P S. [. . .] How I am running on!—But I am so full of things!—I believe I could talk and write forever on what I have picked up over here—and I am so excited over the politics! and now I must take another page, to thank you for the beautiful notice of my little book. If the stories were half as well written as this criticism of them—they deserve it. [. . .]

I do not know what has become of that wretched Bienville—not a word from Mabie, since he arrived. I hope Iberville, will stir Mr Alden with a little more liveliness—He goes soon, accompanied by a map I

5. Jean-François Millet (1814–1875), French painter of peasants in fields, a founder of the Barbizon school in rural France. The mid-nineteenth-century movement emphasized realism in landscape.

found in the Archives—never before published—which should at least make him welcome. By the way such a fine lot of old unknown colonial maps has been stirred up in the Bibliothéque Nationale—I verily believe through all my "fussing," around there about Iberville's maps—Marcel, the Cartographist is giving an exposition of them & although, we got cartographically quite "thick"—he would not pay me the honor of saying I, was the "protoplasmic germ"—in the matter. Marcel, is to write a list & description of these maps, & I am to see if the Mag. of American Hist—will not publish it—And this is goodbye—and—as you see—from having answered my letter—a much newsier one than the first—

Your's—Grace

OLIVIA CLEMENS TO GRACE

Bad Nauheim, Germany, July 1, 1892
Villa Augusta Victoria

Grace dear,
I thought of sending a letter out into the unknown to try and find you. I did not know or did not remember your banker and I did not know where you were gone in England. I thought that a letter sent to your old address in Paris would be forwarded to you and that I was just about to do when your letter reached me.[6]

Oh Grace you can have no idea how perfectly delighted this family are to think that we are to see you and your sister. In spite of the fact that the house keeping will probably go like sixes and sevens[7]—That I am to have Italian servants and cannot speak any Italian—yet, I have dared to ask you and am looking forward with the most intense pleasure to that visit with you. People that have had experience tell me, that house keeping in Florence is perfectly simple, that houses run themselves that servants know their work and do it. It is so much easier for me to believe this than to disbelieve it, as I have taken a house there and have three servants engaged—that I do it, and have faith that it will go comfortably well. If we

6. The letter is missing.

7. An English idiom suggesting confusion or disarray.

can not get anything to eat while you are with us we will go picnicing to Florence.

How I shall *love* to hear you talk once more.[8]

I am here taking the "cure" trying to make myself a very strong woman for next Winter. Mr Clemens has gone to America; he expects to be absent only six weeks, and more than two of them are gone already. Susy and my sister are in Switzerland travelling. Clara is in Berlin pursuing her beloved music. They will all three (my sister Susy & Clara) join me here in about a week.

I have just rec'd a dispatch from Mr Clemens saying he will sail July 5th so that will bring him here a week earlier than I expected him, or even a little more than a week earlier. His dispatch is sent from Hartford so he is there tonight.

Grace if you do not desire to do some travelling in Switzerland I suppose it would be a good deal cheaper for you to sail from England for Genoa. Of course that trip over the St. Gothard is a most wonderful trip.[9] But I believe the trip now to Italy from Eng. by water is a very comfortable one.

Yes you dear I rec'd that beloved enthusiastic letter and how happy I was to get it.

No I do not know London very well and now it is fourteen years since I have been there. How I should love to be going about there with you and your sister. How it would double or even treble my pleasure to have it with you. You must talk it all over to me when you come.

Yes it stirs one, London. Even the names of the streets as one drives along are a great delight.

You are right Mr Clemens' portrait ought not to have had the pipe in the mouth. It was not however planned originally to be exhibited as it has been. It was painted to go into the dining room of the little Inn at Onteora as they have a way of putting up portraits of their guests.[10]

8. Grace's southern idioms and her accent must have entertained them. They teased her about saying "you all."

9. St. Gotthard Pass is a snakelike mountain pass in the Alps.

10. Designer Candace Wheeler (1827–1923), a pioneer in the Arts and Crafts movement, helped create the still-existing Onteora Club, built in 1887. She designed the wallpaper in Mark Twain's Hartford House when she was a partner with Louis Comfort Tiffany. The Clemenses

When Mr Beckwith found that he had succeeded so well he decided that he would keep this one and do an other for the Inn. Of course it should never have been done at all with the pipe in the mouth for any place.

After it was nearly finished I wanted the pipe taken out, but it was too late, it would necessitate changing all the musles about the lower part of the face, but it is a great pity I think. Good night—Grace dear I love you and am so thankful that I am so soon to see you and your sister. I want so much to know her

Always yours
Livy

As Livy implored Grace and Nan to visit, Mimi also pushed them to seize every opportunity that Europe and the Clemenses had to offer.

MIMI TO GRACE
Blowing Rock, North Carolina, July 22, 1892
Valley Vista N.C.[11]

My dearest Grace,
[. . .] Now that Iberville is out of your hands, and off your mind, you must, and I hope will not commence any thing more—you must rest—I know when you get to Florence, you will have entire freedom from work—a visit to the Clemens will be a pleasant ending of your tour—you will have nothing to do, but laugh and grow fat—only think being actually in Italy—realizing in some measure your dreams—is it not all too strange—you & Nannie—I often sit and, try to think it all out, and wonder how it all came to pass—my solution to the proverb is—education and intelligence, energy and persistence, will overcome all obstacles—you have now the reward of all your labor, and all your

visited the Onteora Inn in 1890, as did many other artistic and literary lions, including artist James Carroll Beckwith, who painted Twain with the pipe.

11. May's mountain cottage near Blowing Rock, North Carolina.

self-imposed privation, so my dear children, enjoy every moment that you can. [. . .]

Lovingly
Mimi

Soon a different obstacle threatened the sisters' trip to Florence: cholera.

LIVY CLEMENS TO GRACE

Bad Nauheim, August 30, 1892

Grace dear,

Your letter has given me great pleasure:[12] it seems so good that I am to see you and your sister so soon D. V.

We still hope that we may be able to start toward the south the last of next week but we are not at all certain because of course we cannot send Clara to Berlin until all this cholera scare is past. I hope that this cool weather may make things better but Mr Clemens thinks it will not be at all safe to send Clara to Berlin next week and I am afraid he is right.

Don't take your tickets until the news is better I suppose we might be kept here a month or six weeks if the disease should spread.

As soon as I know when we shall start I will let you hear from me again. I can not but hope that we may be able to go by the first of week after next: in that case we should be ready for you by the seventh or eighth of Oct. I know there is a good deal to do to make the Villa livable and I want it comfortable before you come to us.

As I am not very strong I cannot work very fast, however if we can get away by the fourteenth or fifteenth, reaching Florence by the twentieth to the twenty fourth then we shall be all in readiness. If we are not you will not mind a little picknicing will you?

You are not Grace my dear to bring me any thing from London but your own beloved self and your sister. I want you and that is all, so do not cumber yourself with books or any thing. Only come! We want *you!*

12. The letter is missing.

Sept 2nd
Grace I have been waiting for a day or two hoping that we should hear better news from Hamburg[13] and that I could write more deffinately about our plans, but alas the news is just as bad as ever and Mr Clemens says we must stay right here. Of course he is right I suppose hotels would deny us admission and we should be in a sorry plight if we got away here. Four people were denied admission here yesterday. How terrible it is; One does so deeply pity Hamburg. Of course it is impossible to conceive the terror of it unless one was living in the midst of it; although it seems hideous enough here. Let me know about yourself Grace dear, how you are in body and mind.

We are all well, but one feels at this time that one holds life and health by a very slender thread. I judge you will not think of moving from England until this trouble is past. Mr Clemens says he has been quaranteened once in his life and he never desires the experience again.

Our expenses now begin in Florence, rent of Villa wages of servants and so on. But in this time if ones family are saved alive one will not complain of money losses.[14] With most cordial greeting to your sister know that I am now and always your deeply loving

Livy

P.S. Do write me at once about yourself & your present plan. *Don't* come on to the continent until this sickness is past.

Mimi also feared the reports of cholera that newspapers told.[15] It was in Paris, Berlin, and Hamburg; she was watching Florence, but surely "Mrs Clemens would hardly stay in Florence, and expect visitors if there was so much danger of cholera—the reports may be exaggerated. [. . .] I hope that nothing will interfere with your visit to Florence—it is like a fine dessert or pousse café to your trip."[16]

13. Where cholera was serious at the time.

14. The Clemenses were in financial straits, a condition King knew well in her own life and probably knew about her friends. Olivia's candidness is confirmation of her trust in Grace.

15. Mimi to Grace, Valley Vista, July 22, 1892.

16. Mimi to Grace, Valley Vista, August 26, 1892. Pousse-café is a *digestif* of layered colorful liqueurs to be sipped after a coffee course. In French, literally, "coffee-pusher."

OLIVIA CLEMENS TO GRACE

Bad Nauheim, September 5, 1892

Glorious! Grace dear, the Dr says at present he sees no reason why we should not leave for Florence next week. Of course we do not expect in that case to send Clara to Berlin. We shall take her with us to Florence and later when all this scare is past, send her up to Berlin.

We are rejoiced because our work here is finished and we are a little tired staying here and very anxious to get there. That will only start us from her[e] five or six days later than we expected to leave, so we shall be ready for you and your sister by the fourth or fifth of the month. Or if that in any way inconveniences you we will try to make your rooms ready earlier. I am *so* rejoiced that it has turned out this way. Now I do hope that there will be no contradictory reports that will keep us here.

This change of plan makes numerous notes to write so I must just send this line.

I am *so* delighted that I am so soon to see you

Yours always
Livy.

GRACE TO WARNER

London, September 10 [and 12], 1892

I have been trying and trying for ever so long to write to you—but time is so elusive—and—I get tired—I must be fledging into some thing very literary—for I only write now scrappy, hurried letters—and you see what my chirography has become—I who so hate a weak nerveless handwriting.—[. . .]

We have been here about ten days—and are waiting until it is safe enough on the continent for us to go to the Clemens—They you know, were shut up at some watering place near Hamburg—The last letters announce that they will move in a week. I was very much distressed at their exposure to danger. In a week now—thank Heaven! all fears will be over. [. . .]

Monday evening [September 12]—
[. . .] We stay at the Clemens in Florence until the middle of October—then I suppose we shall spend ten days—in getting through Paris—a few more here—& then the first steamer from Liverpool.—

The last I heard from Mr Alden, he had not received my Iberville—I wonder if he ever did rec. it—I fear he did however & that it is not up to the mark or he would have told me—and Mrs Sangster[17] perhaps that's the reason she does not acknowledge receipt of my MSS—She thinks very likely I shall soon be in N Y—and I counted on having the money to spend over here!—I am almost sorry I promised to go to the Clemens. But Florence was such a temptation—and I long to see them too—and it seemed a pity to deprive Nan of such opportunities—we may never have another chance at Europe. [. . .][18]

Always affectionately
G.

GRACE TO MIMI

London, Saturday night, September 17, 1892

Dearest Mimi.—I commence my Wednesday letter tonight, for if all goes well, by next Wednesday we shall be in Paris on our way to Switzerland—on our way to Italy—The Cholera Scare is about over—and every body starting to move around again. The Clemens left for Florence last Saturday—I shall know Sunday I hope how they fared—& we may start Tuesday morning across the channel again. [. . .]
I believe I told you that the round trip from London and back is $40 apiece & crossing the ocean to New York $58 apiece—I changed my $300 check from Gilder today—$100 to buy tickets—& pay incidentals—$100 deposited at Low's for steamer ticket—$100—for board—and "living"—until we sail—[. . .]

17. Margaret Sangster (1838–1912) was a poet, author, and the second editor of *Harper's Bazar,* serving 1889–1899. The woman's magazine began in 1867 under editor Mary L. Booth.

18. King was mistaken; she and her sisters returned to Europe in 1905–6 and in 1912–13, but neither trip was as exhilarating as this first discovery.

But I tell you—I have earned every pleasure of this trip by the "Sweat of my brains"—I am not quite sure that it is not selfish for us to go on to Florence instead of returning to our posts at home.—and more than once I have been on the point of giving it up. Then I think of the profit in after life—& how much better I shall be qualified to write after it—& the small chance of my ever coming over here again & I gird up my loins & clench my teeth-—& resolve to go on with it—Our visit to the Clemens will terminate about 5th Nov. [. . .] And after this—I'll not want to leave home again for ten years. [. . .]

Nina must not make any preparations for me to go out into society or on anything gay—I am going to settle down to reading study & work—I have seen this folly over here—of our so-called society in N O—the men are all too stupid—the women too vain & frivolous—[. . .] I have seen what real intellectual society is—& I am not going to demean myself any more on the paltry stuff in N O—We will have plenty to talk about & amuse ourselves with—at least for a year—so we can be quite independent of every one.—I think your next letter, after this had better be sent to Mrs. S. L. Clemens, care of Drexel Harjes & Co.—Paris—putting my initials at the bottom of the envelope. We will be with them in 25 days—but I don't know yet, their address in Florence. [. . .] Don't worry about Cholera or any other illness—Nan & I are most particular about our health—& we are prepared for all emergencies. [. . .]

Ever devotedly
Sis

GRACE TO MAY

Lucerne, Switzerland, Sunday, October 2, 1892

[. . .] I am not surprised at the Cholera fears, when I read the sensational paragraphs in the U.S. papers—[. . .] There is really no fear & never has been of a general epidemic outside of Hamburg & Russia—and the most minute precautions are being taken against the outbreak next Spring. As you can imagine even if I had wished we could not for love or money have secured a passage home, during the first panic—& I made up my mind,

> that if I had to stay over here until mid-winter, I would not risk detention in N Y—But I can see, by the letters that there is a good deal of uneasiness about us.—and to tell you the truth if I had not promised the Clemens, & if I did not feel that the visit to Florence, would be of great pecuniary profit to me in my writing I would not go there a step—I am anxious myself to get home—to relieve Nina, & take up my place, in the family work & responsibilities.

Finally, the travelers arrived at Villa Viviani, the temporary retreat of the Clemenses that overlooked Florence. Nan's letter to a friend in New Orleans showed that she, too, had narrative skills.[19]

☙ NAN TO NOTIE MOSS

Florence, Italy, October 13, [1892]

My very dear Notie,

[. . .] I must tell you something now of my life here in Florence. We reached here last Friday night, in quite a rain storm. Mr Clemens met us in the station, put us into his iron carriage and drove us to the Villa. You know the family were all strangers to me, yet while the heat of their greeting was for Grace I too was made very welcome. The villa is in Settignano a suburb of Florence; the house seemed enormous after our stay in Paris. The walls are decorated with large medalions of famous men supported by fat holy looking marble cherubim. This is the decoration of the first sala; the walls are lined with comfortable seats, in the centre of the room is a divan surmounted by a stand of palms.

The Clemens are as you well might suppose charming. She so lovely so perfectly unworldly, he full of sound sense and brimming over with humor: At night when the lamps are lighted he reads aloud—Browning; last night the programme was varied by the reading of one of his own unpublished articles. Every evening we drive somewhere for an hour or two.

19. The Villa Viviani is now an events venue with some features still intact that match Nan's description.

Florence does not seem so pretty to me as many an other foreign city—but probably this comes from the fact that I only see it through a carriage window instead of taking it unaware of slipping upon it from some turn which only a pedestrian ever chances.

[...] There is a large central hall into which rooms open from all sides. I go up a flight of broad stone steps to reach my chamber unless I prefer the secret stairs in the wall, which I generally do. My room opens into Grace's and is an immense affair. Marble floors, high ceiling, and broad windows from which I have a beautiful view of Florence. The villa is surrounded by a dear old garden, where lemon trees in bloom and fruit, magnolias, jasmines, and other tropical plants grow in profusion. A thick grove of elm trees in one corner and as far as the eye can reach, one sees the silvery green olive with its dark fruit. But what to me is most wonderful is the ever shifting lights and shades, and heavenly wonders of Italy! I am almost sorry we go back to Paris and London. I should like to sail from Florence (only ships do not float on the Arno) for then one would be enveloped in this atmosphere of peace and forget for one long week the bustle and commerce of this busy world. Our journey from here will be almost unbroken till we reach Paris for our friends here cannot speak of our leaving them one moment before we are obliged to. I am afraid I have written you what is termed in America a "gushing" letter, but I hope you will pardon me if I have, and try to realize how hard it is for me to keep from boiling over when I have seen so much that is new to me. Grace sends you her love and says she feels even more ecstatic than I do, but that is impossible. We begin our Italian lessons to morrow and I shall feel infinitely better when I can speak a few words of this tantalizing language. I have been writing this letter so long that I quite despaired of finishing it, but a bright thought came to me, so I bounded out of bed one hour earlier than usual this bright Sunday, and after a hearty meal of grapes figs and peaches, gained a few moments of uninterrupted time to give you. Give my love to your mother and kind regards to Mr Moss. With dearest love to you always

Nannie

GRACE TO MIMI, NINA, BRANCH

Florence, October 17, 1892[20]

VILLA VIVIANI

SETTIGNANO FLORENCE

My dearest home-folks—I really am going to try and write a letter to you all, and I shant wait for my wretched old R[ight] H[and] any longer—I have commenced several times, but the appearance of the scratchy date simply put me out of temper—& I told Nan I would not send such a looking piece of chirography to any one—Nan, of course has told you all of our ideal existence here.[21] I can only say of it that it is perfect—& I never again expect to find the like of it on this earth again. As usual I find that any impressions of Florence are totally different from what I expected after reading & hearing so much about it. The city is ugly—built up with brick & stucco—with the few exceptions of the churches and public buildings. The Arno is a thick yellow ugly little one horse creek—the dirt & filth every where are indescribably loathsome—When we drive through it I do nothing but wonder at the fascination the place has exercised over the people for centuries—not to speak of the colony of English & Americans who live here & no where's else—I agree with Mr Clemens that instead of bewailing his exile, Dante should have rejoiced to get out of the place—As for the Biboli gardens—I think my European disappointments culminated yesterday when we drove to them after church—But with all this I could be as great a fool as any one over the place—& I really believe I would go on living contentedly here to the end—what entrances me is the exquisite beauty of line & colour in the landscape—and I believe I should be just as much entranced if every historical association should disappear carrying along with it every work of art. I cannot get my fill of looking out of the windows and it seems to me every look of my eyes brings me a new dose of comfort calm & pleasure—I cannot imagine any one ever quarreling or fighting in this heavenly atmosphere—although the Florentines did such a lot of it—and as for committing the sacrilege of a battle in it, surpasses my comprehension—but I can under-

20. An excerpt was published in "GK and MT," 45. The letter is written with her left hand.

21. The letter is missing.

stand how master pieces of art & literature come here more naturally than mediocrities elsewhere—I am not at all surprised at Dante, Giotto, Del Sarto,[22] Raphael, Fra Angelico—& all the rest—I would be surprised if they had not done what they did.—This is the cream of our voyage. Its well it comes last; nothing else could please after this—

Mrs. Clemens is perfectly lovely to us & I have never seen Mr C so much himself—We all have such a good time together—which never stops until both commence to beg me to stay over the Winter—It is very hard to resist their genuine longing to have us—with the delights of Florence to boot—but I have made up my mind & besides I am more worldly wise than they—& the more I see our perfect passion to be together, talking, reading, and driving, the more convinced I am of the danger of trying to prolong it too far.—Now we do not miss a moment, & the knowledge that we must all separate in a month, keeps our enjoyment up to the pinnacle all the time—Much as we delight in it all for myself I prize it keenly on account of Nan. What a magnificent treat for her! I wonder sometimes if she appreciates how enviable her lot must appear to so many in the world—Mr & Mrs C are delighted with her—& they say they are not going to stop until they know the whole family, & here as in Hartford Mrs C says she is determined to have a visit from them all; and it makes me beam with pleasure to hear her exclaim three or four times a day—"If Nina & Branch were only here!" How I want to know your mother!—Mr C. must meet Branch & make an exchange of good stories. "How can I meet Mrs Mc Dowell?" As for Susy, remembering a long ago invitation, she is always talking of what they will do when they come out in N.O—society.—

Mrs Clemens is in delicate health, but nothing at all serious—The Dr. says she will be as well as ever if she gives up this Winter to rest & quiet. She is a wonderful woman. I am more & more impressed with her fine qualities.—Mr. C. is just bubbling over with fun & devilment. He got off a lot of his good things for the benefit of Nan last night—His take off of Cable is killingly funny to me.

I have received a check from Mrs Sangster for three Bazar letters

22. Andrea Del Sarto (1486–1530), Florentine painter of High Renaissance and early Mannerism.

$120—$40 a piece—just $15 more than I expected.[23] So the seven of them will make quite a nice little sum.—[. . .]

With our usual luck Nan & I are able to give the go-by to the hateful American set—& make what acquaintances we do in the best English & Italian circles. I called the other afternoon, by appointment with Mr Clemens on our nearest neighbor a Mrs Ross the daughter of Lady Duff Gordon[24] and the author of several books. She & her husband live in the old princely Italian style—they own their beautiful villa & the great farm surrounding—& grow wine & olives for the market.—She is handsome dashing & middle aged—has known all the historical celebrities of her time, was evidently a great beauty—besides having a wit—as for the country here abouts, she is intimate with every stone & olive tree—We walked through one salon & corridor after another to get to her drawing room.—the walls all covered with pictures & engravings—& the sides lined with vases & curious bits of furniture. I want to write at least three sheets more, but Mrs Clemens has sent word that she has ordered the carriage for immediately after breakfast so I must stop & dress—The weather is quite cool & Autumnal—except the dampness, the regular October New Orleans weather—My love to everybody & sentiments proper to Emma & Cécile—tell Fred I want to write to him but its so hard to find more in a hand.

Devotedly Sis[25]

Even in a reverie of glorious surroundings and warm friendship, however, business troubles found Grace.

23. King refers to the first three of a series of seven short features ("Letters") she wrote for *Harper's Bazar.* She was later also paid for "Madame Duches de la Pazerio," 3,000 words; "Mademoiselle Blaze de Bury," 3,000 words; "Mr Charles Wagner," 3,000 words (*Harper's* statement, January 5, 1893). On February 6, 1893, Alden sent a check from Harper & Brothers for $175 for the manuscript "Iberville and the Mississippi."

24. Janet Duff Gordon Ross (1842–1927) was a cookbook writer, businesswoman, and sometimes art dealer. Daughter of Lucie, Lady Duff-Gordon (not the British designer). In 1888, she and husband, Henry Ross, bought the Villa di Poggio Gherardo near Florence; she found the Villa Viviani for the Clemenses. Sunday was her day to receive artists and writers.

25. King wrote glowingly of her stay in Florence in *Memories,* 169–80.

GRACE TO MIMI

Florence, October 21, 1892[26]
Villa Viviani

Dear Mimi—

I was astounded yesterday at the reception through the mails of Bienville—a handsome looking volume bound in red. But astonishment unfortunately has been the only pleasant emotion connected with it; for I cannot open the pages anywhere without seeing the most glaring typographical errors, hardly a proper name rightly spelled and words left out of sentences every where—so that whole paragraphs are made perfectly idiotic—Of course the publishers should not have printed it, without my correcting the proofs—but they were so determined, I could do nothing. And—I am humiliated too, by such faults of style & even grammar in it, for which I am solely responsible—that I can't bear to think of any one's reading it. The book seems to have been doomed from the first—and I must say I feel a little bitter, when I think how much Nan's ill temper & peevishness during our first Paris months when I was trying so hard to write it, has contributed to the unvalued, trouble[d], style—Of course she has cured all that by this time, & has learned not to spoil another's pleasure when she is put out—but, unfortunately like all such reforms it comes too late, at least for me. I have written to Dodd Mead[27] to send you the rest of my copies—You can give them in the family only—I intended to send a lot of others to Farrar[28] and the rest who have been so kind in helping me—and I wanted to give Branch as many as he wanted for his country friends—but I must wait until I get home, and make personal corrections of the worst mistakes. So do try and explain the matter to inquirers—& don't blame Dodd & Mead for they have been very polite—& if I can keep them in a good humor they may put out a new edition after a while—If it should be noticed in the Delta[29]—I wanted it

26. The letter is written with her left hand.

27. The publishing house.

28. Edgar Howard Farrar (1849–1922), corporate lawyer and civic leader in New Orleans, trustee of Tulane University, leader in the movement to abolish the Louisiana Lottery. He helped King locate materials for her biography of Bienville.

29. A short-lived newspaper in New Orleans, begun mainly as an organ for the anti-Lottery movement.

stated that circumstances prevented my correcting the proof.—& hence the errors. I shall write to Mrs Baker myself about the T.D.[30]

We are still living in Elysium here—troubled only by the sadness of friends at home. [. . .]

Ever devotedly
Sis

Finally, Grace and Nan departed from Florence. Upon their leaving, Twain gave Grace a copy of his *The American Claimant* with the inscription: "Miss Grace King is requested to try to get as much profit out of this book as the undersigned has gotten out of her & her sister's visit at Villa Viviani—which is requiring the impossible. The Author. Villa Viviani Settignano Near Florence, Nov 10/92."[31]

The dear friends were never to be together again.

☙ JEAN CLEMENS TO GRACE

Florence, Saturday night, November 19, 1892
VILLA VIVIANI
SETTIGNANO (FLORENCE)

Dear Miss King;
There has been a great mistake made in this familly today. In the package that went to Clara containing, that silk shawl for Clara went also Mr Branch King's gloves. Mamma is very much troubled; and while this letter is flying to you, another is flying in the opposite direction to Clara saying that she must send the gloves to your banker in London immediately. I do hope you got to Paris comfortably.

I got a letter from Patrick that made me unspeakably homesick.[32]

With much love to you and Miss Nannie

30. *New Orleans Times-Democrat;* Julie K. Wetherill Baker (1858–1931), poet (as J. K. W.), literary columnist, and wife of editor Marion Baker.

31. Author listed as Mark Twain (Samuel L. Clemens), London, Chatto & Windus, Piccadilly, 1892 (NN-BGC, UCCL 09303, University of California, Mark Twain Papers, The Bancroft Library, Berkeley).

32. Patrick was the Clemenses' coachman.

I am forever yours
Jean Clemens

GRACE TO WARNER

Paris, November 14, 1892
57 rue Boissiere

Your ~~October~~ is fine—splendid! November I mean. It delighted my very soul. I am dashing this off to tell you so—& that we sail for home on the Brittanic on the 23d. Meet us in New York & you shall have my first gushings—& oh!—I have so much to gush about.—arrived here Saturday evening—[. . .] [W]hy why must I leave Paris!—[. . .] I am really wild with all these last excitements—travels & shoppings & theatre—won't you tell Mr Alden when I expect to arrive—I must see him if only for a half hour—

It was a wrench to leave the Clemens and their ideal interpretations of life—But I shall tell you all about them too.

Affectionately Your's
Grace

GRACE TO MIMI

[telegram], December 2, 1892
RECEIVED AT NEW ORLEANS, LA.
S.W. Corner Gravier and St Charles Sts. m: Standard Time 50 6 P
to New York 2
Mrs W. W. King
530 Baronne St. NO

Arrived safe at Marlborough hurrah

Grace

King and Warner somehow miscommunicated and missed each other in New York. Grace also missed Hamilton Mabie about her *Bienville,* Henry Alden about her *Iberville,* and Margaret Sangster of *Bazar* magazine from whom she was to receive a check. Grace waited. No one came but Moses Woodruff Dodd of Dodd, Mead, and she convinced him that *Bienville* had to be reprinted.[33] It was Saturday, then Sunday, and Grace could not afford to stay longer. She wrote Warner "I saw myself losing time & money, awaiting the convenience of a lot of men—which made me furious."[34]

Grace and Nan were home in New Orleans on December 14, 1892.

33. Dodd, Mead republished *Bienville* in 1893.

34. Grace to Warner, December 15, 1892.

CHAPTER 11

ENDURING TIES, 1893–1899

Oh life is so ghastly at times!

—GRACE TO OLIVIA CLEMENS, OCTOBER 13, 1893

Over the next few years, Grace King and Sam and Livy Clemens seem to have exchanged fewer letters.[1] The occasional correspondence expressed sympathies, because troubles and death intervened. Mark Twain was climbing out of bankruptcy in 1895 by way of his world tour; Grace was long familiar with privation. In the words of her protagonist in *Earthlings:* "Poverty makes such cowards of us. [. . .] It destroys even the confidence of youth. We let our lives shrink with our purses. We cannot adapt ourselves to the change from dollar to penny existences. It is not the body that suffers, it is the mind. We hunger not for the food and clothing of the rich, but for their amenities, the consideration, the friendships, the compliments, the caresses, the welcoming attitudes of hosts: the proud among us die famished."[2]

Grace concentrated on work in the final years of the century, but she was not always content. Her series of "Balcony Stories" continued in *Century Magazine,* and Warner declared her "one master in three in this country."[3] However, the collected *Balcony Stories* (1893) in book form sold only hundreds, not thousands. Its dedication read: "To my mother whose balcony stories were the delight of my childhood, these feeble imitations are gratefully and lovingly dedicated." According to May, there was "rapturous praise" in Charlotte over Grace's style and freshness of plot, and May's long-standing book club now proudly called itself the "Grace King,"[4] but the tally of royalties was disap-

1. It is possible that some letters have temporarily gone astray.

2. *Earthlings, Lippincott's Monthly Magazine* 42 (November 1888): 611.

3. Warner to Grace, August 10, 1893.

4. May to Grace, April 7, 1893.

pointing. In the summer of 1893, Grace with Mimi and Nan had a long respite at May's "Valley Vista" cottage on a bluff in North Carolina, and in October, she and Livy Clemens commemorated having been together the previous year.

GRACE TO OLIVIA CLEMENS

New Orleans, October 13, 1893

Home!

This time last year, my dearie—Nannie & I were with you—enjoying that perfect visit—Oh how delightful it was! It is the jewel spot of my European memory—Indeed it glitters like a diamond good to last, all memory to all time!—And where are you now, & the other inevitable question, what are you doing?—If I were Mr Clemens—I would be getting a letter from you very soon now, for you have been constantly in my mind—& almost daily for two weeks I have had my pen in my hand to write you.[5]—But I was so sure you would come over to the Big Fair![6]—and so—I waited & waited.—

We arrived here about a week ago; wonderfully strengthened & refreshed in the body—but all rusty & gone to seed as to mind. Fancy three months with none but the most ordinary intellectual companionship—Even Maman, the best natured of intelligences complained.—May, my usual literary chum as well as sister—was incapacitated from heavy reading by all sorts of miserable little ailments that kept her always within invalid limits. Nannie & I fended[?] the best we could—but dear me! We have been so much together for the last three years that we are getting too much alike—or know each other so well that there are no possibilities of surprises in our intercourse.

I have not heard a word for months from my Northern co-literateurs—We Americans certainly have no genius for friendship—What vast fields of affection we let run to write for most of the merest little cultivation—and though I might just as well try to replace a lost

5. As a native of a city with alternative spiritual approaches, including voodoo, King was likely as indulgent of mental telegraphy as was Sam Clemens.

6. The Columbian Exposition in Chicago, 1893.

toothe as a lost affection—the most of my compatriots seem to go through life growing very contentedly over full sets of artificial friends—[7]

My metaphor is suggested—by a visit today to my dentist—and you must not be surprised if all my thoughts flow odontologically.—for I am of such a sympathetic nature—that the deft actions of my dentist, & his mellifluous tones as he hammered & probed—have won me into seeing his as *the* art par excellence—in the world.—

Nina is still in Milwaukee—we expect her home shortly and try to see the Fair through her experiences—for truth to say, with humiliation—none of us Kings, except her & Branch have seen it—We managed our financial affairs so badly, during the past year, that Providence has deprived us all of at least the profit, of seeing the biggest city & the biggest people on the earth in their native element of astounding the universe.—But how tiresome it all is, in the newspapers & magazines! At least to those who have not been there.

Did you see in the papers of our harrowing, dreadful, terrible storm? All of our poor fishermen & Gulf islanders with their families, swept out of existence—Oh life is so ghastly at times! It sickens me to read the papers—the accounts simply wring the heart[8]—

Dear, do send me a line—Susy, Clara, Jean, Mr. Clemens, yourself—I love you all too much not to pine & long for at least a sign of your well being from time to time—God bless you all—& with dear love to every one of you—

Devotedly Grace.[9]

When Livy answered, she seemed a little more distracted than usual.

7. There is no clear explanation for this censure unless King was feeling overlooked and comparing sedate Yankees with her more demonstrative French friends, whom she had pressured Warner to help.

8. In Louisiana, this hurricane was the Great October Storm or the Chenière Caminada, still ranked third in U.S. history for lives lost in a storm. It was also the subject of stories by Grace King ("At Chenière Caminada," *Harper's,* May 1894) and Kate Chopin (*The Awakening,* 1899).

9. MS, CSmH, UCLC 48926, University of California, Mark Twain Papers, The Bancroft Library, Berkeley.

OLIVIA CLEMENS TO GRACE

Paris, November 5, 1893
Hotel Imperial

Dear Grace,

Here we are in Paris! I wish you were here with us. I think of you a great deal and remember how fond you were of it. I rec'd your last letter since we came and was so very glad to get it. It is now a little more than two weeks since we left Germany and landed in Paris.

I have seen almost no one here, we have a few acquaintances but I have not yet sought them out. We have been trying to get ourselves settled, but we have not yet succeeded.

We came to this hotel expecting to spend the Winter but we found the walls so thin and consequently the noises so very annoying, that it will be impossible for us to get along with it. Then too the food is very poor, so we shall not stay, tomorrow morning I am going to tell the proprietor, this I dread doing so because he has done everything that he could to make us comfortable in our rooms.

This is a dull month I believe generally in Paris and we are having a series of very sombre days.

I judge from your letter that you have not heard that Mr Clemens and Clara are in America, at least they were, Clara is now on the water but Mr C. will remain there for a time yet. Clara returns with Miss Willard the daughter of the lady in whose school she was last Winter.[10]

Susy has begun her singing lessons, and as soon as we are permanently settled Jean will begin School. Susy has great encouragement from The Barroness Cacamaici the daughter of Marchesi[11] She tells her that she has a very charming voice and that all she needs in order to make much of it is more physical strength. Therefore Susy eats much better than when you saw her last and tries in every way to get strong.

10. Clara must have attended the Troy Female Seminary in Troy, New York, founded in 1814 and now the Emma Willard School, named for its founder and women's rights advocate.

11. French-born Blanche Caccamisi (1863–1940) was an operatic soprano and singing teacher, daughter of Salvatore and Mathilde Castrone (Mme. Marchesi). She made her professional debut in Berlin in 1895 as a concert singer and in opera in 1902.

I have been many times moved most strongly to write you but Mr C. and Clara have been gone now for more than two months and that gave me so many letters to write that I had to neglect my friends.

I was indeed sorry to learn of the terrible havoc made in New Orleans and naturally thought first of you and wondered if all was well with you.

I do hope Gracie dear that you are better in health, and so better in spirits I can not bear to have you feel down hearted and feel that perhaps you should like to slip out of this life. Don't do it because we all want you in it.

Susy and I are reading a set of French books The Women of the Tuileries by Saint-Amand. Have you seen them, we enjoy them very much.[12]

Tell me Grace dear what you are writing and what you are reading. I hated to have the Balcony Stories end. What a haunting picture of a self seeking charming old lady you gave us in a Delicate Affair; and poor Pupesse is she still studying her rule for irregular verbs?[13]

How I wish you could come in and have a chat with me, that would be so much better than this slower medium, however this is much better than nothing and I hope you will send me a letter soon.

Please give my love to your mother and Nannie and my most cordial greeting to the other members of your household.

I am still forbidden to make any visits this Winter, but when Mr Clemens comes he will be very glad to call on Mme Blanc.[14]

Believe me as always
your deeply loving friend
Olivia L. Clemens

12. A ten-volume set titled *Famous Women of the French Court* by Imbert de Saint-Amand (1834–1900), published 1892.

13. The titles are the final two stories in King's series of fourteen that Century Company published in book form as *Balcony Stories,* 1893.

14. Marie Thérèse Blanc, the author whom Grace King befriended while in Paris and whose salon she later emulated in New Orleans. Perhaps there is an additional letter from Grace that is missing.

☙ GRACE TO OLIVIA CLEMENS
New Orleans, December 8, 1893[15]

I wrote purposely the other day, dearest friend of mine—to say—a little word—not of apology—for I know you wo'nt stand that—but of the barest statement of my still poverty stricken condition—that keeps me your debtor—in the only particular in which I might repay you, but can't, momentarily—I don't think I ever told you the financial scheme I had to enter last year.—In order to get any returns for my School Hist. of Louisiana—I had to publish it myself—that is with my collaborator. The first edition will more than pay expenses, but I do not get any accounts until Jan 1—After the first edition I ought to get a nice secure little income from it, for many years to come—but—it has, ever since last Jan—kept me in a state of impecuniosity[16]—Of course I am writing all the time—but publishers seem to treat one with the slowness, cautions and reserve of forgers, instead of writers of his.

I have been enjoying Mr Clemens "Esquimaux maiden" & "Reformer" hugely—and May says that his story in the St Nicholas is splendid.[17]

How happy he must be—And ask him please to radiate a little of it my way—Apropos—I think he would enjoy visiting the "Imprimerie Nationale."[18]—I think it is called—where all the government printing is done—& some superb books too—there is a regular day for it. Jean I know would enjoy it hugely—and if Jean goes, she must ask to see the beautiful relief, of horses drinking cut over the door way of what used to be the old stable of the princely establishment—The Imprimerie is in an historic quarter of Paris—near Mme de Sévigné's old hotel, (the Musée Carnavalet)[19] and it is worth reading up in a guide book—and if Mr

15. Written with her left hand.

16. John R. Ficklen (1858–1907), history professor at Tulane University, co-wrote the self-published *History of Louisiana* with King, which was intended as a school textbook. It was used only for a few years, however. When Ficklen died, hundreds of volumes remained unsold.

17. "Esquimaux Maiden" is an attack on American Philistinism; the full title of the other story is "Traveling with a Reformer," both appeared in *Cosmopolitan*. The story in *St. Nicholas* is "Tom Sawyer Abroad."

18. The official printing works of the French government, the Imprimerie nationale succeeded the Manufacture royale d'imprimerie founded by Cardinal Richelieu.

19. Madame de Sévigné (1626–1696) was known for her letter-writing and lived in the building from 1677 to 1696.

Clemens, wants some fun, let him go some morning to the Bibliotheque Nationale, & try & get out a book—There's nothing in the whole world to equal it I am sure.[20]

You will get this about Christmas time—I wish you all—all the merriment I would fain give you—I shall think of you on that day—with all the tenderness that comes from longing love—Keep well, and do run away from Paris if the Influenza come. I am having a mild attack of it now—

Every body sends love to you—I kiss you and love you dear—
Grace.

When Grace had been in Paris in 1892, she had come under the spell of the novelist Madame Marie Thérèse Blanc (Th. Bentzon). Blanc had earlier taken the liberty of translating Twain's favored story, "The Celebrated Jumping Frog of Calaveras County," for the *Revue des Deux Mondes.* Not only was this story dear to his heart as his *entrée* into fame, but in his opinion, Mme. Blanc's act had destroyed the wryness of it. Soon he took the liberty of translating her French version back into English to show what an absurd venture hers had been; the drollness of the story was purely American. Apparently, Grace wrote in defense of Madame Blanc to ask Mark Twain to write a belated apology, but he stood his ground. Friendship had its limits.[21]

S L CLEMENS TO GRACE

New York, April 30, 1894[22]
THE PLAYERS,
16 GRAMERCY PARK

Dear Miss Grace,

Oh, it isn't a bit of use. *I* have not offended; it is Mme B.'s French obtuse-

20. King may refer here to the difficulty of becoming credentialed to use the holdings of the Bibliothèque nationale.

21. Twain answered her translation of 1873 in his "The 'Jumping Frog.' In English, Then in French. Then Clawed Back into a Civilized Language once more by Patient, Unremunerated Toil," published in *Sketches, New and Old* (1875), 28–43.

22. The complete letter appears in "GK and MT," 48.

ness which is to blame. She owes *herself* an apology; I owe her none. If she had been properly constructed she would not have perceived any offence: I didn't construct her, & am not responsible for her defects. Whenever I try to lie in earnest I fail to deceive. If I should try to make her believe I am distressed because I have offended her, I shouldn't "arrive." I have committed no offence, either by fact, act, or intention, & so I know I couldn't successfully pretend to be sorry—for a thing which hasn't occurred.

You see, the whole trouble lies in the French character. It hasn't a shred of humor in it, consequently there is no depth to it; its compass, regulator, balance-wheel, is lacking. When you have hurt a Frenchman, you have hurt a child; you can't reason with him, you can only kiss him & pet him & flatter him.

If I ever run across Mme B. I mean to tell her I was not intending to offend her. I don't imagine it will do any good; but I couldn't say any more & make it sound sincere.

I expect to sail nine days hence & join the family in Paris the middle of the month. I suppose we shall then leave right away for Aix-les-Bains, where Livy will take baths for the gout which is giving her so much pain in her fingers. When I left her the 6th of the present month she was making good progress toward the cure of her other ailments, & Susy was getting stronger and healthier daily.

I send love to you & your sister, & add the hope that we may all foregather again one of these days.

Sincerely Yours
S L Clemens[23]

Livy seemed never to have full confidence in her own letter-writing but was always delighted to receive Grace's newsy ones. She did not conceal the financial straits the Clemenses faced during these years and how they spent money only on the girls but trimmed all extras out of their own expenses. Grace was a safe friend to tell such intimacies; she was not party to the societal expectations of the Nook Farm set and the two women were mutually devoted. Yet, when forced to choose, Livy supported her husband.

23. MS, CU-MARK, UCLC 04727, University of California, Mark Twain Papers, The Bancroft Library, Berkeley.

☙ OLIVIA CLEMENS TO GRACE

Paris, May 16 [to June 3], 1894

May 16th 1894, Paris

Dear Grace,

I was greatly delighted to see your handwriting and yet I was a little scared for fear you might scold because I have been so remiss about writing you. I am always remiss about writing. I suppose if my letters were good things when they are done I should not so much mind the doing them.

June 3rd

So much of my letter was written to you then I was interrupted and have not gotten at it again. On May 19th I went to meet Mr Clemens who had just returned from America. We went together to a little sea-side place where we had been advised, to spend the Summer; Etretat, do you know it?[24]

We found it rather desolate as such places are after the season or before the season.

Finally we decided on a little Chalet that is situated quite back from the coast. The doctor did not want me to be too near the sea; It has a most beautiful view from it's windows and I think we shall be very comfortable there. The people who own it send down for the two months, August and September, their own servants, a cook and a maid so that difficult question is settled for us.

Clara is at present with the people who own the cottage and she says the cook and maid are both good servants. Clara went into this French family six weeks ago in order to try and get the language. I think she has made good progress there. She will remain with them until she leaves Paris for the Summer. She is going the 1st of July with her piano teacher Mme Hopekirk Wilson.[25] She will stay with her and go on with her work during July and August then she will come to us at the sea-side for June. Yes we feel the grind of straightened circumstances but without doubt it is good for us all and wholesome for the young people.

24. Etretat is a high resort beach in Normandy, known for its chalk cliffs. Its beauty attracted artists, including Gustave Courbet and Claude Monet.

25. Helen Hopekirk Wilson (1856–1945) was a British pianist, teacher, and composer of short pieces. She gave an American tour in 1891–92.

How I wish you were here in Paris with us, we could enjoy much together. I have been able to do very little sightseeing and I have taken no french lessons because I could spare that expense. The children must have their lessons, but mine were a pleasure that it was better for me to forego.

I have talked with Mr Clemens about Mme Blanc and I must feel as he does that it is a hopeless case. I have not seen Mr Clemens' article but from what he says I should judge it to be quite harmless. If she takes offense at it I do not suppose we could *make* her look at it differently. Of course Mr Clemens was innocent of intending any affront to her.

Oh Grace dear I do love you and I should like to look into your dear face.

I want to say about the money that I wish you would not send it back to me (if I need it I will call on you for it) and I wish that when you have it ready to send to me that you would just use it to buy something for yourself that you would not otherwise buy. Now my dear *please* do not be annoyed at my saying this and do just what you like.

Susy has been far from well all Winter, but I think she is in better condition than she was in Florence. She has been able to take very few singing lessons, but we hope a great deal from the changes that she is to have this Summer.

I have not yet read Marcella. Susy is just reading it and I am going to read it later.[26]

In deepest love & with a share for Nannie and cordial greeting to the other members of your family

yours always
Livy L. C.

Another letter further reveals the depth of trust between Grace and Livy:

☙ OLIVIA CLEMENS TO GRACE

[fragment, unknown location, June 16?, 1894]

26. *Marcella* (1894), a novel on socialism and wealth by Mary Augusta [Mrs Humphry] Ward (1851–1920).

> We go the first of July to Bourboules for a month. I never heard of the place until the physician recommended my going there. It is almost directly south of Paris in the center of France. It is higher than we are here and the waters are a good tonic. So Mr Clemens, Susy, Jean and I expect to start for there about the 22nd of the month.
>
> This letter so far is surely full enough of the Clemens' plans.
>
> One thing more Mr Clemens fears he shall be obliged to return to America the very last of this month. Our affairs over there are in such a very unfortunate position, that he is obliged to go back and try to get things in a better condition. Yes we are heavy loosers much heavier than I could wish through Webster & Co. Yet why should I wish it, what right have I? We have been greatly favored in our lives, by being exempt from such anxiety. Why should we not take our turn?
>
> We have both of us simply buried money in Webster & Co. so I suppose I ought to be glad that the time came when we simply had no more to put in and the assignment was necessary, but I am not glad. I did wish that it could have gone on. I for myself would have rather mortgaged our house and raised money in that way, but I suppose it was not best, my brother objects strongly to my doing that, he says sell your house when you must but never mortgage it, because then there would be not only the expense of keeping the place up but also the interest on the mortgage.
>
> Although I suppose no better times will come in time to help Webster & Co. still Mr Clemens has great faith in the machine and believes in time it will take us out of all our difficulties. They are now building a machine which is to be tested in [fragment ends]

While the Clemenses battled bankruptcy, Grace accepted requests for more work. "The invitation to write, like invitations at a ball, to dance, seemed undeclinable," she later recalled of those busy years.[27] Letters and checks from editors and publishers Hamilton Mabie, Henry Alden, Samuel Sidney McClure of *McClure's Magazine,* and George C. Brett of Macmillan & Company testify to her modest successes. Yet, Grace often expressed gloom in letters to her sister May. Around them, the times seemed out of joint.

Racial politics became more divisive in the South as whites wrested control

27. *Memories,* 204.

from a short-lived period of equality following the Civil War, and the tone of Louisiana newspapers became blatantly biased. In 1896, the Supreme Court decided *Plessy v. Ferguson* in favor of "separate but equal," but King's letters made no direct comment upon it.[28] She wrote May about local women's aggressive political activism, of which she did not much approve. She joined literary and historical groups but not suffrage ones.[29] Possibly, unsettling local conditions prompted Grace to escape to May's calming cottage and wait for news of friends as she rested.

Grace relied on Warner for news of the Clemenses because travel, illnesses, or other despair seemed to prevent the friends from writing directly. Warner wrote that Sam Clemens was in Hartford in May 1896 but was expecting to join Livy in England in midsummer.[30] And then, while Grace was with May in North Carolina, Mimi broke dreadful but sparse news.

MIMI TO GRACE

New Orleans, August 22, [1896]

Dear Gracie—

We were all shocked this morning to see the notice of Susie Clemens death. I enclose you the clipping thinking maybe, your paper might be delayed—Nan, says she is so much relieved to see; that the poor girl, did not commit suicide, she was so morbid and depressed, poor thing, no doubt excitement brought on Meningitis—I believe—Nan is going to write to Mrs Clemens to day—[. . .]

Lovingly Mimi

At first, the news was confusing to everyone. Nan was shocked and wanted to know "what caused the meningitis." It almost looked "as though she had com-

28. The "separate but equal" *Plessy* decision was not overturned until *Brown v. Board of Education* in 1954.

29. The Portia Club, the first suffrage club in Louisiana, formed in 1892; the Equal Rights for All (ERA) Club was an offshoot in 1896. ERA's emphasis was racially tinged, and the group was against a federal amendment. King's letters do not show that she belonged to either group but do indicate that she spoke once to ERA in 1913 because she needed those women to be "*for* me rather than against me" (Grace to Carleton King, November 18, 1913).

30. Warner to Grace, May 19, 1896.

mitted suicide, dying as she did only a day or two before her mother's return," she added.[31] The rest of the Clemens family had been in Europe while Susy was at home in Elmira and then Hartford. She had wanted to be in her own home when she began to be ill, but it quickly accelerated into meningitis. Livy was cabled but told only that Susy was ill. She and Clara sailed home but were too late to see her alive. Their pastor friend, Joe Twichell, met Livy to break the sad news. The parents remained plagued with "what ifs" and "if onlys." Mimi conveyed all that she could gather obliquely.

MIMI TO GRACE

New Orleans, August 27, [1896]

Dear Gracie—

[. . .] I went around yesterday just before dinner to the Paradises to see if they had got any of the particulars of Susie Clemens death. They gave me all they had which—I send you—Mrs P's mother wrote, that Hartford was in mourning—every one sorrowing for, and with Mrs C.—The remains had been taken to Elmira—Mr Twichell had gone to meet Mrs C.—and break to her the terrible death, which was sudden after all—Mrs Fellow's[32] says that Aug 5th the day fixed for Susie to sail, found her ill, but her friends were not alarmed, the disappointment, to Susie was so great, that her condition became worse—though Meningitis only set in two days before she died. Mrs Clemens, had been written to and she sailed on receipt of the news of her daughter's illness—she arrived two days after her death—Susie died in her own home, attended by the best Dr in Hartford and nursed by her Aunt & Uncle,[33] Mrs Paradise says, no mention is made, of her mind, during her illness—whether she was conscious or spoke at all on any subject—but these as Mrs P. says, her mother was not very intimate with the family, all she heard was from Mrs Dudley Warner—who was excited, and suffering, but who was with Susie according to her statement in pure Yankee phraseology. [. . .]

Lovingly Mimi

31. Nan to Grace, n.d. [August 22, 1896].

32. The Paradises and Fellows are unidentified people who obviously had some connection to New Orleans and Hartford.

33. Theodore and Susan Langdon Crane.

JULIA OLIVIA LANGDON TO GRACE

Elmira, New York, August 31, 1896

Dear Miss King,

My aunt Mrs Clemens has asked me in her present inability to write—to thank you most warmly, in her behalf, for the note of sympathy and love that has come to her from you.[34]

She appreciates deeply your thought of her in her trouble, and the affectionate things you say of Susy. It is a certain help to my aunt to know that her friends are suffering for her.

The end came in absolute peace. My cousin sank into a deep unconsciousness that lasted for fifty six hours, and my mother who was with her, says that she slept until she quietly slipped away.

With repeated assurance of Aunt Livy's thanks, believe me
Very truly Yours
Julia Olivia Langdon

Elmira, New York,
August 31 1896

The closest Livy came to blaming anyone for anything is in her grief-stricken letter to Grace about Susy's death. Who or what did she think had acted wrongly? Perhaps it was the Spiritualism and mind-healing on which Susy had come to rely more than she did on medicine and doctors. It was many months before Livy could bring herself to write to her friend. Finally, word came.

OLIVIA CLEMENS TO GRACE

London, March 9, 1897[35]
Care Messrs Chatto & Windus[36]
110 & 111 St. Martin's Lane
London, Eng.

34. The note from King is missing.

35. In *Memories,* King seems to claim she destroyed this letter from Livy (201).

36. Twain's publisher in England from 1875 forward.

Grace dear,

Your last note of Feb 22nd has just reached me.[37] I rec'd in good time your comforting letter written me in Aug or Sept:

Constantly I have wanted to write you but I have not been able. I am too broken hearted and unreconciled for life seems to me too bitter and too little worth while. I have longed to hear from you again but I could not write.

Every detail of Susy's leaving us seems so unbearable. We left her she was not a child that we should ever have left. We were almost ready to lay our hands on her once more and she slipped away from us. I feel that she was badly managed & that it need not have been. She was my joy & pride. Life is so dull, the poetry seems gone out of it.

I have always had much courage even when things seemed hard but now I have none. I long to be with Susy. I know I am not right minded. I know I am small & unworthy in the way that I take this thing. Grace dear write me when you can & bear with me that I seem so unable to write. By & by if I live I shall come to myself I suppose as others have done under like circumstances.

I love you always and your letters comfort me & it is ever a pleasure to see your hand writing on an envelope. Love to Nannie

Ever lovingly yours
Livy

March 9th 1897

OLIVIA CLEMENS TO GRACE

London, June 27, 1897

Gracie dear,

Your letter has come and with it the check for ten pounds four shillings.[38] But why did you send it? I greatly fear it was not entirely convenient for you and you know you promised not to pay it until it was. I am sorry such

37. King's letter is missing.

38. The letter is missing. It would seem that King borrowed this amount when she visited the Clemenses in Florence.

exagerated reports went to America regarding our condition. As far as our physical needs are concerned we are comfortable, more than comfortable, and little by little we are laying by money to discharge our debt with. So long as we are able to situate ourselves as well as we do now and yet all the time lay by money, from Mr Clemens work, for clearing ourselves, our friends need not be troubled for us.

We are situated 23 Tedworth Square cor Tite St.[39] You asked just where we are: however we leave here in about ten days. Our address is always care Messrs Chatto & Windus.

Of course I cannot at all reconcile myself to going on in this world with Susy gone out of it. She was my great pride and joy always. Now I cannot make anything seem worth while, yet I try to go on as if it were. Oh Grace you cannot conceive what it is to have such a child taken from you. I cannot yet believe it can be true. I loved that child peculiarly perhaps because she needed me peculiarly. Then I went and left her. She seemed so well so much better than she had been for years. The Doctors thought and she thought that a year with my sister at the Farm[40] would be of incalculable benefit to her. Of course we should never have contemplated for a moment her being in that undesirable Hartford atmosphere.

However it is useless to write of it, it is all over. We are powerless and wretched.

What a mystery it all is. What a heart-breaking mystery. It seems impossible to write letters but I love you always. Your friendship is a great deal to me and I owe you *much* much more than you can ever owe me.

Please give my love to Nannie and my kind regards to your Mother and the other members of your family.

Always lovingly your
Olivia L. C.

Samuel Clemens wrote his heartbreak, too, on the first anniversary of Susy's death.

39. The Tedworth location was a more modest dwelling than previous ones.
40. Quarry Farm, home of Susan Langdon and Theodore Crane.

AUGUST 18, 1897 [BLACK-BORDERED PRINTED MOURNING CARD]

In Memoriam.

OLIVIA SUSAN CLEMENS

DIED AUGUST 18, 1896; AGED 24.

In a fair valley—oh, how long ago, how long ago!—
    Where all the broad expanse was clothed in vines
And fruitful fields and meadows starred with flowers,
And clear streams wandered at their idle will,
And still lakes slept, their burnished surfaces
A dream of painted clouds, and soft airs
Went whispering with odorous breath,
And all was peace—in that fair vale,
Shut from the troubled world, a nameless hamlet drowsed.

    Hard by, apart, a temple stood;
And strangers from the outer world
Passing, noted it with tired eyes,
And seeing, saw it not:
A glimpse of its fair form—an answering momentary thrill—
And they passed on, careless and unaware.

They could not know the cunning of its make;
They could not know the secret shut up in its heart;
Only the dwellers of the hamlet knew;
They knew that what seemed brass was gold;
What marble seemed, was ivory;
The glories that enriched the milky surfaces—
The trailing vines, and interwoven flowers,
And tropic birds a-wing, clothed all in tinted fire—
They knew for what they were, not what they seemed:
Encrustings all of gems, not perishable splendors of the brush
They knew the secret spot where one must stand—
They knew the surest hour, the proper slant of sun—
To gather in, unmarred, undimmed,
The vision of the fane in all its fairy grace,

A fainting dream against the opal sky.
 And more than this. They knew
That in the temple's inmost place a spirit dwelt,
Made all of light!
 For glimpses of it they had caught
Beyond the curtains when the priests
That served the altar came and went.
 All loved that light and held it dear
That had this partial grace;
But the adoring priests alone who lived
By day and night submerged in its immortal glow
Knew all its power and depth, and could appraise the loss
If it should fade and fail and come no more.

 All this was long ago—so long ago!

The light burned on; and they that worship'd it,
And they that caught its flash at intervals and held it dear,
Contented lived in its secure possession. Ah,
How long ago it was!

 And then when they
Were nothing fearing, and God's peace was in the air,
And none was prophesying harm—
The vast disaster fell;
Where stood the temple when the sun went down,
Was vacant desert when it rose again!

 Ah, yes! 'Tis ages since it chanced!
 So long ago, it was,

That from the memory of the hamlet-folk the Light has passed—
They scarce believing, now, that once it was,
Or if believing, yet not missing it,
And reconciled to have it gone.

 Not so the priests! Oh, not so
The stricken ones that served it day and night,

Adoring it, abiding in the healing of its peace:
They stand, yet, where erst they stood
Speechless in that dim morning long ago;
And still they gaze, as then they gazed,
And murmur, 'It will come again;
It knows our pain—it knows—it knows—
Ah, surely it will come again.'

S. L. CLEMENS.
LAKE LUCERNE: *August 18, 1897.*

Grace knew death, but not like this. While her friends suffered, her career continued as it had become, including being featured in a "Chautauqua" in Ruston, Louisiana, in 1898.[41] She lodged in a boardinghouse there and lectured from her writings on Bienville, Iberville, De Soto, and LaSalle.[42] One of Grace's champions, Hamilton Mabie, essayist and editor of *Outlook* magazine, enthused that her historical narrative "lives" and "brings the muse of art with it, the elusive quality which cannot be acquired & cannot be imitated; the quality of the born writer."[43] She had no rest, however, for pesky proofs always hounded her. Once, she had corrected galleys while sitting in the pilothouse of a steamer on the Natchez River or while in its bridal chamber, which was hers as the vessel's only passenger.[44] Now from Ruston, she wrote May, "I got off two big batches of proof this morning—but there is another one staring me in the face—perhaps that is helping the heat to make me idiotic—"[45]

And then, by February 1, 1899, she wrote Warner that she was ill: "Malarial fever took me last August—and though it has left me now—it has left me fit for nothing but Malarial fever—the least little work knocks me up—and—I don't know what I am going to do with myself—unless I feel more like myself."

Nevertheless, Grace revived enough to set out with Nina to Canada in July 1899. They visited friends and apparently made a short, perhaps inhospitable,

41. An adult educational movement that began in New York and brought lectures to rural communities, especially in summer.

42. Grace to May, July 20, 1898.

43. Hamilton Mabie to Grace, October 30, 1898.

44. Grace to May, February 17, 1894.

45. Grace to May, July 20, 1898.

stay in Hartford on the return trip but wrote no letters from there. Grace then took a steamer alone from New York and "rolled all the way" to New Orleans. "I hope if my family ever hear of my going to sea again, they will put me in a straight jacket," she wrote Nina from the Mississippi River.[46] Once home, she returned to her "regular routine" and heard again from Livy, this time seeking advice.

OLIVIA CLEMENS TO GRACE

London, December, 1899

30, WELLINGTON COURT,

ALBERT GATE.

Grace dear,

I can not tell you how your letter warmed my heart: how desperately glad I was to hear from you; I felt almost as if I had lost you out of my life it was so long since I had heard from you.[47]

I long for & I need a talk with you. How I wish that I might have it. Possibly you could help me more than any one else, yet I don't know that any one can help me. We feel a great perplexity about where we are to settle down for our old age, for the years that are remaining to us.

We expect to go back to America next Spring or Summer then where? then what? I feel much perhaps most of the time as if I could *not* go back to Hartford. The heartbreaking associations there and all the changes. I still find it very difficult to live without Susy, of course I shall always find it very very difficult. In the old place would it not be still more nearly impossible? Generally the mere thought of the place nearly breaks my heart when I faintly realize that I shall not find her there. I feel even as if the lost childhood of these children that are left to me would be a haunting phantom there. As if I could never get used to the loss of children in the house. Then the great care of that big place—a sort of care that I have been more or less free from for several years—The changes in the friends & the changes which they would find in us. It generally seems as if it would be too heart wringing to be borne. On the other hand it is our

46. Grace to Nina, October 27, 1899.

47. The letter is missing.

old home: can we let it pass into the hands of strangers. Can the house where Susy lived & died go out of our keeping. Jean is so steadily and unwaveringly attached to the place that I feel as if I must take her back to it. I don't know whether she could endure it if we sold the place. Her eyes often fill now at the mere mention of the home & when we talk of selling she looks too wretchedly unhappy. She has made me promise that I will never sell the house without letting her know before I do it. Then of course we can never afford to buy or build as beautiful a house again. A house where we can get as many of the creature comforts. Where we can have as much freedom and luxury as we can have there. Will this at all compensate for the discomforts & for the heart-break. I do not know, I cannot tell.

Do tell me more about Mr & Mrs Warner. Did they seem greatly changed? and not for the better? Do tell me all about it. I feel that Susy Warner has had great trials and that she must have grown finer & sweeter. Oh nobody knows how I dread thinking of trying to go back to the old life, & yet how I dread absolutely closing the book & making it impossible to go back. I suppose no one can help me, yet how does it look to you?

The weather is very unpleasant here now, rain & fog of course this is the time that one must expect it. We are comfortably housed in a very small ~~appart~~ apartment (has it one p or two?) so that sometimes we do feel a little crowded. There is no study for Mr Clemens and he goes down to his publishers for doing his work.

We think Jean is improving in health but it is rather slow and we must stay here on her account until Spring or Summer.[48] The doctor assures us that he can cure her so we must give him a fair trial.

Clara goes on with her singing lessons but she also is far from strong and sometimes I feel troubled about her. She takes singing lessons of Blanche Marchesi and seems to be doing well. You know I am no judge but the judges tell me she has a good voice. Now-a-days she never touches the piano, I feel that she will some day come back to it.

We have seen some thing of Mrs Pemberton Hinks[49] since we have

48. Jean apparently had epilepsy, but Livy did not name it here.

49. Louise Pemberton-Hincks was a celebrated accompanist, sister of Bertha Pemberton, who had played in concert at the Warners'. King knew them from New Orleans.

been here. She lives most beautifully in a large old house with a garden about it, it is a very valuable place. It seems a little strange the way that young Mrs Du Clou[50] lives with them & shares the expenses but I judge it is all right. She is kind but she has not lost all her vulgarisms—perhaps not quite vulgar but a little common, still there is something that makes one like her.

Dear Grace good bye for this time: how I long to see you. Write me before very long. I hope you will have a happy Christmas & New Year. Please give my warm greeting to your mother & sisters & brother, I wish I might know them all. I send a special little message to Nannie, I hope I shall see her again before much more time passes over our heads.

In deepest love
yours
Livy[51]

This letter must have jogged emotions for Grace. The Kings had lost their home in the Civil War and after that had moved often, always in search of a better or different house to rent or, they hoped, to purchase, especially after Uncle Tom's estate was settled back in 1888. His money rescued them for a time, but his business had been liquidated, so Mimi had had to invest her inheritance in Branch's new business. For Grace, a house must have represented the fleeting safety of her youth and some future dream linked to full reclamation of their social status. That childhood solace and her own dear memories of time in Twain's Hartford home could have been on her mind when she wrote a bold answer to Livy.

GRACE TO OLIVIA CLEMENS

New Orleans, December 26, 1899[52]
2221 Prytania St.

Dear, dear Friend—

50. Unidentified.

51. MS, CU-MARK, UCLC 05729, University of California, Mark Twain Papers, The Bancroft Library, Berkeley.

52. A large excerpt appears in "GK and MT," 49.

My impulse was to answer your letter at once—to assure you without loss of an hour—of my sympathy with you—and understanding of your perplexities. But I concluded to wait and think well over what I was going to say—and so to give you—not the result of my feeling—but of my judgment, such as it is—and let me begin by telling you that I have had for the last year or two—to go over the same ground as you—to consider—what plans—I should make—or rather we—in the family should make—towards the establishment of a permanent home—the place as we saw it—that we were to grow old—and die in.—Many things have happened to us—in the past five years—that have made these considerations absolutely indispensable for us.—

My dear—I say—go back to your old home—to the dear beautiful house in Hartford and take up your life again right there—It seems to me—if you and Mr Clemens could do that—it would be a good thing for yourselves—and for us all.—We all saw your life there—the material luxury—the intellectual atmosphere—the good fellowship with all men—the beautiful devotion of husband and wife—the lovely children—radiant—with future promise.—I suppose there was much envy of it around you—I am sure there was—but to me—I can sincerely say—I never saw household—in which there was a nobler striving towards what we all acknowledge—as the best in life.—I had doubts and misgivings—about the development of the rare and difficult characters of Susie and Clara—and at times—I had distressing presentiments—but as with my own family—I consoled myself—with: "We can only do our best—as for the rest—as God—or the great law of the world wills"—well—You had your reverses—and—as in the grand old trajedies—Your fate sought you out—and I truly believe—no one knew as well as I—what you suffered in Susy's death.—There was a sense of humiliation in it—oh! the cup was bitter—bitter—but you had to drink of it—and you did drink of it—

You may imagine—how I felt for you—during that visit of mine to Hartford.—I am glad—you wrote to me as you did—giving me this opportunity of writing to you.—You must not let Susie's home—and the room that she died in pass into the hands of strangers—unless—you have to do it for honour and honesty.—You cannot sell—the lost childhood of your children—as you well put it.—Do you know—that I did not meet a soul there—who did not speak of missing the flitting forms of Susie—

Clara and Jean—running—in and out of the leafy paths between the two houses—(Geoge W's—& your's)—As for me—I could absolutely see the dear little Jean—with her bright cheeks—pretty eyes—and brave frank smile—trotting around—so sturdy—so original—and always—in such pretty quaint dresses.—My dear—if ever there was a home— consecrated by a past, that home is—and you had better meet your future there—whatever it is to be—No matter where you are—that past will follow you—It will pursue you—if you fly it—meet it bravely—it will console you.—And then you must consider—that Clara and Jean—have a right to their home—There they first knew their father and mother—and there—there alone—they can find—and in a way renew—their lost childhood.

Let them have all the benefit they can derive from the inspiration—of that sentiment.—and think too—if grief comes to you again—and you know—it must come again in the course of time—to the family circle—where could you meet it so well—as there.—If you were called to leave your daughters—would it not be a consolation to leave them—in the very stronghold of their family love—and family traditions!—I am jotting down—these thoughts as they come to me—I am a little overawed myself at my temerity—but forgive me—if I seem venturesome.—

Mark Twain—could no where end his days with so much dignity—as in that house in Hartford.—Let him come back to it—holding his fine white haired head high. He has fought a noble fight—and he brings back on his body—only honourable scars from it.—How few in the U.S.—warriors or literary men—can say—the same!

One little practical reminder obtrudes itself here.—and it is a kind of paradoxical one—You can always travel away from your home in Hartford. Whenever you wish—and—you could always let your children—go away from it—as in the restlessness of the young they are sure to want to do—with the assurance that they will want to come back to it—like homing pigeons.—A new place—might not attract them—and then they might turn their longings to some place in Europe—or—indeed—to different places—It is a great advantage that they both unite in Hartford.—When I tell you all this—I do not conceal from myself—a moment—that Hartford is—in itself to me—the most perfect expression of American Philistinism—that I ever came across.—I thought—when I was there—

among your old friends—that I never met more uninteresting people in my life—of a more boring form of uninterestingness.—[53]

Perhaps you will find them better—of course you will—but even then—You must make up your mind—that you will have to lead your life—a great deal to yourself—But you can do that—you have some courage and firmness—in social matters.—I am a coward and weakling—and I am actually terrified when I merely think of Hartford—with this exception always—dear homely sincere Mrs Geoge Warner—and Mr Gay—of all persons!—He came over from Farmington to see me—After having resisted all the inducements to come over and see the grand new dining room—and when Mrs. Susy wanted to show him all her new things—he walked out of the house—saying he had no time to look—that he had only come over to see me.—

I must tell you frankly—if Mrs Warner liked me better—I could judge her more leniently.—She still dislikes me, on account of Mrs Cabell—and Mr Warner—seemed actually to be afraid to show me ordinary politeness. Out of the house he was pleasant and genial—inside—he was affected—cold—critical—and—anxious to get rid of me.—Mary Barton—seems to have the soul—as she has the conduct and appearance of a lady's maid.—Annie Price's quaint and delicate hospitality—is sorely missed—at least it was by me.—Christine and Ellen—are the same—and I could have embraced them—for being so—They shook their heads—and sighed—as they told me—that things were not as in the past.—[54]

Mrs Warner appeared better when staying with us last Spring—than I ever saw her—She was warm hearted and sincere.—But I found her in the Fall—Supercilious—flippant—and like Mr Warner—evidently anx-

53. King's abuse might have been a reaction to the cooler treatment she received from Warner, mentioned later in this letter. She felt snubbed; he treated her well in public but discounted her in his house, perhaps influenced by Susan Warner's lingering pique over the Isa Cabell matter. Instead of a warm reception, King was shown all the new items and decorations in the house. Because she had previously written glowingly of Nook Farm folks, this change in attitude puzzled Livy Clemens.

54. King felt the change in the Warner house without Annie Price, the calming house manager, who now was in Birmingham serving her brother's family. Although her replacement, Mary Barton, was adequate, according to this letter, the kitchen workers also complained that things were different than in previous times.

ious to get rid of us.—The house—is maintained in handsome style—one would say there was every evidence of wealth about it.—Mrs Warner—dominates her set as of yore—but now—she does it—as a great and acknowledged musician.

Ah my dear! They show to me, the want—the actual want—of a grief—or a loss in their lives.—They have grown old—in increasing prosperity—they have *succeeded*—and they are typically American in their enjoyment of it.—As the children say—they "show off."—I was carried—hither and thither to see a new house here—old furniture there—the progress—the increase of wealth every where.—But—it did not interest me. I would have preferred to it all—having Mrs Geoge Warner invited to one meal with me.—But—she seems to be a complete outcast from their hearts.—I did not care enough about it—even to speak of the past.—When Mrs Warner came down last Spring—while she was busily pacing up and down the gallery—with us awaiting the visit of Mr Warner's physician. She spoke about Mrs Cabell—and assured me—that by her part all was forgiven & forgotten—I waived—with all the politeness I could such generosity—and then—I was told—that every body I knew in Hartford—had repeated to the Warners what I said about Mrs Cabell—I would only repeat—that I had really forgotten—all that I said—but—I had only said what I thought was true—and though—I could not approve of people repeating such things—that I did not mind it—it was perhaps better in the end. Mrs. Cabell—is still—the dominant note—in their lives—Mr Charles Clarke spoke to me about her—said—that her influence upon the Warners was still—omnipotent—in comparison with others.—[55]

I stopped here to read over what I have written—It appears—like every thing I write—disjointed and awkward—but I shall let it go—trusting you to understand what I wanted to say.—I can improve one part however—I meant—that as we saw you—in all your prosperity in happiness—in that house—as we know what you have passed through—to see you come back—to the place you started from—willing to accept—proud—to pay the penalties of life—the example would be of benefit to us all—

55. Charles Clark was an editor at the *Hartford Courant.*

And again—you yourselves—as well as the children—could leave that house—easier perhaps than another—should you want to take another jaunt of travelling—as very likely you would.—It would be your place of retreat—your refuge—in a way—that no other place could.—

And again—we your friends—could reconstitute the family there—Susy—your mother—as for your social life—what a host of us—have slept and eaten under that roof.—All of this—makes up life—it is life.—

Mama is not well at all this year—Mrs Gayarré—too—is ailing—and seems depressed.—Branch is getting along fairly well—but he is critically delicate.—Nina—is lingering over the holidays in New York—Her health is not good—and Nina—is one of the disappointed ones in life.—We are very much worried about her.—Will lives with us now.—We are still struggling with him—and for him.—Nan is splendid—hale—hearty—and one great dependence—I am afraid—I am getting to be a kind of lame duck myself.—It is hard for me to be happy and cheerful—I find—that is—to be as happy & cheerful as I want to be for the sake of others.—To tell you—the truth—in your ear—I am afraid of the future—with its inevitable changes—I am afraid—of the past—with more sorrows and griefs in it—but that is only deep down in my heart—my head—I believe is all right.—

Ever with dear love and faithful devotion to you and your's.

Grace[56]

56. MS, CU-MARK, UCLC 46304, University of California, Mark Twain Papers, The Bancroft Library, Berkeley.

CHAPTER 12

MOURNINGS, 1900–1910

It is overwhelming.

—CLARA CLEMENS GABRILOWITSCH TO GRACE KING, APRIL 1910

Letters between Grace and her northern friends became sadder as they faced deaths within their circles. The first decade of the new century carried much loss. Illnesses at home focused Grace's mind on family. Deaths would come and devastate her, as they would the Clemenses. In 1900, Livy had pondered Grace's letter of advice but was still fraught with indecision.

OLIVIA CLEMENS TO GRACE

London, [January? 1900]
30, WELLINGTON COURT,
ALBERT GATE.

Grace dear,
What a wonderful letter you write & how you understand it all! I thank you most deeply for your letter. Whatever you had advised would have comforted me & at the same time would have distressed me, because I am so of two minds.

I opened your letter with fear & trembling and I found myself glad at first that you said "go back to your home": I was afraid you would say don't try to live there any more. Then as you spoke of the difficulties and as I know them I felt faint-hearted, as if I never could even try to go back to the old life. Oh Grace dear I think I have so little courage. Material things have so much power, how every chair & book & corner of the house will make me cry out for what I cannot find anymore on this Earth. Then how difficult to meet the flippancy of those near by.

I cannot quite understand your finding every one there uninteresting—indeed I can well understand your finding many deadly uninteresting—but did you see Mrs Frank Cheney & Annie Trumbull & Miss Sophie Hamerslet? You do not mention Mrs Gay: Was it not a pleasure to see her again?[1] Your letter is a great help & comfort, I have read it and reread it many times.

Dear, dear Grace you are always a help to me & I long to see you. You will come & see me if I go back to Hartford won't you? I am so sorry to know that your Mother and brother & sister Nina are so far from well & strong: and so glad for you all that Nannie is such a strength to you. Do write and tell me all about yourself: What are you doing now-a-days? Are you writing? You say you write awkwardly, I don't find it so: to me no one writes as you do, so forcefully, so picturesquely.

But how I do want to talk with you: to know just what you are feeling and thinking about all sorts of things. What bitter things there are in the world, and how almost nobody escapes. I believe that even Susy Warner must have had much in her life that was bitter and humiliating. Does Mrs Cabell still live with the Warners? I thought she had permanently left them except to make an occasional visit to them. I wonder who the people were who repeated what you said of Mrs Cabell. I thought there were not many that knew & surely we never repeated anything to the Warners. I think however that they know quite well the attitude of all their friends toward her.

One point which I evidently did not make quite clear and [that] is Clara's feeling. She has never felt as sure about going back as Jean. She has not wanted us to sell the place but she has not felt that she could go back. Much of the time she says she feels a great repulsion at the thought of going back. Occasionally she feels that it would be comfort to get back to the old associations, but that is only occasionally. Her state of mind has naturally complicated things & made it difficult to decide what to do. We must either sell the place or go back & live in it we cannot afford to keep it and not live in it. All our debts are now paid except there is a little settlement that Mr C. will make with the bank when it is proved just what he owes them: they released him at a certain sum, something less than he owed but of course he is going to make that right when we get back.

1. Hartford people whom King had claimed to admire.

> My own affairs are looking a little better now & we hope this year to get something from them. Of course we could not live in our old expensive way but I think with care & if we kept no horses that we could live there with our present income. Of course it is a great expense to keep up the place & live somewhere else. I think at any rate that we shall try it for a year & see whether it is wise or not.[2]

But the Clemenses never lived in their "most beautiful house" again.

On Grace's own home front in 1900, her exasperation with family members was as volatile as ever. Mimi's spells of illness were exacerbated by Will's unexplained absences and intemperance. Nan's irritability and Nina's jealousy vexed Grace. "Tolstoi himself could not in all Russia—or Balzac—in France—find a more crazy establishment than ours," she wrote May. "I am sure even in heaven or hell—if I met with any of my family—I would be subjected to their vile tempers."[3] On another day, she might declare that she was living in Paradise, dressing as she pleased, letting her hair down and going bare legged, and taking naps in between working on a long story or on an article for *Harper's* about the Cabildo in the French Quarter, the building in which France and the United States had signed the Louisiana Purchase. Tempers and nervous conditions seemed to afflict the King women, and hard spirits gripped two of the men. Grace was most free when alone, unfettered by restricting garments, and lost in absorbing reading or writing. One of many books she was reading that summer was Marcel Prévost's *Frédérique;* it posed the question of a woman's education and independence. She wrote May that "it is really funny to see how the 'unmarried' woman is asserting herself in literature—It will break up the French restive if the women should learn to resist the men."[4]

While Grace was distracted with these matters, her most consistent mentor died; Charles Dudley Warner was seventy-one.

☙ CHARLES HOPKINS CLARK TO GRACE

[telegram], Hartford, October 21, 1900

2. The letter is incomplete (MS, CU-MARK, UCLC 05728, University of California, Mark Twain Papers, The Bancroft Library, Berkeley).

3. Grace to May, May?, 1900.

4. Grace to May, undated, summer 1900.

POSTAL TELEGRAPH—CABLE COMPANY
10 BM ND JH 12 callwet,
Hartford, Ct., Oct 21—1900.
Miss Grace King 2221 Prytania St.
New Orleans,

Mr. Warner died very suddenly yesterday while down town heart disease.
Chas. H. Clark
12:50 P.M.

GRACE TO MAY

New Orleans, Sunday Morning, [October 21, 1900]

Dear May,
I am in such a rage at that nasty little reporter of the T.D. for getting an interview out of me—under guise of seeking information about Mr. Warner—that I don't think I can write even to you—[. . .] I went down in a wrapper—gave the information—and—this morning—I see the trap I had fallen into.[5]—

Well! Poor Mr. Warner—He certainly was a factor in my life—I had a letter from him in August—the last lines were "dear Grace—I would love to know that you are happy."—I could not sleep much last night after hearing the news—and I cannot keep him out of my mind this morning—[. . .]

Ever lovingly
Sis

CHARLES HOPKINS CLARK TO GRACE

Hartford, October 24, 1900[6]
The Courant
Published by The Hartford Courant Company
Hartford, Conn., October 24, 1900.

5. King apparently said something about Warner's position on annexation of the Philippines.
6. The letter is typed.

JOSEPH M. HAWLEY
CHARLES DUDLEY WARNER
CHARLES HOPKINS CLARK
ARTHUR L. GOODRICH
FRANK S. CAREY
Miss Grace King,
2221 Pritania St., New Orleans, La.

My dear Miss King:—
Much obliged for your letter received today. Please excuse a dictated reply, but I have three days work accumulated on my desk and am very busy beside writing a rather shaky hand at present. Mr. Warner's death was as inexpressibly shocking as it could be. I was just sitting down to dinner with my family when I got a telephone message asking for Mr. Clark of The Courant, and then one of our doctors, after making sure that he had me, said he had Mr. Warner with him in very bad shape, and before I could gather myself together to ask what he meant he said he was dead. He was out walking and taken sick and expired evidently without pain, but all alone and away from home. I got Mr. Twichell and their family physician, Dr. Porter, and went at once and broke the dreadful news to Mrs. Warner, and since then have stayed by her practically all the time until today. She has borne up with splendid bravery, and confessed to me that she had expected this sort of thing, and that every time the telephone had rung for the last two years when he was away from the house her first thought had been that it might be a call for help for him. Her friends have been very kind to her, and it is my hope that she and Mary Barton will live along in the old house.

Mr. Clemens came up yesterday to the funeral with Clara, and he looked very natural indeed and was quite his old self. Talking over the changes in Hartford with me he remarked that the Monday Evening Club seemed to be holding their sessions in the cemetery. We are all hoping that he will come to Hartford this spring, but he didn't promise me that he would.

Please give my kindest regards to all of your family. Your dispatch to Mrs. Warner passed my dispatch to you on the way. I was so broken up Saturday that I could only think of two or three addresses to send to and left the most of them till the next day.

If you are one of those people who regard type-written letters as better not sent, I beg your pardon for sending this, but hope to be forgiven and remain

Yours truly,
Chas Hopkins Clark

P.S. Do not worry about the newspaper business. Nothing will be printed here that will trouble you. A number of other papers have spoken of the attitude of Mr. Warner on the Phillippine question, but they did not know that he had let all those things go overboard in his earnest desire to prevent the election of Mr. Bryan.[7]

Several members of the King family had long ago gossiped about Warner's penchant for frequenting biracial saloons in New Orleans, so the family was probably not surprised that the setting of Warner's death was the home of a mixed-race woman in a neighborhood distant from his house in Hartford. It was his habit when in New Orleans to stay in the men-only *chambres garnies* owned or managed by quadroons.[8] Not much escaped the Kings and their milieu. Grace wrote May: "What an ignoble sort of death it was—but as Branch says Mr Warner was fond of that sort of thing."[9] This kind of cultural knowing had contributed to the earlier rift with Susy Warner over the closeness of Isa Cabell and Warner. If Grace was too outspoken for some of northern polite society, her directness seemed not to trouble Livy Clemens. The two had an almost familial frankness in addition to having good heads for business. Grace also recognized that Livy was the bulwark for Mark Twain and Sam Clemens.

☙ OLIVIA CLEMENS TO GRACE

New York, February 15 [and 24], 1901
14 West 10th Street.

7. William Jennings Bryan, Democratic nominee in 1900 election, fiercely opposed American imperialism; Warner must have supported William McKinley. The Philippine-American War of 1900 occurred after Spain ceded the Philippines to the United States following the Spanish-American War of 1898 and the zeal of Theodore Roosevelt.

8. *Memories*, 100.

9. Grace to May, October 28?, 1900.

Grace dear,
This is the second letter that has been really begun to you and there have been hundreds written in my mind. Your letters are always such a delight to get & I want more. They are a great help to me.

Interupted again and an elapse of several days between this day & my writing of the first part of this letter. I cannot tell you how I long for a talk with you. I know you would say many many things that would help to clear up my difficulties. When are we likely to meet? I am so unsettled in my plan that I cannot say, come to me, for I do not know where I am to be. Jean is not very well and needs the country: Clara is not strong but for her music she needs the city. Mr Clemens enjoys much very much here still for his work he often longs for the uninterupted quiet of the country. So I feel much pulled & very unsettled as to what we are to do. I know that for me Hartford offers absolutely no repose, not as much as a big city because there are no hours in which I am free from interuption. I seem to live all out of doors there and I find myself greatly dreading it. I wonder constantly whether I could make it any different & I fear that I could not. So I find myself occupied with the old questionings.

How foolish it is ever to think much about the future for so many things are decided for us. This Winter & Spring we must be here on account of having Jean under treatment. It may be that next Winter she will still need to be here & then our life will be settled for us.

There are certain atmospheres that I greatly dread in Hartford, you know that it must be so.

Susy Warner is still in the South with Mrs Cabell & is to remain there until April I believe.

The sentiment against Mrs Cabell is very pronounced in Hartford so that people speak their minds quite freely. All the friends who have seen Susy say that she carries herself most wonderfully is very brave & very thoughtful of others.

Dear Grace! What are you doing now What are you writing, what are you reading, what are you thinking? You are a big woman and I love to get your view of things. I am so thankful that you are my friend that you are in my life & that I can hear from you sometimes. This rushing life here seems to give no time for the quiet writing of letters to friends with some exchange of thought in them.

I am reading just now the life of Francis Parkman. I have not got very far but as yet it seems to me to lack human interest.[10]
Now in rereading your letter I see how little I have told you of the things that you ask.

We took a house in New York in 14th street. It is large & bright & sunny & being down town the rent is not as high as it would be up town. We have been quite comfortable, the only difficulty being that it was sometimes hard to keep the house warm. Clara has given two concerts as you have perhaps seen, one in Washington & one in Hartford. She did very well considering that in both places she had a very bad cold. In Washington we were compelled to have the Doctor twice before the performance and in Hartford she was just out of bed after bronchitis. It seemed impossible for her to get rid of her cold: this, added to the fact that she felt that she wanted more lessons before she did much concerting, also the fact that she had a very unreliable agent, decided her to give up her concerts this Winter. We are very glad. We do not oppose her, for of course that is not best, but we are very sorry indeed that she wants this public life.

Mr Clemens is very well & very vigorous, he works a good deal. I am so thankful that you like his attitude regarding the Philippines, many of our friends do not approve, on the other hand very many do & he receives more letters of approval than of disapproval—in fact ten to one I should think.

It is beautiful your description of how you think of me. I wish I had a picture of myself standing behind Mr C. to send you, but I have had none taken since we were in Austrailia & those are all gone. Someday I will try to have one taken for you just as you want it. But I do *hate* having photographs taken.

Good bye my beloved friend
Yours in deepest love
Livy

Feb. 24th 1901

10. *A Life of Francis Parkman,* by Charles Haight Farnham (1900).

Deaths continued to plague the friends. This time, Grace's troubled, alcoholic brother Will apparently committed suicide. As families do, however, the King women reexamined every detail trying to find a reason to believe that his death was accidental. Grace's beloved sister May remained in North Carolina, so questions about Will's demise were puzzled out in letters.

GRACE TO MAY

New Orleans, July 17, 1901

Dearest May, It was almost as if you too had passed from us—not to have you with us to day.—I thought of you all the time—Of course it would not have been right for you to have attempted to come—and I only tell you this to show you how my heart went out to you.

Last night I could not sleep—every time—I closed my eyes—I saw poor Will as Ammen & the policeman carried him into Mrs Gayarre's room—and laid him on the bed—dead—stone cold dead—[. . .] [W]e went over the painful story again—recapitulating it point by point—for Nina's benefit for she did not get up here from the water cure until all was accomplished—How Mimi went to see how Will was—& found he was not in bed—thought he had gone out—saw his hat—ran to the closet, found it bolted—How she called & then beat on the door frantically—& how we tried to get somebody to break it in. Mimi on the gallery saw the night watchman—& we hailed him & brought him up stairs—gave him a hammer—[. . .]—then the discovery—the discussion of cause—[. . .]—at first we had no doubt—but that it was all premeditated—then various doubts—came to weaken that theory—He had not closed down the window—[. . .] There was a half burnt match—on the floor—which might have been used in an attempt to light the gas—[. . .]—Mimi saw him at 11 OC in bed—[. . .] He could hardly have been asphyxiated by fumes from the small burner—in two hours for the closet was open—the key hole open—& a crack in the window—[. . .]

I found that it soothed her to talk so while Nan & Nina saw to all the thousand necessary details—I sat by her & we went over & over the morning tragedy—and Will's life—and all the deaths in the family—[. . .]

We got Miss McGreevy to send us some hats trimmed with crape—&

some black lawn shirt waists—& she pinned Mimi's old veil—again on her bonnet—that was all the preparation we made—[. . .] [11]

Devotedly
Sis

Despite sadness, Grace could not afford to stop writing. She continued with historical and shorter fictional pieces for which she could be paid quickly. Sometimes she made as little as fifteen dollars, as for "The Soul of Things" in *Outlook,* or as much as $120 for "A Destiny" in *Harper's.* But time was robbing her of those who had supported and mentored her. She expressed more weariness than passion when George Préot died at forty-eight.

GRACE JOURNALING, BUT AMONG HER LETTERS
New Orleans, Sunday, September 22, 1901[12]

Mr. Preot is passing away from earth today;—my good friend is breathing his last—he may—at this moment be not of the living—He was the truest, and the most—unselfish friend I ever had.—I can never have another like him—

—All day—as I sit here in suspense—waiting for news of him—I see his kind, good face—always brimming over with good feeling for me—always cheerful—always ready with a humorous turn—a witty reply—[. . .]

I am thankful that I had a long pleasant conversation with him, sometime in June. [. . .] He told me that I had grown so much pleasanter—more agreeable—that I used to be so nervous—striving—never seemed at peace—unhappy—I told him, that I was happier—since I had got rid of all my hopes—and had my future behind me—that I strive no more—for there was nothing more that could give me the pleasure—I sought death—and he became rather sad too—He said my last story was too sad—he asked me why I did not write gayer stories—more cheerful—I

11. The King women looked after the appropriateness of dress no matter what occurred; the crape was a black band indicating mourning.

12. Robert Bush lists this musing among "Notebooks Selections" and includes an excerpt in *GK of NO,* 385–86.

told him I could only write of life as I knew it—but—that I thought that story extremely amusing ("Making Progress").[13] He thought it was the best one that I had written.—

He was the only one who ever helped me in my writing—He was the first one who thought I would write. I remember how much pleased he was with my "Heroines of Fiction" that I read at the Pan gnostics—and how he came around to persuade me to publish it—and to go regularly into writing—

Monday 23rd—Mr Preot died this morning at 8 00. And so—the world feels empty of friends, to me. In comparison with him—the others were not friends—he alone was unselfish and disinterested—[. . .]

By late 1901, Grace had begun a kind of autobiographical novel of women surviving the Reconstruction era; it would later become *The Pleasant Ways of Saint Médard.* The manuscript was rejected several times before finally being published (1916). No doubt, the writing of it caused Grace to contemplate her life and career as she read years of newspapers to prepare, but the fictional form also afforded some distance and license. She continued to write smaller pieces and to read, because "when I run out of ideas nothing starts me off again like reading a good novel," she wrote May. As she was wont to do, she also read volumes of letters, this time Balzac to a Polish countess, Evelina Hanska.[14] And she began to champion the work of friends, as others had done for her, but she had limited success. She must also have kept up with the Clemenses somewhat that year; otherwise her bold request of Mark Twain would have seemed impertinent at best.

GRACE TO S L CLEMENS

New Orleans, November 24, 1901
2221 Prytania St. New Orleans

My dear Mr. Clemens—

A few days after this there will be sent you—a registered letter;—(to the Players Club.) containing the Scenario of a play—which you are to put

13. "Making Progress" appeared in *Harper's Magazine,* February 1901.

14. Grace to May, Good Friday, April 5, 1901.

into the hands of Irving[15]—extracting a promise from him to read it.—I might write you a volume of explanations and apology—but—it would not tell you much more than that fact—
You can imagine the volume—and if you imagine a chain of circumstances—of the most painful kind—fettering a struggling talent; you will not be wide of the truth—of what I might write to you—as the reason why—I am trying to get through you—access—for a young author to Mr. Irving—

The play is withheld—it is still to[o] bulky—for consideration. If the Scenario—finds a reading—the play will soon be sent on—when you read the title: "Dean Swift"—you will see yourself—that Irving is the only man—to whom such a character role, can be submitted—I may say—he—has evoked the character of Swift—from oblivion—as a playing one—Of course—you and I are concerned only in getting the author—to the actor—Mr Phelps[16]—the author—is well known by Walter Page[17]—I state this as a much better endorsement than *my* friendship for him.—
The black [border]—on my paper—is for my youngest brother who died last Summer—tell it—with my love—to your dear wife—my dear dear friend—otherwise—we are all well—Ever your affectionate friend—and admirer

Grace King[18]

Grace seemed to hear from none of the people of Hartford, and she worked closer to home in 1902 and 1903. She confided to May, "I feel loneliness—as if I were playing living—in a big box of a doll house—so small—& retired—and quiet my life is."[19] In summer, instead of going north as she had in other years, Grace, Mimi, Nan, and Nina escaped to North Carolina and boarded at

15. Perhaps King refers to Henry Irving (1838–1905), the famous British actor-manager who was then making his seventh American tour.

16. Probably, Albert Caruthers Phelps (1875–1912), editorial writer at the *New Orleans Picayune* and *Times-Democrat.*

17. Walter Hines Page (1855–1918), southern journalist and publisher.

18. MS, CU-MARK, UCLC 33330, University of California, Mark Twain Papers, The Bancroft Library, Berkeley.

19. Grace to May, January 2, 1902.

spas or mountain resorts. Politics engaged them in New Orleans as always, in particular a streetcar strike that pitted her two brothers on opposite sides of the union. Grace continued her efforts as long-serving secretary and frequent speaker at the Louisiana Historical Society; she wrote short pieces for *Outlook,* the *Youth Companion,* and Doubleday,[20] and she toiled on a biographical sketch of Gayarré. "The best thing he ever did was describing the time & the people of the past. But this of course was what he was least proud of," she wrote May. He "saved every scrap of political writing he ever did—but destroyed his letters & reminiscences of social affairs—He thought he would be known as a diplomat & Senator & speech maker—and he was such a pitiable failure at it!"[21] What was significant to Grace was the personal, the social, and the places and people about which she wrote wherever she was in the world. Letters would have told Gayarré's story with poignancy and truth.

Grace was distracted in early 1903, so "busy trying to think of things to write" that when she was seated next to by-now-famous advice columnist Dorothy Dix at a dinner at Antoine's, she "spent all my time with her wondering what in the name of Common Sense she had written any how."[22] On a more serious note to May about her work, Grace outlined the dilemma of her semi-autobiographical work in progress for Macmillan: "It is hard to combine truth & fiction agreeably & that is my trouble—I cannot free my self from either the one or the other." She fretted not over her descriptions, which she knew were good, but on "the craft of plotting," for she claimed she was going "wobbling around forever in the same place."[23] She worked on that long work in spurts, casting it aside intermittently.

Traumas intruded in the lives and work of the Kings and Clemenses in 1903. Nina came close to a nervous breakdown and had to go off on one of her

20. King received fifteen dollars for "The Soul of Things" in *Outlook* and twenty-five dollars for "Fort Louis of Mobile" on February 14, 1902; seventy-five dollars for "New Orleans, One Hundred Years Ago" in *Youth's Companion,* on March 6, 1902; fifteen dollars for "Spectator" in *Outlook* on July 18, 1902; seventy-five dollars for "The Flitting of Sister" in *Youth's Companion* on July 19, 1902; and twenty-five dollars for "Characteristic American Literature" in *Outlook* on October 24, 1902. Publishers continued to vie for her stories.

21. Grace to May, November 30?, 1902.

22. Grace to May, January 11, 1903.

23. Grace to May, July 26, 1903; Grace to May, August 28, 1903.

repeated water cures. Grace's eldest brother, Fred, was "run over" on the street, a serious accident that caused a broken arm and leg.[24] His wife, Nellie, relied on morphine to curb her frequent serious illnesses. The two moved their troubles into the King household for a time. Meanwhile, the Clemenses were living in smaller quarters in New York and suffering their own ailments, which twenty-nine-year-old Clara conveyed to Grace.

☙ CLARA CLEMENS TO GRACE

New York, June 22, 1903
RIVERDALE
ON THE HUDSON

My dear Grace,

Your letter to my mother[25] came while I was still ill with the "black measles"[26] & it was left in my room for fear of carrying disease to her so that she has not seen it yet at all, but I shall take it to her tonight & explain it all; I shall also tell her that I have answered it as she is not strong enough to begin letter-writing yet. She is better though, very *much* better thank the Lord—& goes to my Aunt in Elmira on the first of July.

Our plans for next winter are not yet settled but we shall probably be in Florence or Pasadena [California] whichever the doctors prefer.

It has been an awful winter—just *full* of illness—Jean was dangerously ill with double pneumonia, Father was six weeks in bed with bronchitis. Jean had measles acutely; I had finally black measles (in their worst form) and all the time Mother was ill, at times alarmingly so.

She does not yet know that Jean was ill for a month with pneumonia & then went South for a few weeks afterwards although the lying my father & I had to do became so complicated that we often contradicted ourselves & each other in the most striking way.

Well dear Grace how are you? And shall we ever see you again? How

24. Branch to Grace, Asheville, September 21, 1903.

25. The letter is missing.

26. Black measles is a severe form characterized by dark eruptions caused by bleeding under the skin.

long ago *is* it since we met I wonder? I hope that you are both happy & well and will not entirely forget your loving friend
Clara Clemens.

Deeper despair was in store, however, and black-edged mourning cards multiplied. On December 5, 1903, Grace's mother, Mimi, died.

[BLACK-FRAMED PRINTED MOURNING CARD IN OLD ENGLISH FONT]

December 5, 1903

Died
On Saturday afternoon, December fifth, nineteen hundred and three at four o'clock
Sarah Ann Miller
daughter of
Branch W. Miller and Anne Eliza De Laybach Kirk
Widow of William Woodson King,
Mother of
Frederick D. King, Branch Miller King, Grace King,
May King McDowell, Annie Ragan King,
Nina Ansley King.

"Oh, Mystery of Mysteries."

Because all the family was gathered in New Orleans, the severe loss of Mimi was not fully told in intimate letters, but Grace mourned profoundly and long in her more self-conscious journals in the following years.[27] As the oldest female remaining, she tried to remain cheery to May even as she wrote that they were "all as dull & stupefied—as when you left. No talking is heard in the house—the only cheery voice that ever was in it—has gone—our voices—are all so common place & flat!"[28] Grace tried to assume Mimi's role in the family, and

27. For King's deep grief, see *To Find My Own Peace.*
28. Grace to May, January 20, 1904.

she, who had resisted church affiliation earlier, was baptized in her fifty-second year, perhaps out of sympathy and to her mother.[29]

Six months later, Sam Clemens was devastated when his dear Livy died after years of debilitating illnesses.

❧ [THICKLY BLACK-FRAMED PRINTED MOURNING CARD]
Florence, June 1904

To whom this shall come:

For what you have said, I thank you
more than I can tell. If I could, I would
thank with my own hand and pen each friend
who has remembered me and mine with
a kindly word of sympathy in this heavy
time, but I am not able to do it. Therefore
I beg that this general acknowledgment may
be accepted as a token of the gratitude, unex-
pressed & inexpressible, which is in my heart.

S. L. Clemens
Florence, Italy June [5,] 1904.

I send my love, Grace King—& hers who is gone, S L C

Grace was pleased that her friend had added a personal note on his card. She wrote Nina, who was at Chautauqua, New York, that she had "got the usual mourning notice from Mr. Clemens but with a nice message—written by himself—upon it."[30]

In 1904, Grace, Branch, and Nan distracted themselves with arranging details of the family tomb and with searching out a house to purchase, at last, for remaining members. Grace followed her ritual of writing short pieces for small pay that provided her personal funds. *Century* paid her one hundred dollars

29. Grace to May, January 26, 1904.
30. Grace to Nina, July 7, 1904.

for a story; *Country Life,* one hundred dollars for two small sketches.[31] McClure accepted one story and rejected another. As she had always done, Grace read volumes of letters and newly published works, including *Charles Dudley Warner* by her Watch Hill friend Annie (Mrs. James) Fields. She thought it "the silliest little book conceivable. Poor Mr Warner—to think of that being the best one can say of him!"[32] She grieved with May over her mother-in-law's death and wrote, "What a year of mourning this has been."[33]

Perhaps a small bright spot in the mourning life of Samuel Clemens was a seventieth birthday party that his longtime publisher, George Harvey of Harper and Brothers, arranged in his honor. Many prominent women attended, but Grace was not among them, although she could also have celebrated her own special day there.[34] The three friends had birthdays on near-consecutive days: Livy's was November 27, (1845), Grace's was November 29, (1852), and Mark Twain's was November 30, (1835).

GEORGE HARVEY TO GRACE

New York, [November 29 or 30, 1905]

To celebrate
the seventieth birthday of
Mark Twain
Mr. George Harvey requests the pleasure of
the company of
Grace King
at dinner on the evening of Tuesday,
the fifth of December, at Delmonico's
at eight o'clock.

31. Grace to May, March 13, 1904.

32. Grace to May, May 15, 1904.

33. Grace to May, May 3, 1904.

34. George Brinton McClellan Harvey (1864–1928), editor and owner of the *North American Review* and *Harper's Weekly,* president of Harper and Brothers. He published a "Souvenir Number" of *Harper's* about Twain's birthday. The *New York Times* reported the following day that almost as many women as men attended the party, including Mary E. Wilkins Freeman, Amélie Rives (now Princess Troubetzkov), and Ruth McEnery Stuart. Apparently, no women had been invited to the sixty-seventh birthday party that Harvey had given in 1902.

Kindly reply to
Franklin Square, New York

The celebration of Twain's birthday might have been a brief respite for him from the black-framed cards of previous years, but that was not so for Grace. She did not attend the party because her most supportive brother, Branch, died quite suddenly on October 22, 1905. She sent a gracious reply to Harvey that matched other expressions of her admiration of Samuel Langhorne Clemens.

GRACE TO GEORGE HARVEY [BLACK-BORDERED CARD]

New Orleans, December 2, 1905
1749 Coliseum Place

My dear Mr. Harvey,
I send my homage to our great writer and my love, to my dear friend. All honour to him who has honoured our Country and gladdened our lives with his genius.

Cordially Your's
Grace King

New Orleans
2 December 1905[35]

With Branch gone, the three unmarried King sisters were on their own in the first home the family owned since the Civil War, and Grace's responsibilities increased. Her concern was focused there. Branch had purchased the Greek Revival house at 1749 Coliseum Place after Mimi's death in the names of his sisters and had also made them beneficiaries of his life insurance.[36] The four

35. MS, CU-MARK, UCLC 34943, University of California, Mark Twain Papers, The Bancroft Library, Berkeley.

36. King listed her address as 1749 Coliseum Place on her stationery, which referred to the green space across the street and gave her location greater cachet. In August 1904, Branch bought the house for $11,500, or $325,625.73 in today's dollars. The family expected to spend an additional

had lived there less than two months when Branch died, and until his estate was settled, the sisters could not afford to—nor did they want to—stay in the house. After several illnesses and delays, they rented it out furnished, steamed out of New Orleans, and spent two years abroad where it was cheaper to live, as the Clemenses had also known.[37] Grace, Nan, and Nina, who with Branch had been looking after Will's son, Carleton, put him in boarding school in London so they could all spend holidays together. While in London, Nina had a nervous breakdown and spent months under a doctor's care, so Grace and Nan traveled only sporadically. The physical pain in Grace's hands also hampered her, but she continued to write fiction and history and often used her left hand to write letters to May.

More deaths followed. In 1907, Grace's coauthor of the textbook *History of Louisiana,* John Ficklen, perished suddenly from a fall. The same year, her dear Parisian colleague Madame Blanc died while Grace tended her in the final days. For Sam Clemens, there was also one more shattering blow. In late 1909, on the day before Christmas, his youngest daughter, Jean, died of a heart attack in her bathtub while apparently in an epileptic seizure. This time the thickly black-bordered mourning card told the darkness sparsely, and it carried no personal note.

[THICKLY BLACK-BORDERED PRINTED MOURNING CARD]
Redding, Connecticut, December 26, 1909

TO ALL FRIENDS WHO HAVE
EXPRESSED SYMPATHY FOR ME
IN MY BEREAVEMENT I
OFFER MY SINCEREST GRATITUDE

$500 on moving and alterations. Branch noted they would immediately save the $1,200-a-year rent for the house in which they then lived at 2221 Prytania Street (Grace to Nina, August 9, 1904).

37. The Kings had hoped to get $150 a month and thought they might get that the next winter. In today's dollars, the $100 they did get is $2,800.07; $150 is $4,200.10. Their monthly expenses to remain in the house would be $200, or $5,600.13 in today's money (Grace to May, January 28, 1906).

S. L. CLEMENS
STORMFIELD, DECEMBER TWENTY-SIXTH[38]

GRACE TO S L CLEMENS

New Orleans, December 28, 1909
1749 Coliseum Place

My dear friend—who was so kind & good time in the old days.—

I have been mourning with you & mourning for you. She has gone where Susie went—to her mother. I cannot imagine her without you—nor you—without her—the beautiful child & girl that I loved so fondly—as all did who knew her.—And now you are left, like some great temple whose altars are empty.—They came into your life—& went away—but the pain and loss of their leaving has been more than made good by the love they gave you—& the love you gave them.

I have suffered too much—myself—to have anything to say about death—life—I only know that while I am suffering it does me o [some] good to be reminded of people who have loved my dear ones—and it was always like balm to hear, that had done good—which can never be forgotten.—The kind—the beautiful hospitality I received from you—& the dear one who then stood at your side—& from the three daughters—imitating with such ineffable child-like grace—their parents—nothing—in all my life—has filled my heart with such grateful memories.

If God—ever turns His ear toward me—he has heard my prayer—to be with you now, that Jean is gone—

Ever your grateful & affectionate
Grace King[39]

38. In 1908, Twain had built a mansion in Redding, Connecticut, somewhat reminiscent of Villa Viviani, which he called "Stormfield" after his short story "Captain Stormfield's Visit to Heaven," published that year.

39. MS, CU-MARK, UCLC 40626, University of California, Mark Twain Papers, The Bancroft Library, Berkeley.

And then, four months later, the last mourning card came. Mark Twain died on April 21, 1910. Only Clara Clemens, now the wife of Russian pianist and conductor Ossip Gabrilowitsch, was left of the small and loving family that had befriended Grace in 1887. To the woman she had called Tety, Clara added a handwritten note to the bottom of her printed card.

CLARA CLEMENS TO GRACE [BLACK-EDGED PRINTED MOURNING CARD]

Redding, Connecticut, May 1910.

For your kind sympathy
and tribute we return
our sincere thanks
Clara and Ossip Gabrilowitsch

"Stormfield"
Redding, Conn.

My dear Grace,[40]
How well I remember those old times & how much Susy & I admired and loved you.

I wish I might see you. The more one loses the more one loves what one still has—& every friend is a blessing untold now. Every single member of my dear family gone!! It is overwhelming. Thanks to the Lord I have a wonderful husband who is my whole support. Lovingly yours
Clara

HENRY MILLS ALDEN TO GRACE

New York, June 20, 1910
EDITORIAL ROOMS, HARPER'S MAGAZINE
HARPER & BROTHERS
FRANKLIN SQUARE, NEW YORK
June 20, 1910

40. Handwritten lines.

Dear Grace,
Your note brings vividly back a Sunday morning on Warner's piazza at Hartford nearly twenty years ago. You were showing me a volume of Villon's Poems. Villon was just having vogue in America.[41]

I am glad you liked the appreciation of Clemens. I had written another—more intimate—in the *Book News Monthly* for March, while he was still at Bermuda. You must read Howell's Memories—those papers—beginning in July *Harper's.*

When I went with my wife to Europe—Feb. 1906, I hoped to be able to see you. We were in London in April, but our time there was so short that we could not take in Oxford, much as we wished to.

Don't you ever come to New York? It would be a great pleasure to see you again. I shall be 74 in November, & the years are beginning to tell. But I have lost none of my love for the friends of earlier years, of whom memory holds—none more fondly than you.

Affectionately Yours
H. M. Alden

WILLIAM DEAN HOWELLS TO GRACE
[London?], August 17, 1910

Dear Miss King,
Your kind letter about my Mark Twain papers followed me here,[42] and made me feel very glad and proud.[43] Nothing could have been welcomer than your praise except the things you tell me those beloved Clemenses said of me. I have always been afraid I was *not* true; now I shall begin to hope I may be.—The longest of the Mark Twain papers is yet to come; I should rejoice if it pleased you most.

41. François Villon (1431–1463), French poet of the Middle Ages.

42. The letter is missing.

43. Howells and daughter Mildred (Pilla) were in Great Britain after his wife, Elinor, died on May 7, 1910. Perhaps King wrote a letter after the first two parts of three of "My Memories of Mark Twain" that appeared in *Harper's Magazine,* July, August, and September, 1910. Harper Brothers published them later that year as *My Mark Twain: Reminiscences and Criticisms.*

After my wife's death, I could not bear to stay at home, and my dear daughter came over with me. I have merely postponed the realization of my loss; that waits my return; but time befriends sorrow.

Thanking you from my heart,
Yours sincerely
W. D. Howells.

CLARA CLEMENS TO GRACE

Redding, July 1, 1910
STORMFIELD
REDDING
CONNECTICUT

My dear Grace,
Your sweet letter came a few days ago[44] & I shall be delighted to send you photographs of father Ossip & me but unfortunately I have not a single one of mother that I can give away for there are only the ones that she gave to Susy Jean father & me. I am so sorry—& it will be a little while before I can send you father's as I have to have some struck off first.

I too have felt that life had been hard on me when it took Susy away (my other half as it were) & then my beloved mother without whom it seemed as if I simply *could* not go on living—but now at last if nothing happens to my husband I have really landed in a beautiful harbor & soon enough to worship every ripple in the delicious blue sun flecked water. Soon father's & Jean's deaths can not take from me this longed for happiness which is actually mine.—

I wish very much that you would let me have your photograph too. Have you the same lovely, curly hair? If you never come North you may see me sometime down in New Orleans when my husband is on a tour.

It would be nice if we could write to each other sometimes so that we do not so completely lose track of each other as we have the past years.—

44. The letter is missing.

With a great deal of love
Your faithful friend
Clara G

☙ CLARA TO GRACE

Redding, August 6, 1910
STORMFIELD
REDDING
CONNECTICUT
Miss Grace King,
New Orleans, La.

My Dear Grace,
It was very nice of you to write me as you did about my husband, telling me all the pleasant things you had heard about him in New Orleans.[45] I am sure, aside from liking him as an artist, you would also like him personally, and I hope that the next time we come to America his concert engagements will take him down again to New Orleans. I will write you a letter myself later on, and tell you some more details about my plans. Meantime a thousand thanks for your lovely letter.

Yours very cordially,
Clara

P.S. Did I tell you that I am expecting a baby about the 20th of this month? As I have not felt perfectly well the last day or two I dictated this letter instead of writing it myself. Ever so much *warm* love to you![46]

Clara's husband apparently attempted a bit of wryness and cheer in his typed announcement of the birth of their child.

45. The letter is missing.
46. The letter is typed, but the signature and the postscript are handwritten.

☙ OSSIP GABRILOWITSCH TO GRACE

Redding, August 18, 1910
"Stormfield,"
Miss Grace King,
New Orleans, La.

Dear Miss King,
I have the pleasure of informing you that I was born in Redding, Connecticut, this morning at 8.15. Mother and I are well.

Very truly yours,
Nina Gabrilowitsch
by o. g.

With the exception of Clara, Grace's contacts had fallen away. She continued her literary business long after her mentors and publishers were gone, but there was little reason or opportunity to revisit the Northeast of earlier years. Face-to-face contact with publishers in New York was no longer necessary. A. C. Armstrong, publisher of her first book, *Monsieur Motte,* died in 1911. His son thanked Grace for her kind letter honoring his father's sincere friendship and agreed that the firm owed her $5.83 royalty, which he enclosed.[47] Hamilton Mabie died in 1916 and Henry Mills Alden in 1919; they had continued to publish some of Grace's short pieces until then.

Grace and Clara communicated at least twice more and once spent time together in New Orleans when Clara's husband was there to perform with the city's Philharmonic.

☙ GRACE TO MAY

New Orleans, January 14, 1915
Thursday Morning

Dearest May,
[. . .] Yesterday I heard that Clara Clemens was here with her husband

47. A. C. Armstrong Jr. to Grace, January 12, 1911.

Gabrilowitsch. I spent the whole afternoon with her, taking tea at the end in the jardín dansant. She is very pretty & just as youthfully affectionate now as she ever was. I don't know when I have had a greater pleasure than in seeing her again—I had Vogue [Flower Shop] send her a pretty corsage of white carnations to wear to the concert—that was superb—one of the triumphs of the Philharmonic. Oh! I wish you and Brevard could have heard him—I like him better than I did Paderewski—his playing is so much more manly—unaffected—not freakish at all—We went to speak to her after it was over & were invited again to tea with Clara this aft.—at the St. Charles. He leaves this morning for Chicago—she goes tonight to N.Y. She was to take tea with us today—but when I saw the disappointment this caused to others, I yielded—so she is coming to see us at 3 OC & we all go to the St. Charles at 4.30—I am glad Nan & Nina will have the opportunity of seeing the queer doings called dancing down there.[48]

And now—tomorrow we can stay at home all day. However I got off my Outlook article all right on Tuesday night—I hope that it will "read" all right—[. . .]

Gabrilowitsch is very jewish looking—but has a remarkably fine face. Clara hates the U.S. & lives in Munich.—of course she is pro-German—& is very much hurt at the hard things she hears about Germany. She does not seem to know or care any thing about the old Hartford circle—I wish that she had been engaged to sing—She seems a little disappointed that she was not.[. . .]

Devotedly Sis

In 1918, Grace typed a letter to her nephew Carleton about having heard Gabrilowitsch play again with the Philharmonic, "the supreme perfection of piano playing and it took me to the highest peak of enjoyment. But the excitement was too great for me and I have been invalided two days from it."[49] She must have written Clara much the same.

48. King probably refers to the Peabody, a popular dance done to ragtime in the 1910s.

49. Grace to Carleton King, March 23, 1918.

☙ CLARA CLEMENS TO GRACE
Seal Harbor, Maine, July 4, 1918

My dear Grace,
You must have thought that I was never going to answer your charming note about my husband.[50]

I am so glad you enjoyed him so much & your note gave *him* pleasure tho, I am sorry that you were ill for I know he would so much have enjoyed seeing you again.

Perhaps you saw by the papers that he accepted the conductorship of the Detroit Symphony orchestra this year, which means that our home will be there for the present. I shall be away a great deal though because I have a goodly number of concerts that require a lot of travelling. I have a new & excellent manager now (Mrs. Sawyer) & she is getting me enough to do. We are working hard & resting at the same time in this adorable place where the air is marvelously bracing. Nina is in *perfect* health & I must admit that we are too.

Are you writing something enthralling now? The short stories you gave me when I left New Orleans were *most* interesting. I love your writing.

Here is a big, warm, hug from me & best greetings from Ossip

Yours lovingly
Clara C.

Years later, Grace heard from Clara again.

☙ CLARA CLEMENS TO GRACE
Detroit, Michigan, November 3, 1930
511 BOSTON BOULEVARD WEST

My dearest Grace King,
Do you ever think of me and the old days? I have a perfect picture in my

50. The note is missing.

mind of just the way you looked, laughed, & generally called forth the admiration of the Clemens children.

I know that it is not well to dwell on the past, particularly when its most loved and vital figures have left this world. But it is nice to imagine that one still possesses some tie with old friends, that one never sees any more.

Are you well? Can't you give me news of yourself and your family? I would so love to feel the mental grip of your hand again if we can not actually meet face to face.

Ossip & I are well and very busy, Nina is starting her sophomore year at Barnard College in N.Y. Does not that sound strange? The days, weeks, months fly fast like pictures flashed on the windows of a rushing express-train. One seems to get nothing done—& yet if one did, one would not breathe more lightly & certainly no imprint would be left on the fickle air. I am beginning to think the best thing is just to live, *feel, smile*,—and nothing else.

The above is my permanent address, for since Ossip has created a wonderful symphony orchestra here & we have bought a house, we shall probably remain in this nest for the rest of our lives.

Lots of love, my dearest Grace—
from your friend Clara C. G.

By 1930, Grace had lost more family members: her dear May in 1920, Fred in 1922. (Nan would live until 1933; Nina until 1942.) She had traveled to the British Isles in 1913 with Nan, Nina, and Fred shortly after the death of his wife, Nellie. Otherwise, she had stayed nearer home. Her attention shifted in later years to overseeing family matters, preserving Louisiana history, and inspiring the preservation of ancient buildings in the French Quarter of her beloved New Orleans.

Until the last, Grace King's letters suggest she was mentally alert. She was most candid with Will's son, Carleton, his taking May's intimate place. She lived a social life consistent with her past and shared the house on Coliseum Place with her fellow unmarried sisters and attending servants. After a short bout of failing health, she achieved a "good death" on January 14, 1932: that is, one at home with family members gathered around to comfort and to witness her final words and the condition of her soul, followed by a proper funeral. She wore a pretty dress on which was pinned her cherished French medal.[51] She was entombed with her parents and family members in Metairie Cemetery, the fanciest burial place in New Orleans.

51. The French government in 1918 had decorated her as an Officier de l'Instruction Publique with a medal of golden palms and purple rosette. London's Royal Society of Arts had added her name to their list in 1912, and Tulane University awarded her an honorary doctor of letters in 1915.

AFTERWORD

Grace King had beheld a literary era. She had finally reclaimed her family's name and earned her own independence by the force of her pen, through fierce determination, and with the aid of influential friends on whom she graced her southern charms. She employed the business savvy she gleaned from males in her family to every area of her life. In a real sense, she was a woman ahead of her time who boldly traveled and achieved a large measure of self-determination. She knew everything and everyone worth knowing in New Orleans and New England, and she wrote about it all: the places and people, politics and proceedings, the food and fashion. Each of her letters contributes to the full context of an enchanting capsule of her time.

Through her own resolve and having encountered and cultivated northern editors and mentors, especially Charles Dudley Warner, Grace gained the career she envisioned. Because everything was personal to her, even her business exchanges included niceties about wives and lives of associates. These further annotate the nineteenth- and early-twentieth-century publishing world, and they show how Grace made her way into it.

Warner was also her primary *entrée* to a unique friendship-of-equals with the Clemens family, an intimacy that gave Grace King an exceptional perspective on their private joys and troubles. She returned their trust with discretion, except in revelations to her family in the confidential letters collected here. In this regard, her fresh voice about Mark Twain and Livy and their daughters has hitherto been largely unavailable to those who might appreciate it most. My hope is that this book fills the void and gains a wider audience for a credible writer and friend and an intriguing woman of note.

Contextual Bibliography and Works Cited

In addition to Robert Bush's many studies of Grace King, other groundbreaking works were David Kirby, *Grace King* (Boston: Twayne, 1980) and Anne Goodwyn Jones, *Tomorrow Is Another Day: The Woman Writer in the South, 1859–1936* (Baton Rouge: Louisiana State University Press, 1981). Etta Reid Lyles gave scholars a new way to place King in her era in "A Transitional Generation: Grace King's World, 1852–1932" (PhD diss., University of Maryland, 1987); Helen Taylor assessed texts in relation to emerging foci in *Gender, Race, and Region in the Writings of Grace King, Ruth McEnery Stuart, and Kate Chopin* (Baton Rouge: Louisiana State University Press, 1989). For understanding Louisiana politics and the Lottery, Joy J. Jackson remains relevant with *New Orleans in the Gilded Age: Politics and Urban Progress 1880–1896* (Baton Rouge: Louisiana State University Press, 1969). Twenty-first-century scholars make their own discoveries in King's works as they build on Bush, Kirby, Jones, Lyles, and Taylor but rarely contradict them. Mary Ann Wilson's exploratory essays include "Grace King: New Orleans Literary Historian," in *Louisiana Women: Their Lives and Times,* edited by Janet Allured and Judith F. Gentry, 137–54 (Athens: University of Georgia Press, 2009); James Nagel reexamines several texts from King's *Balcony Stories* in *Race and Culture in New Orleans Stories: Kate Chopin, Grace King, Alice Dunbar-Nelson & George Washington Cable* (Tuscaloosa: University of Alabama Press, 2014); Rien Fertel studies King as a historian and historical figure who influenced the image of New Orleans in *Imagining the Creole City: The Rise of Literary Culture in Nineteenth-Century New Orleans* (Baton Rouge: Louisiana State University Press, 2014); Catharine Savage Brosman provides historiography in *Louisiana Creole Literature: A Historical Study* (Jackson: University Press of Mississippi, 2013). Recent essayists offered new perspectives on Grace King's stories in a seminar, "Grace King of New Orleans: Beyond Local Color Fiction," at the International Conference at Université de Lorraine, Ile du Saulcy, Metz, 2014.

Recent studies of Mark Twain's friendships with and reliance upon women form context for this project. Laura Skandera Trombley writes of Twain's immediate and extended family of strong-willed women and how they influenced his creativity in *Mark Twain in the Company of Women* (Philadelphia: University of Pennsylvania Press, 1997). Trombley also examines the role of Isabel Lyon, his overpowering personal secretary, in *Mark Twain's Other Woman: The Hidden Story of His Final Years* (New York: Knopf, 2011); Karen Lystra writes about the same complicated alliance in *Dangerous Intimacy: The Untold Story of Mark Twain's Final Years* (Berkeley: University of California Press, 2004). Elizabeth Wallace considers the friendships of the aging Twain with innocent vacationing girls in *Mark Twain and the Happy Island* (New York: McClure, 1913); Benjamin Griffin transcribes family writings that reveal the private side of Twain in *A Family Sketch and Other Private Writings*, by Mark Twain, Livy Clemens, Susy Clemens (Berkeley: University of California Press, 2014). Resa Willis captures the trusting friendship between Grace King and Olivia Clemens in *Mark and Livy: The Love Story of Mark Twain and the Woman Who (Almost) Tamed Him* (Abingdon, UK: Routledge, 2004), and Steve Courtney makes accessible a significant male friendship in *The Life and Times of Mark Twain's Closest Friend, Joseph Hopkins Twichell* (Athens: University of Georgia Press, 2010).

WORKS CITED

Bush, Harold K., Steve Courtney, Peter Messent, eds. *The Letters of Mark Twain and Joseph Hopkins Twichell.* Athens: University of Georgia Press, 2017.

Bush, Robert. *Grace King: A Southern Destiny.* Baton Rouge: Louisiana State University Press, 1983.

———. "Grace King and Mark Twain." *American Literature* 44, no 1 (March 1972): 31–51.

———. *Grace King of New Orleans: A Selection of Her Writings.* Baton Rouge: Louisiana State University Press, 1973.

Fertel, Rien. *Imagining the Creole City: The Rise of Literary Culture in Nineteenth-Century New Orleans.* Baton Rouge: Louisiana State University Press, 2014.

Grace King Papers (MSS #1282). Louisiana and Lower Mississippi Valley Collections, LSU Libraries, Louisiana State University, Baton Rouge.

Heidari, Melissa Walker. *To Find My Own Peace: Grace King in Her Journals, 1886–1910.* Athens: University of Georgia Press, 2004.

Hooker, John. *Some Reminiscences of a Long Life.* Hartford: Belknap & Warfield, 1899.

Karson, Robin S. *A Genius for Place: American Landscapes of the Country Place Era.* Amherst: University of Massachusetts Press, 2007.

King, Grace. *Memories of a Southern Woman of Letters.* New York: Macmillan, 1932.

Mark Twain Papers. University of California, Berkeley.

McCrory, Thomas J. *Grand Army of the Republic, Department of Wisconsin.* Madison: Prairie Oak Press, 2005.

New Orleans Daily Picayune.

New Orleans Times-Democrat.

Pfeffer, Miki. *Southern Ladies and Suffragists: Julia Ward Howe and Women's Rights at the 1884 New Orleans World's Fair.* Jackson: University of Mississippi Press, 2014.

Powell, William S. *Dictionary of North Carolina Biography.* Chapel Hill: University of North Carolina Press, Vol 5. November 9, 2000.

Scharnhorst, Gary, ed. *Mark Twain on Potholes and Politics: Letters to the Editor.* Columbia: University of Missouri Press, 2015.

Twain, Mark. *Mark Twain's Travels with Mr. Brown.* New York: Knopf, 1940.

A Note about the Grace King Papers

The Grace King Papers have been a part of the archival holdings of LSU Libraries' Special Collections since 1954. This rich, extensive collection documents the life and work of one of Louisiana's most significant writers. Like many archival collections, the Grace King Papers have their own story to tell, and they have been preserved thanks to the intervention and stewardship of many people.

LSU history professor Edwin Davis encouraged his student Grace King Coxe, who was heir to Grace King, to preserve her aunt's legacy. Coxe gave LSU Libraries King's papers, along with those of King's father, William Woodson King; and her adviser, the historian Charles Gayarré. Together these collections amount to over 20,000 items. They offer a distinctive history of a once-prominent family and an intimate look at the life of a unique southern woman author.

In a tragic turn, only six years after Coxe deposited her aunt's papers at the LSU Archives, she died in a fire that destroyed her home in Denham Springs, Louisiana. Her husband and children survived. The collections would likely have been lost forever had Coxe not donated them to LSU Libraries when she did.

The Grace King Papers and Grace King Selected Papers consist of correspondence, literary manuscripts, photographs, and business papers. They document King's career, travels, social and family life, and personal interests. Some letters detail her association with the Louisiana Historical Society and its publication, the *Louisiana Historical Quarterly.* Correspondence with prominent American, European, and Canadian contemporary authors includes letters between King and Charles Dudley Warner, Samuel Clemens, Richard W. Gilder, Francis Parkman, Hamilton Mabie, H. M. Alden, William McLennan,

Walter Page, and Charles L. Norton. The collection also contains documents pertaining to recognition of King as a writer.

Through Miki Pfeffer's use of these materials in *A New Orleans Author in Mark Twain's Court,* we gain insight into a writer who both embodied and resisted the ideals of white womanhood of her day.

GINA R. COSTELLO
Associate Dean, LSU Libraries

The Grace King Papers and Related Holdings:

Grace King Papers, Mss. 1282, Louisiana and Lower Mississippi Valley Collections, LSU Libraries, Baton Rouge, La.

Grace King Selected Papers, Mss. 1282, Louisiana and Lower Mississippi Valley Collections, LSU Libraries, Baton Rouge, La.

Charles E. A. Gayarré Papers, Mss. 1282, Louisiana and Lower Mississippi Valley Collections, LSU Libraries, Baton Rouge, La.

William W. King and Family Papers, Mss. 1282, Louisiana and Lower Mississippi Valley Collections, LSU Libraries, Baton Rouge, La.

Index